AF206966

In and Against Development
Volume 1

Critical Reconstructions of Political Economy, Volume 5

Studies in Critical Social Sciences Book Series

Haymarket Books is proud to be working with Brill Academic Publishers (www.brill.nl) to republish the *Studies in Critical Social Sciences* book series in paperback editions. This peer-reviewed book series offers insights into our current reality by exploring the content and consequences of power relationships under capitalism, and by considering the spaces of opposition and resistance to these changes that have been defining our new age. Our full catalog of *SCSS* volumes can be viewed at https://www.haymarketbooks .org/series_collections/4-studies-in-critical-social-sciences.

Series Editor
David Fasenfest (York University, Canada)

Editorial Board
Eduardo Bonilla-Silva (Duke University)
Chris Chase-Dunn (University of California–Riverside)
William Carroll (University of Victoria)
Raewyn Connell (University of Sydney)
Kimberlé W. Crenshaw (University of California–LA and Columbia University)
Heidi Gottfried (Wayne State University)
Alfredo Saad-Filho (King's College London)
Chizuko Ueno (University of Tokyo)
Sylvia Walby (Lancaster University)
Raju Das (York University)

IN AND AGAINST
DEVELOPMENT

VOLUME 1

From New to Newest Development Economics

CRITICAL RECONSTRUCTIONS OF POLITICAL ECONOMY
VOLUME 5

BEN FINE

Haymarket Books
Chicago, IL

First published in 2025 by Brill Academic Publishers, The Netherlands
© 2025 Koninklijke Brill NV, Leiden, The Netherlands

Published in paperback in 2026 by
Haymarket Books
P.O. Box 180165
Chicago, IL 60618
773-583-7884
www.haymarketbooks.org

ISBN: 979-8-88890-786-3

Distributed to the trade in the US through Consortium Book Sales and
Distribution (www.cbsd.com) and internationally through Ingram Publisher
Services International (www.ingramcontent.com).

This book was published with the generous support of Lannan Foundation,
Wallace Action Fund, and the Marguerite Casey Foundation.

Special discounts are available for bulk purchases by organizations and
institutions. Please call 773-583-7884 or email info@haymarketbooks.org for more
information.

Cover design by Jamie Kerry and Ragina Johnson.

Printed in the United States.

Library of Congress Cataloging-in-Publication data is available.

Contents

Preface

As this is now the fifth in a Series of Volumes on the *Reconstruction of Political Economy*, it has been increasingly difficult to find something new to say in each successive Preface, and to avoid repeating myself. So, in keeping it short and referring the reader to the earlier Prefaces:

- Thanks to all who have contributed and encouraged along the long way in bringing this Volume to fruition, especially co-authors.
- It has been a long slog teasing out revised versions from multiple drafts even of previous publications.
- Repetition has been unavoidable, especially so that individual Chapters can be standalone.
- I am heavily concerned that my highly constrained personal circumstances, and some degree of vanity and its indulgence, are reflected in even conceiving of this project of reproducing journal articles and the like from my past. Nice, though, to have a review at all, not least a generally favourable one, of the first two Volumes from Jamie Morgan (2024) even though I have not been entirely kind on his earlier, 'balanced' take on economics imperialism (Nielsen and Morgan, 2005) – there is no balance, you are either against it or you are for it. Otherwise, you get rolled over or, arguably worse, incorporated and complicit.
- I hope, not least with overall Introductions to the Volumes, and Postscripts as Preambles to individual Chapters, to have offered some rationale beyond vanity and indulgence for these Volumes. Through my own scrutiny and reproduction of my own endeavours, this offers the prospect of rescuing some of the past trajectory of scholarship, and its changing character and emphases (and things were not always as they are now even in my own lifetime as a political economist, and memories can be short and false in the rapidly moving fashions that are characteristic of academia). I have also sought to situate my own scholarship, and that of others, in its broader material, policy and ideological contexts, with lessons on how to survive, and even prosper, as a political economist in an increasingly hostile environment for such within the discipline of economics (although prospects are more favourably housed within other disciplines, even management and business studies, with corresponding migration of personnel, analyses, publications and teaching).
- Overall, as an academic, one of my main goals for the past thirty years has increasingly been to marry my own contributions to the reproduction of future generations of political economists who actively both command

the mainstream critically and offer and develop alternatives from political economy. A bonus, if not an imperative in and of itself and as an element in understanding the world, is for achievements in these respects to engage in and with corresponding activism across ideological and policy spheres.

— In the latter respects, I can afford, or have no choice but, to avoid both indulgence and immodesty. Whatever I have touched has gone belly up, Cassandra-like, with prognoses and proposals observed only in the breach (if as yet to be proven correct in adopted retrospect) — even a partial list is long and depressing: the (UK's) Alternative Economic Strategy of the 1970s, the British coal industry (with one stunning exception, Fine, 2023c and O'Donnell, 2023, the British nuclear industry, privatisation, the Greater London Council (but do not overlook the employment of women drivers on London Transport and fuller access across plastic as opposed to glass employment barriers, etc, for which I can claim no credit other than being there), industrial policy, social policy, the (UK) Nation's Diet, post-apartheid South Africa, finance, and, last but by no means least, development.

CHAPTER 1

Introduction: Towards a History of Development Economics

Postscript as Personal Preamble

This is the fifth Volume in the series *Critical Reconstructions of Political Economy* that seeks to situate the reproduction of some of my earlier contributions of journal articles and the like in their own and the contemporary context. It is also the first of two Volumes on development economics. As such, it displays considerable resonances with the previous Volumes, especially the first three, because of its heavy framings of development economics (and studies) around the application of economics imperialism to development, with a particularly important role played by the World Bank, as primarily covered in the sixth Volume (and second on development as already indicated).

In one respect, though, this opening Chapter does not follow the pattern or tradition established in those Volumes that came earlier. It does not attempt to survey the development literature. There is a personal and logistic reason for this. Just before this series of books was conceived and initiated, I was asked by two former (successful) PhD students of my longstanding collaborator, Dimitris Milonakis, and with both of whom I had frequently interacted, to contribute on the economics of development to a proposed volume to be edited by them. Without this book series on the go, I found time to draft something straightaway and sent it off to them, and then forgot about it, even its existence. On looking through my records for files on development to feed into this, and the following, Volume, I turned up the contribution (Fine, 2024d). Still unpublished, I chased up the editors and, to my surprise, plans were well in hand for their volume to appear with my own contribution put on the back shelf for being more or less ready to go. I could not use it for this Volume as it both had yet to appear and was neither a journal article nor, prospectively, an unpublished piece.

So, insofar as I have a recent account of my views already in hand of what I have to say about development, it can be found in this previously mentioned contribution. Even so, I could still have offered an introduction that included some sort of updating or additional take on the fields of development economics and studies. I deliberately chose not to do so, and probably would not have done so even in the absence of having most recently drafted my thoughts elsewhere (although I do offer an acronymic summary of my views at the end of this Preamble).

Such reluctance points to the main rationale for this, and the following, Volume not offering an overview of the fields of development economics and studies. In a nutshell, by virtue of both subject matter and, for development studies if not economics, approaches, they have become so sprawling that they defy any sort of systematic framing of, and explanation for, their evolving substances. This is not to suggest that they do not have trends and fashions, and that these respond to material and intellectual developments (most obviously, currently for example, the pandemic, the environment, financialisation and, if to a lesser extent, social reproduction, intersectionalities and decolonisation of the subject matter with whatever degrees of energy in teaching and research). Indeed, the list of these borders on the innumerable – which is precisely the point. Rather, it is at least as important to explain why development economics/studies should be so sprawling as it is to try and make some organised sense of the sprawl.

I begin with development economics. And I do so by pointing to the reproduction below of an earlier contribution of more than a decade ago as the main substance of this opening Chapter. The piece first appeared in *Third World Quarterly* (Fine, 2009) at a time when my own thinking on development and economics imperialism was about to reach a tipping point. For, as elaborated in the earlier Volumes on economics imperialism, I had identified two stages in its development: the first, or old economics imperialism, associated with Becker presumed perfectly working markets as the basis on which to understand economic and non-economic phenomena; but the second, or new economics imperialism, associated with Stiglitz, understood the economic and non-economic as responses to market imperfections (informational for Stiglitz but otherwise for others). Both phases, though, shared a common commitment to relying upon production and utility functions, optimising individuals, and identification of the efficiency properties of equilibria.[1]

With Stiglitz at the forefront of market imperfections economics (imperialism) and his becoming, in the mid-1990s, the Chief Economist at the World Bank,[2] the scene was set for development economics to come under the spell of the new phase of economics imperialism, and for it to be implicitly

---

1 These have been designated as technical apparatus, TA1, and technical architecture, TA2, or TA^2 in combination.

2 To a large degree, the role of Stiglitz inspired my initial understanding of, and interest in, economics imperialism as a revolution taking place within economic and its extension to other disciplines and subject matter (Fine, 1997a).

acknowledged as such with Stiglitz's launch of the post-Washington Consensus (PWC), as documented at an early stage in Fine et al. (eds) (2001) and through the lens of social capital in particular (Fine, 1999 and 2001a). Previously, the old phase of economics imperialism applied to development (perversely, denominated as the new development economics to distinguish it from the old/classic development economics that it displaced) had been heavily promoted from the World Bank by Anne Krueger alongside the Washington Consensus during the 1980s.[3]

As a result, at the time that it was drafted, I had come to the conclusions that economics imperialism was alive and well, had passed from its first to its second phase, that it had been applied as such to development as new and 'newer' (as I dubbed it) development economics, but that both economics imperialism (and, by implication, its application to development) had nowhere further to go upon the presumption that its core framings around utility and production functions, etc, remained sacrosanct. As a result, I saw no potential for economics imperialism to progress further in terms of its analytical framings other than blundering onto ever more applications of market imperfections and their consequences for, and treatment of, the non-economic. I conjured up the image of zombieconomics to characterise what the discipline had become – both alive and dead, or undead, at one and the same time.[4]

But I was wrong. I had unduly placed some faith in the ability and integrity of the mainstream to retain some resemblance of attachment to analytical rigour, particularly in light of its priding itself on its axiomatic approach. With zombieconomics, in shifting from perfect market to market imperfections there was nowhere further to go if remaining faithfully committed to TA[2]. The qualification is vital, for it has not been observed. For zombieconomics was given a new lease of life by complementing it, inconsistently, with whatever else it cared to draw upon from across the social sciences, especially around behavioural assumptions that departed from given preferences and their optimisation. As covered in great detail in Fine (2024b), this involved the "suspension"

---

3   Whilst I refer to the old, new and newer economics imperialism (Becker, Stiglitz, and beyond, see below and Fine, 2024a and b), it is necessary to dub these as new, newer and newest when applied to development, respectively. Note the same conundrum applies to cliometrics as new, newer and newest economic history (Fine, 2024c), and, if less clear cut, for institutional economics, welfare economics, economic sociology, industrial economics, etc.

4   I was not happy about the epithet post-autistic for mainstream economics, because it was both an inaccurate description and, as the parent of a special needs child, offensive to those characterised as autistic. Interestingly, and commendably, the mainstream took a similar view but without consideration of addressing the substantive reason for the offence, https://gregmankiw.blogspot.com/2007/12/autism-and-economics.html.

of TA^2 – it is both there and not there at the same time – by setting it aside or complementing it. In other words, so confident had the mainstream become in its TA^2 that it could combine it with all sorts of considerations (bringing them back in) even though these had to be set aside in order to justify and construct it in the first place. And, crucially, this has opened up the newer phase of economics imperialism (and newest phase of development economics) in which more or less anything goes in terms of subject matter and explanatory factors. Hence the sprawl in the newest development economics.[5]

Before addressing the parallel sprawl in development studies, observe that, as indicated, whilst the piece that follows was first published in 2009, it was revised two or more years later as an intended contribution to an Aporde volume on development economics.[6] The earlier contribution was longer but the later one benefitted from recognising that development economics had crossed the rubicon from its newer to its newest version. As a result, there is a tension in the pieces combined, despite their considerable overlap, since the revised text both draws upon, and was initially entitled in terms of, zombieconomics, but it also acknowledges the new lease of life from 'suspension' although that term is not explicitly deployed.

As documented in Fine (2024b), this tension between the newer and newest in the piece that follows conforms with the timing of my identification of the transition between the two phases of economics imperialism. A lot of other things were going on at the same time as well, reflected to a greater or lesser extent in my own work and thoughts, and reference is made to them even though this may now appear to be odd for their now having passed from attention or for being able to be taken for granted. Longstanding was what I have described as the dual retreat from postmodernism and the extremes of neoliberalism (in ideology, scholarship and policy practice). This dovetails with the impact of the later Global Financial Crisis (GFC) of 2007/8. There is also discussion of the work of David Harvey, Bob Brenner and Amartya Sen in light of their influences at the time (plus discussion of Walter Rostow for his significance for economic history, Fine, 2024c, economics imperialism and development) as well as more idiosyncratic reference to Sir Josiah Stamp (with implications for financialisation and Polanyian double movements) and the

---

5   Significantly, explicit acknowledgement of the presence of economics imperialism across the social sciences in general, and across development economics/studies in particular, has declined over the last decade even though its presence has extended and deepened. This contrasts with an earlier period in which both proponents and critics pointed to the rise of economics imperialism (Fine, 2024a–c for this "watershed").

6   https://www.aporde.co.za The volume did not, however, reach fruition.

issue of interdisciplinarity by comparative scrutiny of consumption studies, management studies and social capital.

This is an appropriate point at which to move to the sprawl that is development studies. To a large extent, this is longstanding because of both the wide varieties of subject matters associated with development (for example, deriving from the notion of modernisation and its critics) and from the corresponding wide range of disciplines from across the social sciences, and more, that are drawn to apply themselves to development, each with their own methodologies, methods, conceptualisations, theoretical framings, and subject matter.

Here, though, I begin by highlighting two mutual and reinforcing factors that have conditioned, even intensified, the sprawl that is development studies. The first is economics imperialism in general and in its application to development studies via (new, newer and newest) development economics. Indeed, it is more or less immediate that, as economics imperialism enters its newer phase (of suspension) in general, and the newest development economics in particular, that it should itself sprawl across development studies and inspire corresponding sprawls in response from its understandably prompted critics in reaction.

So (mainstream) develop economics contributes to the sprawl of development studies without in any way at all filling out the field and dominating let alone eliminating alternatives. Yet a second, major factor is the role of the World Bank as a self-proclaimed knowledge bank in which the scope of its attention has been extended far beyond the economic to all things social – in other words, development studies. Unsurprisingly, the increasing reach of the World Bank in these respects, its adoption and promotion of the new, newer and newest development economics, and its powers of agenda setting in developmental and policy discourses create a perfect storm for consolidating the sprawl that is development studies, and to influence its variegated content and evolution to a greater or lesser extent.[7]

These remarks are borne out indirectly by two recent personal experiences, each involving a contribution to an edited volume. One is to the fourth edition of The *Companion to Development Studies* (Dauncey et al., eds, 2024; and Fine, 2024e). The other is the Companion to the World Bank (Vetterlein and

---

7 For a recent valiant effort to place order upon the sprawl, see Sumner (2024), delineating four contemporary approaches (that need to be more in dialogue with one another): development and aid; the global; the critical; and a renewal of the classical development studies for contemporary times emphasising systemic relations of disadvantage and the importance of the historical.

Schmidtke, eds, 2024; and Bayliss and Fine, 2024).[8] The development studies volume contains a first part with thirteen chapters on different approaches. The other eight parts (with almost a hundred chapters in total) sprawl over topics such as the global, language, poverty, modernity, legacies, nationalism, civil society, NGOs philanthropy, gender, corporate social responsibility, ethics, religion, social capital, children (and youth and ageing), identities, sustainability, decolonising, peace, conflict and wars, migration, urban, slums and gentrification, and so on. The World Bank volume covers disciplinary perspectives, conflict, law, environment, education, health, politics, corruption, ethics, housing, community, development, gender, institutions, human rights, and so on.

Only in the second of my two Volumes on development economics do I focus on the World Bank's economics and, inevitably, its love-love relationship with economics imperialism and, ultimately, the newest development economics. This first Volume is focused around contributions on development economics as economics imperialism and corresponding criticism of it with the posing of alternatives, to some degree on the terms that take the mainstream as critical point of departure. Thus, for example, drawing upon increasing returns to scale or externalities does not break with the mainstream but it does pose awkwardnesses for it to some degree as well as stretching towards taking a more fundamental break and critical path that is systemic, structural or transformational, etc, on whichever term you can take your pick.

In this Volume, the focus is in part upon the nature of economics imperialism, how it has evolved, and how it relates to development economics, not least in the body of this Chapter that follows. An early contribution to (new and newer) development as economics imperialism appears as Chapter 4, in which the shift to Washington Consensus and from it to post-Washington Consensus are assessed by reference to Kuhn's notion of paradigm shift.[9] But the Volume begins with two Chapters on the work of Amartya Sen.[10]

These are drawn from contributions that were first drafted when I was just getting up a head of steam on economics imperialism. Accordingly, the first, on his entitlement approach, especially to famine and food, situates its literature review on the tensions between the microeconomics of entitlements and the macro- or systemic nature of famines (rather than entitlements versus availabilities). This firmly places it in the potential terrain of economics imperialism

---

8   See also the variety just around development and governance in its own dedicated handbook (Hout and Hutchison, eds, 2022).

9   The same is done for economics imperialism more generally in Fine (2001c).

10   For personal connections with Sen as my Ph.D. supervisor, see Preamble to Chapter 3 and Fine (2001b).

but Sen himself is not so readily pigeonholed. He has always both deployed the mainstream and critically exposed its weaknesses, in part by doing both together. As a result, Sen is sometimes dubbed as belonging to the mainstream and at other times seen as departing from it. Both are true, and there is no point suggesting he is one or the other (although my own inclination is to see him more as critic).[11] Indeed, as argued in Fine (2018a), Sen's own trajectory from entitlements to freedom and democracy has seen the waning of his star from within mainstream economics, including within development economics if not studies, as his concerns have departed considerations that fit within mathematical formulations (as was so with his social choice theory and work on inequality as well as the axiomatics of entitlement sets). This is especially so of his contributions to ethical concerns (whether around social choice, inequality, entitlements, capacities and freedoms) as addressed in Chapter 3. Here, in departing from Sen to a large degree, it is concluded that the ethics of provisioning needs to be located in relation to how provisioning takes place prior to, or in conjunction with, who gets what, and this is also vital in understanding whether and how particular ethical issues are raised and framed (and can be critically assessed as such).

The following three Chapters are not so much exposure of economics imperialism as applied to development as opposed to taking it where the mainstream itself does not care to roam. What they share in common is to draw out what are unpalatable conclusions for the mainstream from mainstream analyses themselves. Chapters 5 and 6 do this for trade theory, demonstrating the weaknesses of the arguments for free trade on theoretical and empirical grounds once the slightest semblance of realism is introduced. Chapter 7 is much more wide-ranging, and recent, seeking to locate developmentalism in the age of financialisation, ranging over industrial policy, the developmental state, and the requirements for bringing about the systemic change that underpins development.

In the Volume that precedes this one, concern with how to contextualise the current period, and address social provisioning within it, is summarised through a sequential formula of determining factors (although analysis itself needs to revisit and refine these conceptualisations as they are developed).

---

11 But see Ragkousis (2024) for the uncomfortable attempt, inspired by the Critical Realism approach to economics, to fit Sen into the Veblenesque notion of neoclassical. He does so by exaggerating the evolutionary aspect of Sen's work and overlooking its other framings, in order to explain why Sen should be embraced by both mainstream and heterodoxy. See Chandra (2024, Chapter 10) for a recent narrative of some of Sen's scholarship and its influences.

Without going into the details covered there, first up is globalisation (GLOB) to situate, for example, national aspirations for development within those forces that promote or impede it at grander and unavoidable levels (for better or for worse). Second is neoliberalisation (NL) as the current stage of capitalism which is, third, underpinned by, but not reducible to, financialisation (FINN). Financialisation itself is associated, often seen as synonymous, with Commodification, Commodity Form and Commodity Calculation, CCFCC, given the corresponding presence of monetary motives and ethos. These, in turn, give rise to different systems of provision, SoPs, straddling the roles of public and private sectors, with corresponding Social Norms (SNs) of who gets what and how, with the formation of material cultures (MCs), around how these are understood and contested. The corresponding levels and rhythms of capital accumulation give rise to economic embedded within social reproduction (ER&SR). The overall result is for outcomes that are variegated, volatile and conducive to vulnerabilities (V^3) especially in light of mounting economic and social crises, growing inequalities and inequities, and swings in popular sentiments and politics in the wake of the demise of progressive organisations and movements, the rise of social media and authoritarian centralism increasingly exercised in more or less competent and corrupt elites attached to large-scale capital in general and finance in particular.

So, here, in a nutshell, we have it as GLOB, NL, FINN, CCFCC, SoPs, SNs, MCs, ER&SR, and V^3. Further, three, logically sequential, phases of NL can be identified – the original 'shock therapy', followed by Third Wayism to ameliorate the consequences of the therapy whilst allowing the treatment (accumulation led by FINN) to be sustained and, currently, continuing and increasingly overt state intervention and support (despite laissez-faire neoliberal ideology that has always been observed in the breach) to promote faltering FINN-led accumulation through forging collaboration between (large-scale, global) finance and corporations. In practice, these phases can overlap, be accelerated or delayed, and arise unevenly across (national and/or regional) location and issue. Last, if once again not necessarily with perfect fit across time, place and application, the three phases of neoliberalism correspond to the three phases of economics imperialism in general and the new, newer and newest development economics in particular (with an ex ante economics imperialism period corresponding to Keynesian interventionism and welfarism and the old or classic development economics).

There we have it. The rest, as they say, are the details and the (present as) history.

1   The Paradoxes of Development[12]

Whilst the history of development studies has been written a number of times and from a number of perspectives (Corbridge, 2007), the same is less true of development economics. This is remarkable in at least two respects: first, development economics has changed beyond recognition within my own lifetime as an economist (and I am not so old); second, in violation of the law that history is written by the victors, most reflections on the evolution of development economics have originated from the vanquished, and/or those who regret the direction it has taken and who wish to restore the methods, substance and pre-occupations of what has gone before and been discarded. In short, there is a new (as well as a *newer* and *newest*) development economics that is distinct from and usually ignorant of the so-called old or classic development economics that preceded it, symptomatic of casual neglect of its own intellectual precursors. Whatever has happened to development economics, it tends, with minor exceptions to be mentioned later, to be disinterested if not uninterested in its own past.

There is a second paradox associated with the history of development economics. This is that, around the period of the post-war boom, from the 1950s to the 1970s, it was relatively stable and self-confident, especially in its orthodox version which used induction to identify and explain theoretically the sequence, patterns and processes of development on the basis of historical experience – the generation of agricultural surplus for investment in industry, demographic transition, urbanisation and formation of a class of wage labourers, and so on. This is not meant to imply that the old or classic development economics was without controversy, which raged around balanced versus unbalanced growth, the presence and virtues or not of urban bias, the shifting patterns of inequality over time and their relation to savings and investment, and so on. Since then, however, it has been subject to remarkable changes in fashion and orientation, and become almost restless in its search for new and challenging subject matter (from corruption to violence, from good governance, through institutions to social capital). Despite this, though, the new neoclassical economics approach to development economics is marked by a recognisable uniformity in methods and theory. It unambiguously derives from a confident and broader "mono-economics", a stranglehold on the discipline

---

12   Originally published as Fine (2009) and, as mentioned, this version also draws upon an intended Aporde volume from 2012, entitled "Towards a History of Development Economics," that never appeared but thanks to Nicolas Pons-Vignon for detailed comments on the later version.

that has excised alternative methods and theories and, yet, perceives development (and economy and society more generally) as falling within its universal
scope of application. By way of corollary, or third paradox, the new development economics has ranged across a wider range of subject matter at the same
time as its explanatory principles have become narrow to say the least, irrespective of their validity on a narrower terrain.

2   From Economics to Economics Imperialism

In this light, it is first necessary to locate development economics within the
broader scope of the discipline of economics itself for the two have gone from
occupying parallel universes to becoming more or less synonymous with one
another. It is also important to locate (development) economics in relation
to other disciplines. And, unlike history in the making, this can be done with
the benefit of hindsight and by starting with the here and now and travelling
backwards to reveal how we got where we are (see Milonakis and Fine, 2009;
Fine and Milonakis, 2009; and Fine, 2011 for fuller accounts).

First and foremost, as a discipline, mainstream economics is increasingly
subject to an esoteric and intellectually bankrupt technicism that is absolutely
intolerant of alternatives and only allows them to survive on its margins. The
technical apparatus that this involves, utility and production functions, are
well-known to students of economics at every level of the discipline, as is the
methodological focus of relying upon optimising *individuals* in single-minded
pursuit of self-interest. This apparatus is embedded within formal mathematical models centred on (deviations from) efficiency and equilibrium, and reputedly tested against the evidence statistically through econometrics. Despite
its considerable and longstanding methodological and theoretical fragilities,
especially from the perspectives of other social sciences, there is no sign that
this situation of mono-economic dominance within the discipline is liable to
change as a result of internally or externally generated critique. Indeed, mainstream economics continues to strengthen its stranglehold through research,
publications and training with Americanisation to the fore. Insofar as there
are disputes within economics, it is on the basis of very narrow differences
across a much wider acceptance of core methods and techniques. It is salient
to observe how little the mainstream's influence has been shaken by the global
crisis since 2007.

Second, and perversely, the influence of neoclassical economics on other
social sciences is currently stronger than at any other time. This is a consequence of a new and virulent form of 'economics imperialism' that takes

neoliberal, free-market dogma as its point of departure. An old form of economics imperialism, most closely associated with Gary Becker, presumed that more
or less all economic *and* social phenomena could be explained by reference to
the more or less perfectly coordinated rational, optimising behaviour of individuals (Becker, 1996 for example). By contrast, the newer economics imperialism, with Joe Stiglitz to the fore, whilst emphasising that markets work well
in general, also accepts that the economy is subject to market imperfections
(see Chang, ed. 2001 for a selection of Stiglitz's writings on development).[13]
In order to address these, institutional (or non-market) outcomes evolve, but
they may themselves be subject to imperfection. So, in contrast to neoliberalism, the mainstream can now claim that it takes history, culture, institutions
into account seriously as joint, potentially favourable, determinants alongside
the market. And this opens up the traditional subject matter of other social
sciences as economists claim to be taking their concerns seriously albeit on
their own methodological, theoretical and conceptual terms.

   This involves, on the one hand, an extraordinary reductionism of the social
to informational or market imperfections and pursuit of self-interest while, on
the other, considerable scope for inscribing (bringing back in) the *social* by
plunder of concepts and insights from other social sciences (ranging from trust
and customs to institutions, etc.). Despite the absolute dominance of methodological individualism in its current form and the widespread belief in the
harmonious, if at times flawed, properties of free market capitalism, there is
no unified ideology within mainstream economics which could be compared
to post-war Keynesianism (or, indeed, mid-nineteenth-century free trade
Ricardianism). Rather, orthodoxy is more a matter of adhering to technique
and adopting a certain approach in resolving theoretical and empirical problems. As a result, its postures are contingent on the incidence and nature of
market (and institutional) imperfections. This has the further result that, both
in popular and academic discourse, the diffuse nature of the new orthodoxy
makes challenges to it more difficult and less influential (unlike potential for
unifying opposition to the challenge of neoliberalism that is readily perceived
as more or less narrow-minded dogma).

   Third, in the realm of methodology, the social sciences remain generally
hostile to the methods and postures of mainstream economics, when they
are explicitly confronted rather than informally incorporated. Nevertheless,
rational choice adherents have made much headway in sociology, political

---

13   See entry on him by me (Fine, 2006a, in Simon, ed. 2006) and also Fine and Van
       Waeyenberge (2006).

science, history, and elsewhere. As a result, the depth, extent and nature of the influence of economics imperialism by topic and discipline are diverse, not least in light of longstanding traditions, content and dynamics of the other social sciences. In addition, the openness of the other social sciences to economic arguments also reflects the current intellectual retreat across the social sciences over the last two decades from the excesses of both postmodernism and neoliberalism, although the latter's presence and continuing influence occasionally remain strong. This is because of a renewal of interest in how the world is materially organised, not least with the emergence of concepts such as globalisation. Thus, the current intellectual environment is one in which the social sciences are more open to economic arguments in seeking to address the nature of contemporary capitalism. Yet this also opens the way for economics imperialism. On the other hand, there is less appeal of orthodox economics arguments as far as other disciplines are concerned where the social and the systemic are genuinely taken as starting points, as in attention to relations, structures, conflict, power and critical interest in the meaning of concepts deployed both by scholars and to the objects of their scholarship (issues entirely unknown to mainstream economics and much political economy as well).[14]

Fourth, over the post-war period, economics began by being dominated by an uneasy analytical compromise between Keynesianism (and a concern with systemic behaviour in the limited form of orthodox macroeconomics) and general equilibrium theory and microeconomics, in which deviation from conditions for perfect competition might warrant intervention by a benevolent state. But the so-called formalist revolution in the 1950s within economics witnessed the heavy promotion of mathematical methods and microeconomic principles, not least as a foretaste of what was to come. At the time, though, microeconomics and formal methods were perceived to be of more limited application and scope, with the exception of Keynesian macroeconomics (and the IS/LM model in its standard form), where economy-wide considerations were to the fore that might selectively involve account of non-economic factors such as institutions, policy, politics, culture and ideology.

---

14   Note that Deane et al. (2023), in a post-pandemic context, suggest that for development economics to renew its incorporation of the systemic, there is the need at least initially to be aware of the discipline's past contributions and achievements. They "call for the re-integration of these alternative perspectives into the development economics curriculum – it is not always necessary to reinvent the wheel, and there is a rich existing literature for lecturers and students of development economics to draw from", p. 64. For development studies, post-pandemic, see Wiegratz et al. (2023).

This compromise between formal and informal methods and across micro and macro was rudely shattered by the collapse of the post-war boom in the 1970s and the emergence of a particularly virulent form of monetarism (the New Classical Economics) in which it was presumed that the state was, at best, ineffective and, at worst, a source of inefficiency. This all went hand in hand with strengthening the role of microeconomics (and methodological individualism) both within the discipline and in pushing the cruder and earlier forms of economics imperialism in which the non-economic is understood not as the result of market (and institutional) imperfections but as the functioning of the market by other means as in public choice, property rights or human capital theory. As was (in)famously and typically put by the Nobel Prizewinner for economics, James Buchanan (1984, p. 14), "We commence with individuals as utility maximizers ... his utility function. This function defines or describes a set of possible trade-offs among alternatives for potential choice, whether the latter be those between apples and oranges at the fruit stand or between peace and war for the nation".

During the Keynesian period, though, mainstream economics had retained some idea of the limitations on the scope of application of both its micro *and* its macro principles, within economics itself let alone in extension to other disciplines. This left considerable scope and respect for applied economics to prosper with empirically rooted inductive analyses to the fore across a range of topics that seemed to lie outside the domain of mainstream economic theory. From the 1970s, such analysis has been displaced by new theoretical fields, and empirical methods, as in the new institutional economics, the new growth theory, the new economic geography, and the new welfare economics, in which market and institutional imperfections are now used to substitute universal theoretical principles for empirical investigation other than through statistical testing.

In short, the new form of economics imperialism and the economic theory on which it is based, with emphasis on market and institutional imperfections, can be caricatured as "zombieconomics" (Fine, 2009). This is because it is both alive and dead at the same time. It is alive in the sense of not only aggressively and crudely, if not savagely, occupying its own territory and subject matter to the exclusion and absorption of competing paradigms but also through its increasing appetite for the flesh of other disciplines that it both infects and converts to its own nature with only limited traces remaining of what has been destroyed. By the same token, it is intellectually dead, having nothing new to offer other than parasitic extensions of its principles to new applications.

3   From Pre-Washington Consensus ...

This brief overview of the post-war history of the discipline in general offers insights into the evolution of development economics in particular. For sake of convenience, the evolution of development economics is divided into three periods. The last two, associated with the Washington Consensus and the Post-Washington Consensus (PWC) are familiar and recent enough to be instantly recognised and also to have been heavily scrutinised and debated (Fine et al., eds, 2001; Fine and Jomo, eds, 2006; Bayliss et al., eds, 2011; and Marangos, 2009). Their correspondence with broader disciplinary changes within economics is more or less immediate. As a product of the 1980s, the Washington Consensus is a reflection of the rise of neoliberalism and the analytical preoccupation with the pursuit of self-interest, most obviously in terms of the notion of rent-seeking and, subsequently, corruption and governance especially in relation to the problems posed by the transition economies. Development economics for the Washington Consensus is simply the application of the crude, treatment of the non-market as if it were reducible to market economics, and gave rise to what has since been termed the new development economics in which formalism also played an increasing role. By the same token, the PWC is based on what I term the *newer* development economics since it applies the (market and institutional imperfection) information-theoretic approach to development with Stiglitz to the fore. As he puts it in the Stiglitz Report (2010) in critique of the orthodoxy, p. 60, "this standard view ignored key advances in economics in the last quarter century – and especially results relating to the inefficiency of markets when it is recognized that information is always imperfect and asymmetric".

With the shift over the past two decades from one Consensus to the other, it is natural to understand the old development economics as constituting part of a *Pre*-Washington Consensus. This too can be pinpointed in terms of its location within the earlier character of economics as a discipline. As a specific field, it is generally recognised to have emerged after the Second World War as a response to decolonisation. As a result, it is not surprising that it should stand apart in method and content from the theoretical designs of standard micro and macro, as did other applied and historical fields. It was not subject then, at least initially, to the designs of the formalist revolution. Indeed, the old development economics was concerned with how economic rationality (especially entrepreneurial spirit and culture) might become adopted within developing economies (thereby accepting that all behaviour is not necessarily rational, especially prior to development) and how broad economic and social transformation could be brought about, especially through the agency of the state. Toye (1993, pp. 30–31) describes the old development economics in the following terms:

> The original theory of socioeconomic development that accompanied the post-1945 decolonization of Asia and Africa rested on the idea of modern society as the goal of development. Modern society supposedly had typical social patterns of demography, urbanization and literacy; typical economic patterns of production and consumption, investment, trade and government finance; and typical psychological attributes of rationality, ascriptive identity and achievement motivation. The process of development consisted, on this theory, of moving from traditional society, which was taken as the polar opposite of the modern type, through a series of stages of development – derived essentially from the history of Europe, North America and Japan – to modernity, that is, approximately the United States of the 1950s.

Thus, the old development economics was concerned with broad socio-economic processes and structural change as opposed to a theory of choice based on economic rationality. By the same token, the old development economics was inductive rather than deductive, seeking out empirical regularities in the transition from traditional to modern society. And, in conformity to the hegemonic Keynesianism of the time, the old development economics laid considerable emphasis on the role of the state as agent of change (as opposed to focusing on the optimising behaviour of a representative individual). Such features of the old development economics are in part brought out by a commentary on Simon Kuznets, Nobel Prize winner for economics and leading empiricist in the study of economic history and development. For Huff et al. (2001, p. 719):

> Modern economic growth, Kuznets (1971, p. 346) points out, requires a modern nation state to serve as a clearing house for institutional innovations and to possess the ability to act as "an agency for resolution of conflicts among group interests; and as a major entrepreneur for the socially required infrastructure".

Such postures could not sit comfortably within the standard analysis of mainstream neoclassical economics.

Significantly, then, the rise of the old development economics had a close connection to a certain style of economic history in subject matter and, especially, US personnel reflecting their location within economics departments and the continuing presence of those trained in the institutional tradition. This is most apparent in the work of possibly the most prominent of economic historians at the time, W.W. Rostow. His Stages of Economic Growth: *A Non-Communist Manifesto*, emphasis added, carried a message to the world that could not be clearer in the wake of the launch of the Sputnik in 1957 and the perceived threat of Soviet economic and technological catch-up. Whilst Rostow's ideological credentials could not have been stronger in support of US hegemony, and his volume was to go through three editions and sell three hundred thousand copies, his own stance on economic history was not supportive of the single-minded theory and numbers characteristic of the emerging cliometric (or new economic history) school – a progeny of the old economics imperialism from the late 1950s that sought to explain all economic history on the basis of optimising individuals and deductive methods. Rostow's schema for development followed a stylised induction of stages of economic growth from the experience of the developed countries. Whilst in part relying on standard growth theory, for Rostow, the ultimate causes of such growth are situated in a framework of modernisation, of breaking up of traditional societies and, correspondingly, of major shifts in political, cultural and social variables that are not reducible to the economic.

This is a consequence of the then established style of economic history to which Rostow adhered, but it also reflects a keen commitment to distance his approach from the "economic reductionism" that he attaches to Marxism. Indeed, his book's last chapter is devoted to a critique of Marxism for its economic reductionism (making up 15% or so of the main body of the text). The (mis)representation of Marx should not be taken too seriously except as a fascinating ideological text, reflecting (lack of) scholarly values of the time in this respect, but the nature of his construct of Marxism is instructive (Rostow, 1990, p. 149):

> The first and most fundamental difference between the two analyses lies in the view taken of human motivation. Marx's system is, like classical economics, a set of more or less sophisticated logical deductions from the notion of profit maximization.

Ironically, this is a better description of the economics imperialism of the present day. Indeed, Rostow (1957, p. 510) stated his preference for interdisciplinarity "because I was repelled by Marx's economic determinism". In contrast (Rostow, 1990, p. 149):

In the stages-of-growth sequence man is viewed as a more complex unit. He seeks, not merely economic advantage, but also power, leisure, adventure, continuity of experience and security; he is concerned with his family, the familiar values of his regional and national culture, and a bit of fun down at the local ... In short, net human behaviour is seen not as an act of maximization, but as an act of balancing alternative and often conflicting human objectives in the face of the range of choices men perceive to be open to them.

In short, from its own perspective, Rostow provides a manifesto of sorts more against neoclassical economics than Marxism by seeking to retain the notion of a more rounded individual. His antipathy to the idea that history can be reduced to the optimising individual could not be plainer. For, "The theorist has generally been uneasy if not awkward if forced to work outside Marshallian short-period assumptions; the historian – like the human beings he writes about – cannot avoid working in a world of changing tastes and institutions, changing population, technology, and capacity" (Rostow, 1957, p. 514). Thus, the old development economics carved a place for itself, like much applied economics more generally, outside the domain of both microeconomics and macroeconomics. In part, this reflected an acceptance that development was to be construed as something more than the economic as traditionally conceived, with a corresponding deference to the limited applicability of depending exclusively on "rationality" and needing to incorporate the insights and methods of the other social sciences to explain development fully.

4   ... to Post-Washington Consensus

Significantly, the nature of the old development economics in scholarly content and ideological thrust set some of the context for the nature and influence of more radical alternatives with which it contested. At the time, this was especially associated with dependency and world systems theory, drawing inductively upon global, not national, starting points for understanding a continuing division of the capitalist world into developed and underdeveloped countries, with the former exploiting the latter through various mechanisms of surplus transfer (initially lower wages and hence export prices but subsequently incorporating debt and technological dependency, for example). Such approaches are notable for their emphasis upon structures and corresponding terminology – developed/underdeveloped and core/periphery. Ultimately, though, their declining popularity and influence resulted: in part from internal theoretical weaknesses (if dependent countries produce cheaper, why not produce everything there with more, not less, development); and in part from the unavoidable success of admittedly select members of the periphery, especially East Asian NICs, necessitating a refined terminology to allow for semi-periphery, and so on.

In short, such radical alternatives both prospered and were stretched by theoretical and empirical anomalies, complexities and diversities (even more so with the rise of China today, for example). But as some sort of critical mirror image of the old development economics, all was to change with the rise of the new development economics at the time of the collapse of the post-war boom and the rise to prominence of neoliberal ideology. Heavily inspired by the IMF/World Bank Washington Consensus, the new development economics emphasised the virtues of the market and the vices of the state in promoting economic development. But it did much more than this by incorporating development economics into the mainstream, with little or scant regard for the significance of non-economic factors (except as impediments to development). In the first issue of the *World Bank Research Observer*, Anne Krueger, the Chief Economist at the World Bank and the force behind its adoption of the Washington Consensus, asserted: "Once it is recognised that individuals respond to incentives, and that 'market failure' is the result of inappropriate incentives rather than non-responsiveness, the separateness of development economics as a field largely disappears" (Krueger, 1986, p. 62).

This set the standard for what was to follow. For, as it was put at a later stage (Agénor and Montiel, 1996, pp. 11–12):

> We do not believe that economic agents in developing countries behave differently from those in industrial economies, in ways that are inconsistent with the rational optimising principle of neoclassical microeconomics; rather, we believe that they behave similarly to their industrial counterparts, but operate in a different environment.

In other words, economic principles are universal; only the environment in which they prevail is subject to variation. In this way, an establishment-driven challenge was made to both method and content of the old development economics. By driving to the extreme of neoliberalism in ideology, policy, and scholarship, it provided the basis for a mild reaction against the idea that markets work perfectly whilst allowing those universal principles to be uncritically taken for granted (see Rodrik, 2007, p. 3).

In this light, the 'newer' development economics does not fundamentally break with the methodology of the new even though it is more state-friendly and emphasises the significance of market imperfections. Rather, on the continuing basis of methodological individualism, it seeks to address (lack of) development in terms of market and institutional imperfections. Indeed, development becomes an ideal application for economics imperialism, with formal models of economic and social change and structure being subject to econometric testing. Such testing is itself the way in which the inductive methods of the old development economics have been displaced in incorporating empirical evidence.

5   Twixt Development Economics ...

The result has been, at least within economics, to collapse the distinctions between economics, economic history and development studies. In principle, this is no bad thing. It is essential that all three be studied together as development is irreducibly both economic and historical. But, in the hands of the newer development economists, both development and history provide the raw materials by which to provide narrative for the universal methodology of mainstream economics and data by which to test hypotheses. This can come in the purer form of continuing to rely exclusively upon imperfectly informed and institutionalised but optimising individuals, or other behavioural assumptions and institutional contexts can be taken as given as in what might be termed the newest development economics, in which, to some extent inconsistently, other behavioural assumptions are appended to rationality on an ad hoc and selective basis (as has happened more generally with behavioural economics across the discipline of economics).

One leading example is provided by Krugman (1992), whose mathematical models involving increasing returns to scale are perceived by himself to have rescued the old development economics from its technical deficiencies and lack of persuasion. That the classics might have rejected such methods rather than being incapable of them does not appear to occur to him. But this does serve as a warning of the extent to which the newer economics imperialism both appropriates and distorts the content of what was once standard but is now perceived to be heterodox.

Significantly Krugman deploys the same principles and methods to appropriate economic geography, explaining core and periphery relations and uneven development without any reference to the role of the state, let alone policy making (see the remarkable Fujita and Krugman, 2004). Paradoxically, if from only a slightly different perspective, similar methodological criticisms apply to the appropriation of economic geography in the physical determinism of

Jeffrey Sachs' work, where the flagging of policy is at the opposite extreme to Krugman's absolute neglect.[15] This is illustrative of the more general process of subsequently bringing back in, on a selective basis, what was first left out in establishing the technical apparatus of the mainstream. It is equally to be found in the new growth theory, the new institutional economics, and so on. But it also goes hand in hand with marrying such pure use of the technical apparatus with other, more or less arbitrary elements of the 'irrational', accepting for example that individuals may have other motives or be bound by exogenously given institutions, customs or habits. These range from freakonomics to neuroeconomics, but also include the new economic sociology, which more seriously and critically takes the technical apparatus as point of departure (Fine and Milonakis, 2009).

Typical, in so far as this is possible in an environment of such idiosyncrasy, is the work of Bates et al. (1998) in their *Analytic Narratives*. On the analytic side, there is little novelty other than the scope of the approach in covering both history and development. For, p. 8:

> Institutions ... induce choices that are regularized because they are made in equilibrium ... Behavior becomes stable and patterned, or alternatively institutionalized, not because it is imposed, but because it is elicited.

But there is a wish to "blend rational choice analysis and narration". Thus, p. 10:

> Our approach is narrative; it pays close attention to stories, accounts, and context. It is analytic in that it extracts explicit and formal lines of reasoning, which facilitates both exposition and explanation.

It also 'focuses on choices and decisions', p. 13. But the narrative plays no analytical role, simply serving to determine which model or game should be considered to be appropriate and which equilibrium results. This is hardly a recipe for studying change, let alone endowing it with a genuine historical and developmental content.

Yet, to a large extent, the previous account is deeply rooted *within* the evolution of development economics to what should be its familiar current state and prospects as far as orthodoxy is concerned. But the nature and significance of development economics, as it has become, is only fully gauged by locating it across a broader intellectual context and developments within the economy

---

15   See, for example, Sachs (2005) and Unwin (2007) for a critique.

itself. For the latter, for example, it is already apparent how decolonisation, post-war boom, and the Cold War provided the context for the modernisation ethos of the old development economics (as well as alternative critical approaches based on notions of underdevelopment). By the same token, neoliberalism and, ultimately, the collapse of the Soviet bloc have paved the way for both Washington Consensus and PWC. And the nature and role of development economics looks different from outside the field itself, especially from within development studies which is equally subject to change both on its own terms and in relationship to development economics.

For, first and foremost, development studies has increasingly drawn upon, indeed has been formed out of, the study of development *within* disciplines as in the geography of development, the sociology of development, and so on. In this respect, its scholarship incorporates a range of methods and methodologies far wider than, and generally along the lines of opposition to, those offered by mainstream economics. Not surprisingly, the division between development studies and development economics has tended to mirror the differences or hostile relations between the other social sciences and economics more generally around the validity or otherwise of methodological individualism of a special type and reliance upon more or less sophisticated statistical regressions.

Second, this *multi*disciplinarity has provided the opportunity and motivation for *inter*disciplinary study. Third, the range of topics studied is far, far broader than those that come under the rubric of development economics (although open to economics imperialism). Fourth, greater reliance upon inductive use of case study evidence (as opposed to statistical manipulation of large data sets) has meant that development studies has placed much greater emphasis upon specificity, context and meaning as opposed to ignoring these or taking them as unproblematic. This has, in the extremes of postmodernism, allowed critical theory to be exclusively concerned with the deconstruction of the meaning of concepts as opposed to attaching the generation of those meanings to (the study of) material practices themselves – how do the poor perceive themselves as opposed to what causes their poverty (and, equally, influences their own perceptions). Such limitations of deconstruction of the poor has to some extent conceded the terrain around analysis of material practices (including policy) to those who are entirely without critical sensibilities in the postmodern and, often, any other sense. But parallel universes for how the world is and how it is perceived is not inevitable, universal nor unchallenged, and the balance across these issues is shifting unevenly and variously across the social sciences. Indeed, whilst the rush from one post-ism to another continues to prevail, the increasing significance of attempts to come to grips with the material and the critical as mutually conditioning is one of the most marked and encouraging intellectual developments around the turn of the millennium, both within development studies and the social sciences more generally other than for mainstream economics itself.

Last, the presence of critical scholarship within the constituent disciplines of development studies, and within development studies itself, has been married to a more aggressive motivation around the object of study, ranging from the wish to do good (or better) through to systemic critique. Of course, these are not absent in development economics but they are of a much lesser degree of depth and breadth, almost inevitably as a result of the method and substance of what is involved. To put it polemically, if you were genuinely concerned about development and the poor (or the economic more generally), the last thing you would study is economics. There is, to use the vernacular, sample selection bias in who studies what, how and with what results, with radical and critical scholarship being attracted away from economics.

Before pursuing these points further in the next section across the evolution of development studies (in relation to development economics), two further general remarks are helpful. The first concerns interdisciplinarity and a general presumption that this places a discipline or field such as development studies at a disadvantage in the light of what is presumed to be parasitic dependence and dilution.[16] This is not my own experience, and outcomes are much more complex and mixed, accidental even, to be reduced to simple prognostications about the relative merits of inter- as opposed to intra-disciplinary study – although, in principle, if rarely in practice, wide-ranging critical incorporation across disciplines is imperative for knowledge and conceptualisation. Consumption studies, for example, was long at the forefront of critical theory, but this did not prevent it from being unduly captured by the extremes of postmodernist interpretative discourse at the expense of what has now become a much more promising attention to the material culture of consumption.

Management studies, on the other hand, might be seen to be the most self-serving and shallow of disciplines, dictated to by powerful corporate interests and vocational motivation. Yet, in the UK, the Organisation of Critical Management Studies is reputed to include one-third of all academics, had its origins in Marxist labour process theory, and displays a bewildering array of the most advanced and trendy critical methods and topics. This reflects the peculiarities of the timing and mode of forming of management studies in

---

16   Although, since the time of writing, interdisciplinarity has been on the uptake, at least in principle.

the UK but it demonstrates the extent to which the strength of critical scholarship is not confined by multidisciplinarity even in the most unlikely fields (although I am mindful of the extent to which 'distance', intellectual and/or geographical, from the USA is a significant factor in both of these examples, and the same applies to development studies).

Second, then, the evolution of a discipline needs to be placed in a broader context than in its own inner development, as is brought out, even if in an extremely limited way, by Kuhn's notion of paradigm as being attached to a community of scientists which might be broadened to encompass practitioners in the widest sense. This all suggests that the location of radical alternatives to development economics (with a basis within approaches drawn from heterodox political economy) has increasingly shifted out of development economics itself (where it has been marginalised) and into development studies and, as a consequence, is as much influenced by that discipline, and its set of constituent disciplines, as heterodox economics itself. And development studies has also evolved both in relation to development economics and to the broader intellectual, material, ideological and policy environments. Across both disciplines, it is imperative to recognise that the relationship between rhetoric, scholarship and policy in practice is not necessarily consistent although there are connections between them, and they also shift over time and across topic (Fine, 2010a; and Bayliss et al., eds, 2011). Thus, at the grand level, neoliberalism as rhetoric has been about leaving things to the market; in scholarship it has ranged from neoclassical monetarism to the mutually inconsistent neo-Austrianism; and, in practice, it has always been about heavy state intervention to promote private capital in general and finance in particular. By the same token, if overgeneralising, the shift in scholarship and rhetoric from Washington Consensus to PWC has in practice been accompanied by a hardening and stretching of the traditional Washington Consensus interventions (Van Waeyenberge, 2007 and 2009).

6   ... and Development Studies

Now consider the rise of development studies in the period of the Pre-Washington Consensus. The contribution set by the old development economics offered both a standard for the prevailing orthodoxy and what was primarily a critical scholarship on systemic grounds as point of departure. Development studies was heavily influenced by the political economy of development, not least with varieties of dependency or world system theory to the fore, raising systemic concern over the causes of lack of development as well as, or even in place of, how to bring it about. By the same token, such political economy was significant at the very least in providing a backdrop to the study of non-economic issues in development, with modernisation as a potential critical point of departure in ranging across the social sciences. In retrospect, the location of the study of development outside of economics, especially in the United States other than in the hands of applied or heterodox economists or economic historians, is a telling factor in the evolution of development studies in the Pre-Washington Consensus period.

The contrast with the Washington Consensus and subsequently is striking. First and foremost, and both characteristic and causal, has been the emergence of the new (newer and newest) development economics, the application of economics imperialism to development where previously the influence of orthodoxy was at most reflected in a predilection for formal methods, whether mathematical models or the search for empirical regularities that could be attached to development.

Second has been the decline of the political economy of development through a pincer movement that has in general, if not universally, pushed it towards the margins. For the rise of the new development economics was promoted and accompanied by an increasing intolerance within the discipline to any heterodoxy, whilst development economics became less of a separate field and more of an application, like most other fields, of pervasive and uncritically deployed methods and principles. By the same token, the decline of heterodox political economy deprived the other social sciences of core critical economic content. This itself dovetailed with the rise of postmodernism, general hostility to (economic) reductionism, and emphasis on the discursive and its deconstruction at the expense of material realities (Schuurman, 2000 for a discussion). There was, in a sense, an unwitting conspiracy to fill out the analytical space through an extraordinary alliance around two totally incompatible approaches to subjectivity – that of neoclassical economics that was fixed within the individual and in meaning (utility of given goods) as opposed to the interpretative capacities and relativism of the knowing, feeling and inventive agent.

Third, whilst it is totally inappropriate to look back nostalgically upon an unblemished golden age of scholarship in the Pre-Washington Consensus, donor agencies, the international financial institutions, and especially the World Bank, have now become increasingly dominant in setting the agenda for development studies. This is less so than for development economics, but the latter in the hands of the World Bank has increasingly set the orthodoxy from which critical dissent takes its points of departure. This might be seen as the form taken by, or the surrogate for, Americanisation of development studies as a discipline given its formal absence as a discipline in the United States, with pride of place being occupied by mainstream economics across the disciplines. Further, this has not simply been a matter of influencing or determining intellectual boundaries, weight and momentum, but has also been accompanied by the dull compulsion of incentives around publish or perish, policy considerations, consultancies and research grants.

And the compelling motivational counterpart to such factors has been an increasing focus upon policy – or, more exactly, economic and social engineering as the goal of development studies in addressing everything from poverty to governance. This places critical scholarship, one that seeks to understand before (or in place of) intervening, in a dilemma if the oppositional extreme of descent into a purely discursive critique is to be avoided as opposed to offering materially and systemically grounded proposals for alternatives that neither border on unrealistic demands nor idealise the popular, resistance or social movements as such. Interestingly those technical 'engineers' of development, those who deliver projects on the ground, and who acknowledge the political role of their interventions, have necessarily found themselves isolated, not only from orthodoxy for its wishing not to raise such issues, but also from its critics who wish to raise nothing else.[17] In other words, the World Bank has both increased its influence on the social science of development and the influence of such social science (and economics within it) on development thinking. This has been at the expense of (progressive) practitioners on the ground, in the sense of those with technical expertise who deliver development policy, unless these be conforming social scientists. Policy debate has increasingly been about ideas, the knowledge bank, as opposed to delivery.

Fourth, this has all been associated with the decline in interdisciplinarity in development studies, especially where interaction with the economic is concerned. The exception that proves the rule is where economics imperialism is involved. For this has had the effect of appropriating the economic within development economics as well as within development studies more generally. Where the other social sciences have found this unacceptable, the response has tended to be one of retreat into intra-disciplinary concerns at the expense of the economic, especially under the influence of postmodernism, as in the sociology, politics and meaning of development for which the economic can become an ever-distant backdrop if present at all.

Fifth, to the extent that development studies constitutes an uneven scattering across disciplines and topics, albeit with occasional concentrated effort

---

17   For an interesting personal account, see Biggs (2008).

and focus driven by academic or other fashions, this has had the further effect of creating more intensive divisions and dissonance across rhetoric, scholarship, policy and realism. The roots for this lie primarily within the World Bank where the incidence of inconsistencies are pervasive, mixed and shifting but, crucially, overlaid by an extraordinary expansion in its activities as researcher, trainer and proselytiser. This trend is quite distinct from its search to lead policymaking through leverage of its own loans and self-appointed role as knowledge bank (Bayliss et al., eds, 2011). The consequence has been that in place of the amorphous but at least single notion of modernisation, there has been the proliferation of developmental terminology, from good governance through to corruption, each element of which has to be critically unpicked across rhetoric, etc, to make any sense of what is being said or, possibly more important, being done. And the corresponding attention to individual topics and fashions is increasingly removed from broader understandings of what development is and how it is to be achieved (as opposed to piecemeal remedying of failure to achieve).

This is, however, to have moved past the Washington Consensus to the PWC. For the former, the rhetoric of leaving as much as possible to the market responded to its own developmental failures, the missed decades, by explaining how this was the consequence of not adopting its policies in practice. For the PWC, it has been more of the same but with a more constructive gloss and state-friendly stance even if with preference for the market wherever possible. But, despite the foregoing, it is important neither to overlook nor to dismiss the role played by dissent from the development studies community (as well as recognising the channels into which it has been steered).

In the 1980s, two main elements in such dissent were offered by notions of the developmental state and adjustment with a human face. These are indicative of the trends we have identified. The developmental state literature has been fragmented into two schools, the economic and the political, with one emphasising the need for policies to correct, or create, market imperfections, irrespective of the politics of implementation; the other examining the conditions under which the state is capable of acting developmentally without regard to the policies themselves. Based on this, a more than creditable critique was launched on the Washington Consensus, not least in light of the East Asian Newly Industrialised Countries. But the developmental state literature was already in decline by the mid-1990s, prior to the Asian financial crises, and was considerably outflanked by the PWC that simply ignored it and pretended to have invented something similar in its own watered-down and piecemeal version of interventionism (see discussion of the developmental state in Chapters 7 and 8).

Adjustment with a human face offered an equally commendable critical function along the lines of 'it's hurting and it ain't working', at least for the poor, across an increasingly wide range of diverse topics. Significantly, in parallel with such contributions, again analytically and critically diluted by PRSPs, MDGs and the like, has been the impact of the work of Amartya Sen, possibly the most prominent of interdisciplinary economists, certainly so for development. To a large extent, though, this has been the result of his considerable intellectual powers and energy. His contributions have been mainly confined to straddling the boundaries between economics and (moral) philosophy. Further, the passage from social choice theory through famine, entitlements, capabilities, through to freedom, ultimately (Sen 1999a) has been marked by some reliance upon the analytical framework of microeconomics (or at least tensions between the micro and the macro), a remarkable absence of causal content, and, despite his work on famine, a lack of engagement with the specific and contextual content of the separate elements that make up entitlements, capabilities and freedom (with the suspicion that the entitlement approach to food, however appropriate, has informed a broader application). The result has been to place, in practice if not in principle, limits on the extent and nature of interdisciplinarity and the depth and breadth of critique to be found in development studies arising out of Sen's work (Fine, 2004b).[18]

This has been especially so for the period of the PWC and corresponding Comprehensive Development Framework, CDF, launched in 1997/98. Within a decade of its launch, albeit with continuing tensions, the PWC has made remarkable strides in reconstructing the relationship between scholarship, rhetoric, realism and policy in practice. It remains crucial not to overgeneralise and homogenise across different areas (Bayliss et al., eds, 2011; and previously Fine et al., eds, 2001). But, for the scholarship, the newer development economics has been extraordinarily successful in opening up development to mainstream economics in six distinct but complementary and mutually supportive ways. First, it allows a much wider set of economic issues to be addressed as a consequence of explanation based on market imperfections. Second, it allows a much wider set of non-economic issues to be incorporated through appeal to imperfect institutions. Third, the application of these principles is not contingent upon any detailed knowledge of development, development studies, or particular countries or regions other than through access to readily available data sets. Fourth is the expansion of such data sets and the capacity to handle

---

18   See also Corbridge (2002 and 2006), the latter being his entry on Sen in Simon (ed.) (2006).

them. Fifth, the market/institutional imperfection approach is far more palatable to other social scientists than neoliberal alternatives. And, sixth, research funding has been increasingly associated with the World Bank as a source of both support and legitimisation.

In case of rhetoric, and more in the purveying of knowledge and command of training of development professionals, the putative role of the World Bank as knowledge bank has been particularly prominent. It has, of course, been accompanied by a more state-friendly stance in principle in case potential correction of market and institutional failures can be demonstrated to be beneficial. But the underlying logic is one of promoting the market or globalisation. The extent to which this rests on a realistic assessment of the consequences involved, both in depth and breadth, is a matter of concern in light of burgeoning problems, the environment for example now increasingly sandwiched between limited progress on poverty (especially in Africa) and the threat of financial crises as the new kid on the block. And there is an equally cavalier attitude towards causation. Questions of class, power, the systemic and conflict continue to be notable for their absence, apart from the occasional exceptions that prove the rule as with the assault on conflict inspired by Paul Collier (Cramer, 2006 for a critical assessment).

7   Future Prospects

But this is neither a full nor, thereby, a balanced picture of the current state of play and prospects. For, there are a number of decisive positive features within development studies, with corresponding implications for renewal of the political economy of development. First is its genuine multi-disciplinarity and, on occasion, interdisciplinarity. This means that development studies is irreducibly attached to methods, issues, theories and concepts that zombieconomics is incapable of appropriating and/or dominating. Thus, the fate of development studies does not lie in the hands of (development) economics but is dependent upon developments within its other constituent disciplines and how they respond to economics imperialism through their own disciplines irrespective of development and also directly through responses to development economics from alternative perspectives.

Second, again over generalising, there has been, across the social sciences other than economics, a dual retreat from the extremes of both neoliberalism and postmodernism as analytical agenda-setting devices. This is apparent in the equally general, if not universal, interest in addressing the material realities of contemporary capitalism. What is the world in which we live and, in particular, why does it generate such poverty and inability if not unwillingness to deal with it? Significantly, the most important concept bearing on this issue to emerge over the last twenty years (and no longer than this) is globalisation. Crucially, it has been won away from its neoliberal project (the state is withering away and this is a good thing) and is now attached to a bewildering array of studies appealing both to the systemic operation of capitalism on a world scale and, yet, demonstrating the continuing salience of the nation-state, its interventions and the importance of specificity (Fine, 2004a). Inevitably, such developments have engendered both a renewal of interest in political economy and, to a greater or lesser degree, an antipathy to economics imperialism both within development studies and more widely.

The result for development studies as a whole and within each of its contributing disciplines, and across topics, is that the outcome is uncertain depending upon how the intersections of the conflicting intellectual trends identified are handled. The same applies to interdisciplinarity more generally. In the case of social capital, for example, as I have argued extensively, there has been an extraordinary degradation of social science as this concept has exploded in its scope of application. And, as far as the World Bank and development studies are concerned, this has been particularly unfortunate in being at least complicit with economics imperialism, overlooking the systemic, and often proceeding as if globalisation, class, power, meaning and conflict had never been heard of.

Third, however, account must also be taken of the material circumstances under which development studies will evolve in the coming period. Although this is generally understood in terms of globalisation and neoliberalism, variously interpreted, the defining characteristic of the current period is one of financialisation. It is not simply that there has been a growth and proliferation of financial services, but these have penetrated into, and mediate, an ever-increasing array of our economic and social lives. Financialisation is both in the vanguard and the beneficiary of privatisation, commercialisation, (neo)liberalisation, commodification, and so on. This is not to say that financialisation is either all-powerful or homogeneous in its effects. Quite the opposite, which is why, for example, there should be a renewal of interest in Polanyi's double movement,[19] not least as the financial and other crises of the last decade or

---

19 The concept of the double movement usefully refers to the continuing tension and conflict between the efforts to establish, maintain, and spread the self-regulating market and the efforts to protect people and society from the consequences of the workings of the self-regulating market. For Polanyi, this entailed special attention to money (finance), land and labour. This is unnecessarily restrictive as is the framing within a dualism

more seemingly threaten the well-being of developed as well as developing worlds.

This also suggests that, crudely overgeneralising, neoliberalism should be understood as having entered a second phase. The first is appropriately understood in terms of shock therapy, particularly for those developing countries undergoing adjustment under the Washington Consensus, and not to be confined to the transition economies of Eastern Europe. For the intent was to release market forces, or private capital in general, as much as possible, and finance in particular. This first phase has now run its course and is giving way to a second phase with two closely related elements. One is to temper the worst excesses of the first phase, thereby presenting itself as more state-friendly and humane, the social market but the market nonetheless. The other is for the state to intervene to allow for the continued progress of financialisation. This is transparent for those who care to see in case of the extraordinary interventions that are being used to prop up the financial system, not least with huge subsidies from the state – while those who have suffered the damage, as home-owners for example, must pay the price. But also, as privatisation has begun to falter, especially in the (poorest parts of the) developing world as is recognised by a World Bank apologetic for its previous dogma on the issue, so policy becomes a matter of the state supporting the private sector to deliver rather than conceding to it. The same is true of public services more generally as the era of user costs and subsidy elimination has given way to a stance of public–private partnerships (Bayliss and Fine, eds, 2008).

The analytical and policy dilemmas posed for development studies by this situation is beautifully if inadvertently and implicitly anticipated by Sir Josiah Stamp. Apart from serving on the Board of the Bank of England, he was reputedly the second richest man in the UK in the 1930s as a result of his financial and other interests:[20]

> Banking was conceived in iniquity and was born in sin. The bankers own the earth. Take it away from them, but leave them the power to create money, and with the flick of the pen they will create enough deposits to buy it back again. However, take it away from them, and all the great fortunes like mine will disappear and they ought to disappear, for this would be a happier and better world to live in. But, if you wish to remain the

---

between market and non-market ethos as opposed to contradictory outcomes across economic and social reproduction.

20   See http://en.wikipedia.org/wiki/Josiah_Stamp,_1st_Baron_Stamp for this quote and background information on this remarkable individual.

slaves of bankers and pay the cost of your own slavery, let them continue to create money.

A moment's reflection will reveal the striking affinity between this judgement and dependency theory, once notions of core–periphery are replaced with those associated with banking versus the rest. There is not only the moral opprobrium associated with surplus (wealth) transfer but also the presumption of a mechanism by which such transfers are realised (dependency of some sort as opposed to the flick of the pen) and irrespective of efforts to the contrary unless they run very deep (sufficient detachment from the world system or abolition of the right to create money).

It is not my intention to dwell here upon the strengths and weaknesses of dependency or world system theory but only to bear them in mind as we interrogate Stamp's posture. An illustration of the parallel is provided inadvertently by Biel (2000). The potential promise of utilising finance is mirrored in the idea that, "NICs do at least represent some real change", p. 190, so that, "some parts of the South could take advantage of weaknesses in the North's control mechanisms and gain some degree of real autonomy", p. 191. And, for taking it all back again, "the colonies were fashioned in such a way that they would permanently service the accumulation needs of the fully capitalist economies", p. 12. Thus, pp. 81–82:

> import substitution did have a flaw from capitalism's point of view ... if consumption of the product was local, wages would eventually have to rise to provide additional demand, and this would eventually contradict the whole assumption upon which internationalisation occurred, namely cheap labour. The development potential of the model was thus limited; it would work for a while, but then would have to be scrapped. And this is exactly what happened. At the end of the 1970s, the dominant forces in the world economy turned against import substitution as vigorously as they had once propagated it.

But, whether for finance or underdevelopment, despite its power as metaphor on its own terms and as a starting point for investigative purposes, there are more questions raised than answered. First of all, for finance at least, the metaphor refers exclusively to the redistribution of wealth. Even so, what are the mechanisms by which wealth is retrieved through the capacity to create money? What are the implications for the nature and rate of accumulation, and the levels and distribution of employment and/or rewards among those outside the banking system? And what is the broader impact on social and economic reproduction?

On these issues Stamp's quote is simply one of silence but they are decisive for the fate of development studies, and its constituent disciplines, in the coming period. For if, as suggested, financialisation is the defining systemic feature of the current period, then explicitly or implicitly by default, some stance must be taken on the role of finance in whatever is being addressed. This is obviously so for systemic study itself, not least with financial crises on the horizon, the rise of China, the increasing indebtedness of the USA, and so on. But Stamp, suitably refined and qualified, offers an investigative edge in the study of environmental controls for example. Is this to be another opportunity for financialisation with the bizarre prospect of burgeoning future trading in not producing something? To understand how such fetishised markets could arise with what effects, what they are and what they mean surely depends upon a political economy of capitalism and of finance that draws upon an interdisciplinarity in which development studies could and should be in the lead.

This is especially important for policy purposes, and the analytical frameworks that inform policy. The sub-prime mortgage crisis has revealed not only how vulnerable is the global financial system in its proliferation and extension of interacting markets but how support for these in times of crisis commands government intervention and resources at the expense of those activities that finance is putatively deemed to support. To be parochial and polemical, would not the funds dedicated by the Bank of England to the rescue of Northern Rock have been better spent in financing the building of tens of thousands of homes directly? But what is true of housing and those previously dependent upon the sub-prime market is of much wider and more general relevance to all other aspects of economic and social reproduction throughout the world of development and development studies. It is important both to emphasise the heterogeneous if pervasive impact of financialisation and the variety of mechanisms through which its incidence is felt, as well as the need to anaesthetise or isolate progressive interventions from its global reach.

What role can political economy play within development studies as the latter addresses the second phase of neoliberal financialisation? The prior question is the nature of the political economy to be deployed itself. This requires a judicious mix of both abstract theory and contingent context, with characterisation of the current period of contemporary capitalism combining both. Consider, for example, the work of Bob Brenner. The first Brenner debate on the transition from feudalism to capitalism centred on the significance of class conflict, and the relative importance of production as opposed to exchange, following the earlier Dobb-Sweezy debate.[21] Does the external intervention of commerce bring about the dissolution of feudal relations and the emergence of capitalism, or are these the consequence of the dynamic arising out of internal class conflicts? As such this ongoing debate continues to have immediate implications for development understood in part in terms of how capitalist relations of production are established and evolve within developing countries.

The second Brenner debate, concerning the explanation for the failure of sustained recovery from the collapse of the postwar boom, is removed from such considerations in a number of ways.[22] Brenner does not deal with development even indirectly since his preoccupation is with a tripartite competitive conflict between US, Japanese and European (predominantly German) blocs of capital. This is in itself questionable given the internationalisation of capitalist production (and inter-affiliate trade) of multinational corporations. But Brenner does usefully point to the error of posing working class militancy and advance (for money and social wage) as the source of the malaise (slower growth, investment and productivity increase) in the capitalist world over the past thirty years in contrast to its performance over the postwar boom (when living standards were, of course, rising rapidly). Both militancy and rewards to labour have at most been limited.

In rejecting class struggle between capital and labour as the immediate cause of the slowdown in contemporary capitalism, Brenner switches attention to intra-class conflict, between capitalists, as the decisive factor. In particular, he argues that incumbent large-scale capitals have occupied existing market demand and deterred new entrants and investment, including their own. The implication, if not drawn by Brenner himself, is that developing economies will be constrained as much if not more by such incumbents. This is all, however, fraught with both theoretical and empirical weaknesses. Theoretically, it views the restructuring (and expansion) of capital as contingent upon a simple process either of self-expansion within an individual sector or entry by new investment from another. But the restructuring of capital is levered by other mechanisms as well, not least acquisition and mergers as well as through state intervention (to the point of nationalisation during and/or underpinning the postwar boom). At an empirical level Brenner would presumably have difficulty explaining the success of the East Asian NICs, as well as the extraordinary success of China that has shot to prominence since Brenner's investment overhang hypothesis was first put forward. Of course, as with Biel, this can be

21   For an overview of all of this, see Aston and Philpin (eds) (1985).
22   For a relatively recent critical account covering what follows, with both general overview and reference to a particular sector, see Fine et al. (2005).

dismissed, or embraced, as exceptional. But, as has been argued, Brenner's account is also shown to be wanting when shifting from (developing) country to sectoral level. For the steel industry, while exceptionally favourable to Brenner in principle in view of its heavy levels of fixed investment which are thereby equally favourable to incumbents, has experienced extensive changes in technology, location of production, sourcing of markets, and emergence of new entrants (Fine et al. 2005).

As a result, if only by way of omission, Brenner has usefully pointed to the significance of the levers for the restructuring of capital as underpinning the slowdown of accumulation. As already observed, these depend not only upon intra-class relations between the productive capitals directly engaged but also upon the financial system and the state as agent of restructuring. The impact, indeed the nature, of neoliberalism has been for financialisation to have substituted the expansion and extension of financial markets at the expense of industrial restructuring. Moreover, the thrust of neoliberalism has also been to constrain state restructuring of industry in deference to financial interests as well as at the expense of the more general role that the state can play in furnishing the economic and social provision that supports growth and development.

In these respects, David Harvey's work is more penetrating (especially Harvey, 2003 and 2005). Rooted in a continuing commitment to Marxist political economy, he has, in particular, attached the fate of development to the notion of 'primitive accumulation', extending it by use of the term 'accumulation by dispossession'. This is the means by which to address a wide range of phenomena from plunder through to privatisation of public services. In addition, he has posited the notion of a 'fix', especially a spatial fix, as a way of mediating between abstract theory and concrete developments (the geography of underdevelopment, for example) as accumulation proceeds.

But there is no need to confine ourselves to spatial fix or otherwise. Presumably there are also gender, labour, class, race, environmental, cultural and any other number of fixes as the preconditions for, and consequences of, continuing accumulation. To the extent that emphasis is placed upon one or another, this presumably reflects either the object of study or the judgement of what is of more general significance in the current conjuncture. Further, the idea that accumulation by dispossession, especially out of the noncapitalist world, is what sustains capitalism is open to an inverted interpretation. Capital accumulation is not dependent on accumulation by dispossession but the latter is liable to be intensified when accumulation through its own inner momentum is constrained. Such is the nature of the contemporary 'financial fix', to coin a Harvey-like phrase, in which the surplus available to reward and to sustain financialisation is limited by the slower pace of real accumulation induced. Financialisation both reduces the surplus produced and appropriates more of it, inducing accumulation by dispossession as a reaction as much as a motive force.

Otherwise, Harvey's accumulation by dispossession would appear to be a generalisation of Rosa Luxemburg's discredited under-consumptionism as an explanation for imperialism, in which the need for non-capitalist markets is perceived to be essential for capitalism. This is not to deny that accumulation by dispossession is both important and inevitable for contemporary capitalism, only that its significance cannot be derived as a sine qua non of capital accumulation.

This meandering across some recent contributions to the political economy of contemporary capitalism (and the implications for 'development') means that general prospects across the social sciences, and for specific topics within and across them, remain extremely open, with the major exception of orthodox economics which continues to be remarkably unmoved by its failure to predict, even allow for, global crisis. The same potentially bright prospects apply to development economics and development studies, and interdisciplinarity, more generally. But, in this, the PWC has very little to offer analytically, and in other respects, as a result of its methodological individualism that has sought to pick its way simplistically and piecemeal between the potential benefits of globalisation and its admitted downsides.

More constructively, then, the following can be posed as essential to a political economy of capitalism with corresponding implications for the role it can play for a political economy of development studies (Fine, 2004a), with the notion of 'glocalisation' symbolising the necessity of attending to global forces and local responses and outcomes. For the need for such attention to the political economy of capitalism, as a global system, with uneven and diverse outcomes that cannot be reduced to universal and narrow economic principles, has been strengthened by the global crisis, its consequences, the rise of the BRIC economies, etc.

In this light, a first requirement is to incorporate an appropriate value theory, one which addresses issues of class, power and conflict in the context of capital accumulation. Development is, after all, about capitalism as a world system and is not reducible as such to a matter of efficiency, equilibrium and optimisation within particular parts of that system. Nor can it be reduced to the extension of microeconomic principles of perfectly (or imperfectly) working markets to as broad a range of economic and social phenomena as ingenuity will allow through economics imperialism. Second, attention necessarily focuses on the relationship between classes and the state and how they resolve and sustain the conflicts associated with a system of accumulation.

Third, what is the role of the financial system in the processes of accumulation and economic and social reproduction? Fourth, what are national differences in systems of accumulation, and how are they to be identified and related to (fractions of) classes and their conflicts and reproduction? Fifth, why are sustained periods of economic growth punctuated by crises? Sixth, what is the relationship between economic and political systems and how can they be addressed by a genuinely interdisciplinary approach? Seventh, what is the relationship between economic, social and cultural factors and processes? And, eighth, what is the impact of the new world order, US hegemony, and the factors associated with 'globalisation' upon the prospects for growth and development, not least in the wake of the financial crisis of 2007 onwards? No doubt each of us could add other issues to this list which should itself change over time. But without a political economy of capitalism, the prospects for a prosperous and progressive development studies remain bleak.

CHAPTER 2

Entitlement Failure?

Postscript as Personal Preamble

With the exception of contributions on or around South Africa, I now realise in looking back that my piece on the entitlement approach to famine, pioneered by Amartya Sen, was the first that I published in the field of Development Economics/Studies. Sen was the supervisor for my PhD on social choice theory for which he had long been the leading scholar in following upon Arrow's Impossibility Theorem.[1] The prompt to engage with development at all at that time came primarily out of my work on South Africa, not out of any personal connection to Sen, who had some prominence in development if not on the same scale as social choice. I do remember during my time as his research student discussing many issues with him, unrelated to my PhD research, including some grand posturing on development as imperialism and the like (mindful that we were at the London School of Economics – where Thatcher was only on the horizon but development was heavily monopolised by Basil Yamey and Peter Bauer, neoliberals on toast well before the term entered popular discourse). Sen dismissed my piece as "hot air", which both took me aback as being unusually unkind but, equally, determined my resolve that no one else would ever have occasion to say the same to me again. I hope to have succeeded, at least in (spoken) word if possibly not in thought.

So, insofar as I engaged with development through the entitlement approach, it was at most due to Sen because of his, and my own lingering, interest in social choice theory from which it derives at least in part. Much more important than Sen as such, let alone development, was my interest and contributions in consumption studies in general and food studies in particular. At the time of publication, I had already been involved in developing the system of provision approach to consumption with application to the food system or, more exactly as I insisted, food systems in light of the differences between dairy, meat, sugar and so on. As a result, I was necessarily interested in famine alongside all other material and cultural aspects of food.[2] So this was the main

---

1 See Arrow (1951) and, for a heavily updated retrospective, Sen (1970/2017) with Fine (2018a) and Fine and Mendes Loureiro (2021) for some commentary.
2 For most recent account, see Bayliss and Fine (2021).

rationale for closely examining the entitlement approach although it may have conformed with influence from Sen and development more generally.

As reported on more generally in the Preface, in searching for the best text from which to reproduce this piece, I found that copying and pasting from the published pdf gave too much gobbledygook. So, I went back to search through my original files and dutifully found a version with which I was prepared to work, taking the most recent available in the folder. As normal, in part to incorporate copy-editing corrections, I compared the text against the published version and, to my astonishment, found that an entire section, the Introduction, was missing from the original. This led me to renew my search across my folders from twenty-five years earlier, leading to the discovery of the Word version of the published text, more or less, from 1997 as opposed to the first version from 1994.

This is all a bit of a dull narrative until the substance of the Introduction is scrutinised. For it very explicitly contextualises the entitlement approach in the context of economics imperialism although the term exclusively used is colonisation (of other disciplines and subject matter by economics) alongside revolution in and around economics – with reference to the piece, published in the same year, that explicitly references the revolution in economics (in its title) (Fine, 1997a).

From a personal point of view, the redrafting of this piece between 1994 and 1997 pinpoints the beginnings of my dedicated attention to economics imperialism. The micro, at the narrowest extreme, is about individualistic access to food. The macro, at the broadest extreme, is about any social and/or historical factor concerning generalised access to food. Such self-indulgence aside, there are a number of more general implications.[3] First, and significantly, the article itself, as opposed to its introduction, remains organised around the insight that the literature around famine and (critique of) the entitlement approach, is struggling to reconcile the analytical relationship between micro and macro considerations. In a sense, the micro/macro conundrum is a telling tension within the literature but it is also a proxy for what is a more general framing, from the later introduction, around economics imperialism for which the reduction of the macro to the micro is an imperative (at least in the first two phases of economics imperialism).

Second is to remark, given the new introduction could be added to an otherwise largely intact original text, that the observation and critique of

---

3 These are discussed more fully in Chapter 1 with the more general propositions over the nature and evolution of economics imperialism covered in detail across Fine (2024a–c).

economics imperialism (for development) at the time could occur without explicit reference to it. Everyone knew that the new development economics, associated with the World Bank and the Washington Consensus that derives from the 1980s onwards, pioneered by Anne Krueger, was both reductionist as economics and of development more broadly. No need to call it economics imperialism.

Third, my attention to economics imperialism runs in tandem with, if not just ahead of, its second, newer, market imperfection phase, pioneered and launched in the context of development by the Post-Washington Consensus and Joe Stiglitz, in 1997/98.[4] Significantly, the new development economics did not originate with Chicago, which prided itself on and promoted economics imperialism, although there is no reason why Chicago could not have sought to appropriate development if it had displayed any interest in doing so. But, precisely because the imperfect markets/institutions PWC was presented, and seen, as a critical reaction against the perfect market/anti-interventionist WC, close attention to economics imperialism in development has remained muted in being named as such across the WC/PWC transition.

In all these respects, development as economics imperialism has common features with the new, newer and newest economic history. It escapes what I have termed the watershed in attention to economics imperialism, in which it was heavily noted and contested until the second decade of the new millennium, at which point its vanguard was no longer occupied by Chicago-style, first phase, market perfection, old economics imperialism. For both economic history and development, there was no such watershed since the incidence on them of economics imperialism was either taken for granted (especially by its critics) or simply overlooked both before and after the watershed that did apply to other topics and disciplines for which the presence of old-style Chicago-inspired economics imperialism was decisive in allowing later versions of economics imperialism to be seen to be other than imperialistic.

Indeed, proponents of the second phase of economics imperialism have been wont to proclaim their opposition to economics imperialism (in the form of being interdisciplinary) and, thereby, to be willing subjects of what has been dubbed reverse economics imperialism. This has intensified during the third, newer phase of economics imperialism in which the other social sciences are plundered at will to supplement, or even displace, core economic analyses as if this represented subordination of economics to the sociological, the psychological or whatever. Significantly, though, this later phase of economics

---

4   See Stiglitz (1998a), with Fine et al. (eds) (2001) for critical assessment.

imperialism was not even imagined at this point as I could not see beyond the core techniques of the mainstream, more widely applied, across the social sciences in light of market imperfections and responses to them. Accordingly, as late as Fine (2009), I still saw economics imperialism, in a development context, in these terms – as zombieconomics with no further avenues to pursue other than through feeding on market imperfection versions of the world.[5]

Last, and by no means least, with the benefit of analytical hindsight, it is now possible to give a far more complete characterisation of the entitlement approach (debate/literature). To do so requires the acknowledgement of *four* phases of economics imperialism, not only old, new and newer but also what I have termed its pre-history.[6] I had thought of this as having been confined to the journey from the marginalist revolution of the 1870s to the formalist revolution of the 1950s. During this time, lingering attachments to the perspectives of nineteenth-century political economy persisted in varieties of ways and unevenly as core microeconomic principles became established and accepted, increasingly at the expense of earlier conceptualisations. In a sense, the pre-history of economics imperialism is the mirror image of economics imperialism, or economics imperialism in reverse (if not to be mistaken with reverse economics imperialism – the claim that economics is being colonised by the other social sciences). It involves the gradual exclusion of the social and the historical and the methods and conceptualisations of other social sciences rather than, as with economics imperialism, these being selectively reintroduced on the basis of now well-established framings from mainstream economics.

Understandably, I have taken the pre-history phase of economics imperialism to be located chronologically prior to the formalist revolution. But, especially given what has been argued to be the variegated nature of economics imperialism across subject matter, time and context, this is not logically so. Different aspects of economics imperialism's three (or four) phases, and their combinations can arise at any time.

This is exactly the way in which to understand the entitlement approach. Despite grounding his entitlements within the technical and individualistic terms of neoclassical economics, albeit with access to food extending beyond the market alone, Sen's departure from the Food Availability Decline (supply) approach drew upon social and historical factors – classes and the media for example, quite apart from the power of the state and the role of monopolistic,

---

5   Nonetheless, the third phase of economics imperialism was already being acknowledged at this time, see discussion in Fine (2024b).

6   For full accounts, see Fine (2024b).

speculative trading – that sit uncomfortably within more or less pure models of supply and demand, potentially embracing characteristics of the third phase of economics imperialism. This is a result both of his own scholarly orientation and the nature of the subject matter. By the same token, much of the contributions to the debate offered an even stronger reaction against the sorts of reductionisms involved in treating famine as a matter of (individual) entitlements.

As with other contributions around other topics, I have sought to review subsequent literature. A search revealed very little to review so I went no further. There is an enormous amount on famine and also on entitlements, with Sen extending the latter to other provision than food leading to the capability approach and then to freedom, all of which has been most prominent.[7] But the entitlement approach to famine as such was more of a moment.[8] I suspect it did much to kill off simplistic versions of the food availability decline approach but as an obstacle to, or stepping stone for, economics imperialism applied to development, it necessarily played more of a symbolic than a substantive role.[9]

1   Introduction[10]

The purpose of this Chapter is primarily to re-examine the famine and entitlement literature in the light of its position more generally within the development of economics. This introduction begins by setting the context and rationale for such an endeavour. For recently (Fine, 1997a), I have argued that mainstream economics is currently undergoing revolutionary change.[11] Although the core, formal models of general equilibrium remain as strong and as central as ever, economics is increasingly colonising the subject matter of

---

7   For a broad take on the origins and evolution of the capability approach, see Erasmo (2024).

8   Note that Jaspars and Kuol (2024) open their abstract of the introduction to a special issue on the topic, "Over the past decade, famine and food insecurity have increased, yet there have been few articles with a critical analysis of their social and political dynamics." Interestingly, their overview makes no reference to Sen.

9   It would be interesting to conduct a comparative study of the entitlement approach to famine and the nature and impact of (civil) war studies, based on greed versus grievance (Collier and Sambanis, eds, 2005a and b; with Cramer, 2006 for a more measured view). How did they impact study of their respective topics, and how did they relate to economics imperialism and development.

10   Originally published as Fine (1997b). Thanks to John Sender, other colleagues at SOAS, and anonymous referees for comments on earlier drafts.

11   See also Fine (1998a, Chapter 4).

the other social sciences. In some respects, the process represents a reversal of the transition from classical political economy to neoclassical economics in which the marginalist revolution of the 1870s separated the economic from the non-economic and set the latter aside altogether or as exogenously given. Whether in more general formal models or in more informal approaches, economics is now able to address politics, the household, institutions, the state and so on.

Conceptually, these developments have been spearheaded by two separate techniques although each has in common the neoclassical version of rationality associated with methodological individualism.[12] The first, for which someone like Gary Becker is a leading practitioner, involves extending the range of behaviour explained by utility maximising individuals to terrains that were previously thought of as inappropriate since they did not fall within the orbit of the market. The second technique, for which Joe Stiglitz is an able representative, is more innovative. It overcomes what was, from the perspective of social sciences, a profound weakness of the methodological individualism of neoclassical economics – namely, its inability to explain the existence of social structures, institutions, 'non-rational' behaviour, etc. By appealing to asymmetries and imperfections in information and rejecting the costlessness of making (market) transactions, it has been possible for neoclassical economics to explain why optimising individuals might create institutions, etc even in the context of an otherwise perfectly working market. The result has been the blossoming of the new institutional economics and the new political economy, but also a range of other applications as in the theory of financial institutions, segmented labour markets, and the correspondingly increasing presence of neoclassical within development economics.

If the preceding paragraphs provide an account of how economics is stretching its scope of applications, it is equally important to recognise that its reception is both mixed and uneven. For some disciplines, it has forged alliances with early, sympathetic settlers, as in rational choice politics. For economic history, the separate discipline of cliometrics has been established alongside more traditional methodologies. Not surprisingly, the world of post-modernist consumption and discourse theory remains untouched – neoclassical economics remains uninterested in the deeper meaning of both objects and subjects. In most areas, however, there is a steady forward march, in which resistance is encountered and overcome even if old traditions continue to leave their mark

---

12   Continuing reliance upon individual rationality in the form of utility maximisation signifies that the current revolution in economics does not represent a restoration of classical political economy.

on the outcome – examples are provided, for example, by the now general use of, or reference to, human capital and the new household economics.

A standard and prominent example of such revolutionary change is to be found in the new rural economics. Indeed, the area has been most prominent in pushing forward economics as a theory of institutions because of the models developed both for the institution of sharecropping and for the peculiarities of (informal) rural credit markets. It is worth quoting from a leading text to reveal the salience of the points made previously. First, the rural is simply an extreme example of more general economic problems. Second, these problems are ones of (divergence from perfect markets in) making market transactions in the context of imperfect information (Hoff et al. 1993, p. ix/x):

> In choosing the title for this book, we initially hesitated to treat the Economics of Rural Organisation as a separate area of specialisation within economics. One could argue that there is a general theory of information and missing markets applicable to all economies. But in the rural sectors of developing countries ... the problems of imperfect information and missing markets are especially acute. There the obstacles to perfect markets arising from imperfect information are compounded by rudimentary transportation and communication infrastructure, weak legal systems, and conflicts between statutory and customary property rights systems.

Finally, it is accepted that, "this book emphasises information constraints and transaction costs, rather than political constraints on the development of the rural sector", p. x.

No such limitations or boundaries are, however, evident in the text edited by Bardhan (1989) as he takes a variety of more informal contributions to "lump them together" as the Coase-Demsetz-Alchian-Williamson-North (CDAWN) school, p. 4. Significantly for the discussion below of the relationship between micro and macro analysis, he perceives CDAWN and more formal models as a source for Marxists "in building firmer micro foundations for their theory of historical materialism", p. 5. This indicates that the forward march of the new economics is not confined to, nor does it undermine, the use of formal mathematical models. Rather, these co-exist alongside their more informal and often eclectic application to the institutions or other social factors under consideration.

Despite the high academic profile of the new theory of rural organisation and institutions, it is remarkable for the extent to which it has developed completely in parallel with what is an even more prominent literature in the same area – that of entitlement and famine that was inspired by Amartya Sen from the early 1980s. This literature has had a major theoretical, empirical and policy impact – as is most marked by the recent World Food Summit held in Rome in November 1996 under the auspices of the FAO. Relative to its previous counterpart in the deliberations of the World Food Conference of 1974, emphasis has shifted from expanding production of food to a much broader concept of food security that involves access to, and not just the supply of, food. The influence of the entitlement approach has been profound. Yet, in the new neoclassical literature, as in the books referenced above for example, entitlement and famine might just as well not exist. By the same token, in the entitlement literature, reference to the new neoclassical literature is equally notable for its absence.

This raises a number of questions, none of which is satisfactorily answered by the false suggestion of an insurmountable analytical incompatibility between the two sets of literature. First, then, why have the two literatures overlooked one another? On the one hand, a possible answer is to be found in the tying of the entitlement literature to famine. For the latter, within a neoclassical perspective, there is something unsavoury, if not unrealistic, about individual optimisation resulting in outcomes that involve death. On a purely technical matter, it is necessary to weight death according to a level of utility. If, as seems reasonable, it is set negatively infinite, it would appear to be impossible to explain how famines occur since no one maximising utility would choose death (and negative infinite expected utility) even with a low risk. More generally, the new developments within neoclassical economics remain profoundly uncomfortable with questions of power and conflict let alone instances where rational economic agents die or are killed.[13]

On the other hand, the entitlement literature has placed some distance between itself and neoclassical theory because of the very terms in which it is expressed. Of course, entitlement can be interpreted in individualistic terms in a variety of contexts. But, outside the famine literature, it is equally associated, for example, with a social welfare system (entitlement to benefits), with

---

13   See, for example, the responses by Williamson (1993) and Stiglitz (1993) to the relatively mild suggestion from Bowles and Gintis (1993) that exchange is not only institutionally driven but also "contested". For Williamson, p. 107, "The power hypothesis is typically vague and often reduces to an ex post rationalization ... Although I seriously doubt that power qualifies for main case standing in the commercial arena, I agree that it can sometimes be brought in as an auxiliary hypothesis." For Stiglitz, p. 111, "There are good economic reasons, beyond the exercise of 'power' (whatever that much-used term means) for the existence of hierarchical relationships."

the legal system (entitlement to property rights), and with ethical principles of justice (entitlement to human rights). Sen's own work, and presumably his judicious choice of the term, has been motivated by concerns with poverty, social choice, capabilities, inequality, and moral philosophy, all of which are notable for forging a relationship between the individual and the social, an issue on which focus is placed below. Further, Sen's high status with, but not centrally within, mainstream economics and his interdisciplinary concerns, unusually catholic for an economist, have placed a protective belt around the entitlement literature from the marauding of unreconstructed neoclassicals.

A second question is one of where does the entitlement literature fit into the revolution or current developments in economics, given that it does not incorporate the new neoclassical rural theory. Is it nonetheless a part of the revolution or a pocket of resistance against it? The latter cannot be taken for granted since the presence of methodological individualism, for example, outside of, and not prompted by economics is possible as in the political theory of collective action associated with Mancur Olson. Locating entitlement theory in this broader context, then, is the main concern of this Chapter. In particular, the entitlement literature is assessed through its treatment of the relationship between macro and micro, the individual and the social, for these constitute the watershed which the revolution in economics takes as its point of departure from its own past in colonising the subject matter of other social sciences.

The next section, however, begins by briefly examining the more conventional way of approaching the entitlement literature – in terms of its relationship to its own point of departure, the food availability decline approach to famine. The third section establishes the tension between micro and macro in the entitlement approach. It does so in a number of subsections, dealing in turn with the definitions of entitlements and famine themselves, the position of classes and economic theory within the approach, and issues of method.

The fourth section addresses an apparently separate issue – how does the entitlement approach relate specifically to food. The study of famine can be seen as belonging to the broad field of food studies. Whilst this is a disparate and far from coherent discipline, Fine (1993) has argued that its insights need to be coherently organised around two distinguishing themes.[14] These are, first, the formation of integral food systems that forge socioeconomic processes into definite, possibly shifting, structures linking production to consumption through the chain of intermediate activities. Second, food systems

---

14   See also Fine et al. (1996). For later work, see especially Fine (1998d) and Bayliss and Fine (2021).

are specifically distinguished from other systems of provision that source consumption by the nature and extent of their dependence upon the 'organic' content of food. One issue with which to address the entitlement approach is the extent to which it develops a theory that is specific to, rather than simply applied to, food.

However, by focusing upon the specificity of food, a suggestion is made on how to address the micro/macro tension within the entitlement approach. It is through more emphasis being placed upon contradictions attached to underlying structures and processes (i.e. the macro level) than to their complex outcomes in the form of individual entitlements (the micro level). As the entitlement approach has its roots at the micro level of the *individual* incidence of starvation, it is concluded that it can at best point to the directions to be taken by macro analysis. In this light, the final section concludes that the entitlement approach is best seen as an *investigative* method rather than as providing a *causal* theory. Consequently, whilst flirting with methodological individualism, the entitlement approach offers, as in its past, the basis on which to resist the encroachments of neoclassical economics into other social sciences and a platform on which to provide an alternative.

2   The Entitlement Approach as Such

The entitlement approach to famine has now been heavily debated for well over a decade.[15] The literature has been characterised by a number of features, often overlapping within individual contributions. First, there are those that have sought to develop and to apply Sen's original ideas whether empirically or theoretically.[16] Second, there are those who have sought to dispute Sen's empirical account of the causes or absence of famines.[17] Third, there have been theoretical criticisms of the approach from a variety of perspectives. At times, the debates have been fierce, generating more heat than light. Indeed, in assessing the literature, Gasper (1993, p. 709) has pointed to the considerable confusion over basic concepts within the literature, explaining it by reference to "the vagueness and multiple associations of the term 'entitlement'".

---

15   For an overview of the literature on famine, see Devereux (1993a). See also Raikes (1988) and Bush (1996).

16   See especially Drèze and Sen (1989 and 1990a–c).

17   See Bowbrick (1986 and 1987), Allen (1986), Nolan and Sender (1992), Nolan (1993) and, in response, Sen (1986, 1987a, 1992 and 1993).

More recently, Osmani's (1995) magisterial assessment of the entitlement approach offers a review of the literature in which he identifies two different tensions within the literature: one is between the status of food availability decline (FAD) and entitlement analysis considered as hypotheses and as approaches; the other is between earlier and later, more sophisticated presentations of Sen's initiating position. On the first count, he considers that the entitlement literature has inevitably suffered from its intellectual origins, as being seen as an alternative to its alter ego, FAD. Suitably caricatured, FAD implies that, whatever has caused an acute decline in the supply of food, this is a necessary condition for famine to emerge. Put the other way around, in normal circumstances, a growing supply of food (relative to population) is sufficient to guarantee absence of famine. As the argument remains at the level of the aggregate supply of food, it does not address problems of distribution in any sense. Essentially, it presumes – without justification nor analysis at more disaggregated levels – that trickle-down advantages accrue to the vulnerable from whatever increases the aggregate supply of food.

Osmani's meticulously careful discussion essentially comes to the conclusion that, possibly understandably, misinterpretations of Sen have arisen in the past as a consequence of Sen's wish to rebut the FAD theory of famine, with its inevitable dependence upon aggregate falls in the supply of food. However, on the second count, Sen has contributed an *approach* to famine. As such, it allows for no hypotheses, or causal hostages to empirical fortune but, rather, incorporates FAD as a hypothesis as a special case.[18] Accordingly, the entitlement approach is not an alternative hypothesis to FAD in which, for example, increased inequality in the distribution of the same, or even more, food is seen as the cause of famine. Sen's contribution is to provide an approach to, not a theory or hypothesis about, famine. Consequently, for expositional purposes, it might have been better if FAD, whether interpreted as approach or hypothesis, had not been the intellectual point of departure for Sen's approach. Indeed, Osmani contends that, as a result of its generality, the entitlement approach is able to incorporate a range of explanatory factors that may or may not have been overlooked by Sen himself but which cannot, thereby, be taken as indicative of fallacy or inadequacy of the entitlement approach, as argued by many of its critics.

There is much agreement between Osmani and the present contribution in terms of his assessment of the evolution of the entitlement approach. His

---

18   Thus, Osmani would presumably disagree with Swift's (1993) assessment that only Sen has inspired any worthwhile *theory* of famine.

position, however, in distinguishing between approach and hypothesis, and in emphasising the former of the two as attached to entitlements, is profoundly methodological in content. As will be shown, in this respect, he is less careful and more superficial in his discussion in sharp contrast to the main thrust of his argument which is painstaking. Often relying upon questionable, even erroneous and inconsistent methodological assertions, he seems to overlook that differences in method are as contested as approaches to famines themselves, and that this may inform the debates over the entitlement approach as much as the misunderstandings and tensions that he suggests. Indeed, not surprisingly, it is precisely in the context of method that different emphases in the tension between macro and micro analyses are heavily involved. This is the basis in this Chapter for suggesting a different interpretation of the literature, that it reflects tension between pitching analysis at the micro and macro levels.[19] Further, Osmani's own stance is a perfect illustration of this micro/macro tension and of the alternative, or even complementary, assessment of the literature offered here. Thanks to the strengths in his expositional clarity and synthesis, his contribution will frequently be referenced in what follows, even if critically, in order to clarify sharply the alternative approach to the literature offered here.[20]

3   Is the Entitlement Approach Micro or Macro?

3.1   *Establishing Entitlements?*

The entitlement approach is unambiguously microeconomic in being built upon the modern technical apparatus attached to the general equilibrium theory of neoclassical economics, both in form and *initial* content. For Osmani, p. 267:

> It requires us to undertake a detailed and disaggregated study of how the
> supply side, as well as the demand side, affects the endowment sets and

---

19   Previously, Woldemeskel (1990) has considered that Sen has a demand-based account which moves the discussion of famine from a macro- to a micro-level.

20   Osmani's contribution, whilst not receiving his formal blessing, might be thought to be a fair representation of Sen's own views, less because it appears in a *Festschrift* honouring him and more because it has been commented upon by Sen, even if with the usual disclaimers, and is most supportive of his position. Below, unless otherwise indicated, reference will be to Osmani (1995).

entitlement mappings of different people ... In short, the entitlement approach calls for the use of the general equilibrium method.

It starts with the endowments of the "individual", although there is potential ambiguity around the level of disaggregation – whether it be to the household or to genuine individuals. Osmani observes, p. 254:[21]

> The basic unit of analysis is an individual person. For practical purposes, however, the analysis can also be conducted at collective levels such as household, group, or class by using the standard device of assuming a 'representative individual'.

Dependent upon the shifting marketability of these initial endowments and the terms of trade, the individual endowment may not provide for a non-starvation (exchange) entitlement. Consequently, the entitlement approach is concerned with the micro(-economic) capability for survival.

This immediately places into question what is meant by a famine, since it is plainly social in character, something other than a number of individual cases of starvation. As Sen (1981, p. 39) himself observes, "famines imply starvation, but not vice versa", but the highly common "'regular' starvation has to be distinguished from violent outbursts of famines". Famine would appear to involve geographical and chronological concentrations of death in which social arrangements, broadly conceived, for individual food availability have failed, Osmani, p. 256:

> A *famine* occurs when a large number of people within a community suffer from such entitlement failures at the same time.

Even at the starting point, then, in the definition of famine itself, a tension between macro and micro emerges. Just as a war or a battle within a war cannot be interpreted as a large number of individuals engaged in single-handed combat, so famine is not simply large numbers of deaths by starvation. To elaborate a definition in more detail, however, is impossible without straying into causal factors, something which might be considered to violate the entitlement approach which requires inadequate entitlement to food to be identified prior

---

21   This already raises a tension in the compatibility between macro and micro analysis with methodological implications, since many would eschew, for example, the notion of class as a 'representative individual'. Indeed, the intent of the latter concept is to avoid macro analysis other than by treating it as equivalent to relations between individuals.

to its causes. For the approach defines famine as individual deaths in order to be able to explain this outcome by generalised individual entitlement failure.[22]

More nuanced definitions of famine seek to locate it in a much broader context, thereby eschewing generalities. Devereux (1993a, p. 19), for example, after a careful review of the literature, resorts to the notion of an insider definition:

> Famine victims, who have a broader and subtler conception of famine than do outside observers, must be consulted if a precise and, above all, useful definition is to be found. The views of famine 'insiders' are worth incomparably more than those of textbooks and dictionaries.

To employ postmodernist vernacular, this implies that the notion of famine is socially constructed in meaning and cannot be reduced to objective numbers of individual deaths by starvation. More specifically, Dyson's (1993) appeal for careful and more broadly-cast empirical analysis of the incidence of the demography of famine is based on the suggestion that falls in food entitlements lead to a redistribution of deaths by time and place (seasonally and through migration) as well as affecting fertility.[23] He can conclude, p. 25, "It is clear that excess mortality is not an inevitable component of famine".

Even putting aside these conundrums, it is important to note how rapidly the analysis moves from the level of individuals to representative individuals and how the notion of entitlement is broadened to incorporate other forms of generating entitlement than through the market exchange of endowments alone. Sen (1981, p. 159) refers to a relation between people and food in terms of a "network of entitlement *relations*", emphasis added to highlight a profoundly social concept. He specifically includes rewards to labour in various forms, own production, inheritance or the transfer of assets, and the social security net provided by the welfare system (which may incorporate a famine relief component). As Sen recognises, this does entail limitations in terms of both ambiguities and scope of definitions of entitlements, p. 48 forward, such as the

---

22   See also Macrae and Zwi (1994, p. 7) who surmise from the literature, "Definitions which identify famine with widespread starvation deaths conceptualise famine as an enviro-economic event culminating in an *individual* biological crisis, and that this ignores the essentially *social* nature of the disaster." (emphasis added).

23   Nor is the relationship between famine and mortality even positive (Dyson, 1993, p. 25), "The sometime role of drought in triggering famine but actually improving mortality, and conversely rainfall in breaking famine but actually raising death rates, deserves particular emphasis in view of the special prominence of malaria throughout much of Africa today." See also Seaman (1993) for a discussion of the complex relationship between famine and the causes and incidence of mortality.

fact that property rights may not be well-defined and, thereby, open to conflict, and property rights may not be observed in practice because of illegality (looting or riots) or exercise of violence. As will become apparent, the ambiguity in property rights is not resolved by pressing legitimacy into service as a criterion; it does not necessarily help us to identify entitlements in practice, nor shifts in the distribution of property rights as opposed to shifts in the nature of those rights themselves.[24]

Now much of the literature has played, often implicitly, upon the potential ambiguity in the definition of entitlements. Sen is perceived to have relied upon too limited a scope in the definition of endowments and in the transformation of endowments into entitlements, the so-called E-mapping. Particular attention has been paid to Sen's central concern with legally sanctioned access to entitlements, and how this is undermined by a variety of other means of access to food. There are five separate issues, or distinctions, involved here, although they overlap and each is complex and multi-faceted.

First, as has been at least implicitly recognised in the literature, and explicitly by Osmani, the entitlement approach involves a division between those entitlements that are included (often the legitimate, for example) and those that are not. The boundary between the two can be moved, especially to generalise the approach by incorporating more factors. This constitutes one plank in Osmani's case for the generality of the entitlement approach and of its being robust against criticisms of excluding various considerations.

The second distinction, however, is between what is endogenous and what is exogenous. As an approach, the entitlement framework does not have to provide a definitive and fixed position on this division, although it often does so in practice. But it is not neutral on the matter. For, in examining individual entitlements, there is the need to take many factors as exogenous, certainly to the individual if not always in aggregate (if taken as the sum of individual behaviour). Yet, to define individual entitlements, the macro framework must be given even if, drawing upon the first distinction, the more factors that are taken into account in defining entitlements, the broader is the potential scope of the endogenous at the expense of the exogenous.

The third distinction concerns the micro/macro division itself. For many of the factors that are taken into account and/or as exogenous are macro or social factors. Fourth, there is the division between proximate and more fundamental causal factors, between the immediate reasons for lack of entitlement and

---

24 This is especially important if famine is seen as due to sudden shifts in entitlement arrangements, rather than in the entitlements themselves, as discussed in Devereux (1993a, p. 79) for example.

deeper explanations which, once again, tend to lean away from the individual and towards the social (and historical). A closely related but separate fifth distinction is one of chronology or the presumed association of proximate with short-term as opposed to long-term factors.

Shifting the boundaries in the entitlement literature has, for example, been captured in the literature through critical reference to the passivity characteristic of the victims of famine in Sen's analysis (de Waal, 1990; Duffield, 1993; and Watts, 1991). More generally, shifting the boundaries around, and undermining the notion of entitlement, has been prompted by the notion of 'coping' strategies. This is an unfortunately inappropriate term since it conjures up the image of the latter-day, working class housewife attempting to eke out a living for her family on an inadequate wage or share of wage. In practice, however, the entitlement literature has given a content to the notion of coping that strays far from individual or household 'making-do' in strained circumstances and is highly social.

Swift (1993), for example, refers to "local collective coping" and provides a box distinguishing between "African" and "Indian" models of food security drawing upon differences in local redistribution, moral economy, civil society and armed conflict, quite apart from formal anti-famine policies, food production and availability, infrastructure, and implementation capabilities of government and NGOs. Adams (1993) also refers to the moral economy of Mali in terms of its social practices and institutions. Devereux (1993b) identifies a number of coping strategies, although more along the lines of smoothing consumption over time even to the point of starvation to guarantee community survival (on which see later).[25] In short, as Davies (1993) suggests in her abstract:

> There is a tendency for 'coping strategies' to become a shorthand for a complex web of processes at work, making for great confusion in identifying what is being talked about.

---

25   See also Devereux and Naerra (1996) for a discussion of Namibia, where coping strategies are perceived in terms of shifting diet (to include reliance upon wild foods) as well as shifting demographics. For Duffield (1994, p. 51), apart from reducing food consumption, "coping strategies can involve labour migration, petty trading, the accumulation of debt, gathering wild foodstuffs and, as a last resort, the sale or pledging of such subsistence assets as livestock, land or jewellery, often at rock-bottom prices." Note that Jaspars and Young (1995) find that the children of the wealthy can be as malnourished as those of the poor if wealth is in the form of illiquid assets.

At the extreme, coping is confronted by conditions which are deliberately and socially engineered to undermine entitlement. As Duffield (1993) observes, the underlying entitlement relationship can even be one of the deliberate extermination of opponents, in part through famine, with the conscious exercise of power to gain advantage. It is worth briefly dwelling upon the extensive war and famine literature because both empirically and analytically, it has been perceived to be the weak point of the entitlement approach. The empirical grounds are simple enough. The incidence of recent famines, especially in Africa, have been almost exclusively associated with wars.[26] From this, however, it is often presumed that the entitlement approach simply fails, as in Solway (1994) for example. But why should this be so, especially if the boundaries of what constitutes entitlement are broadened sufficiently?

The answer is not, then, to be considered in the range of factors incorporated but in their incompatibility with the individualistic element within the entitlement approach. Thus, relative to the entitlement approach, the analytical problems posed by war are not simply the disruption of agricultural production, local economies, trade and aid, and the creation of new patterns of demand for food and refugees, as suggested by Devereux (1993b). Rather, as for Keen (1994), famine can be deployed as a weapon of war to benefit the economic and political position of some groups at the expense of others, the continuation and intensification of longstanding conflicts over resources. It reflects the political making of markets rather than their failure through differential access, often officially sanctioned by force as in cattle raiding.[27]

Nonetheless, war only serves to bring out in sharp form the social content of famine that is irreducible to individual entitlements. Violence or coercion more generally can be attached to famine or hunger, not least in intra-household distribution. For Patnaik's (1991) analysis of India, famine is immanent as a result of long-term and uneven patterns in the creation and extraction of agricultural surplus, whether to benefit pre-independence Britain or post-independence industrialisation and urbanisation. Similarly, the distinction between long-run

---

26 See also Macrae and Zwi (eds) (1994), Keen (1994), Gasper (1993), de Waal (1990 and 1993), Nolan (1993), Watts (1991) and Bush (1996).

27 See Keen (1994, pp. 119–21) for an account for Southwestern Sudan with cattle prices moving dramatically and locally against owners forced into starvation selling. Keen notes parallels with Sudan with famine as weapon benefitting some at the expense of others for 1983–85, Ethiopia (cattle raiding, perverse beneficiaries in relief relative to need and migration), 1967–70 Nigeria/Biafra (ditto), 1968–73 Sahel (incidence amongst nomadics), 1845–89 Ireland (landlord clearances), 1932–34 Ukraine (targeting of wealthy), and 1992 Somalia (as consequence of elite in-fighting).

and short-run factors, often closely associated with systemic as opposed to proximate, is indicative of the tension between macro and micro.

Apparently more mundane than war or systemic tendencies and structures, but potentially important in defining the boundaries of entitlements if food relief is considered as an entitlement or part of the E-mapping, is the availability of transport or infrastructure more generally. If this extension of entitlements is sufficiently widely interpreted, it can incorporate the freedom of the media (which is perceived to act as a stimulus to government action)[28] or the choices enshrined in deep-rooted institutional, religious and cultural practices as suggested by Woldemeskel (1990). Gore (1993) pursues this line furthest, suggesting that, "command over commodities depends upon something more than legal rights", p. 433. He is particularly concerned with social mores which may constrain or promote entitlements in practice, irrespective of their ideological role, suggesting that Sen, "underestimates the role of socially enforced moral rules in constraining and enabling command over commodities", p. 443. Thus, food riots can be a legitimate, if not legal, form of access to entitlement.[29] Gore concludes that Sen's approach is helpful as a starting point for "extended entitlement analysis" only if it recognises how legal rules work out in practice, taking account of their interplay with socially-enforced mores which might lie outside the law.

Now Sen's initial contributions were already capable of incorporating an extension in the scope of factors influencing ultimate entitlement. The extended entitlement mapping adds to exchange entitlement in as many ways as are specified, irrespective of the ones specified by Sen himself and irrespective of whether these are the most important ones for famine in general or for the famines that he considers himself. This, then, is not the main point to be emphasised here. Rather, as observed above, the greater the number of forms of entitlement that are specified, the more the individualistic basis for defining, or analysing, entitlements is undermined. This is partly because the non-exchange forms of entitlement tend to be social in character – as in the welfare system, let alone food riots and moral economy. In addition, the interaction between the various components of extended entitlements renders their definition at the level of the individual (household) not so much ambiguous as impossible. A weapon, for example, is an endowment that has an exchange value with an equivalent in food; but it can also gain a purchase on access to food through (collective) violence as well as redefine property rights and

28   See Ram (1990).
29   See Serulnikov (1994).

ownership, but only contingent upon the shifting social conditions in which it is wielded.

Thus, whatever the scope of entitlement analysis, it depends analytically upon a structural separation between the individual's characteristics (including marketable endowments and other sources of entitlement) and the social mechanisms, market or otherwise, that provide for an extended entitlement mapping. In general, the network of entitlement relations and the individual entitlements within them cannot be defined independently of one another. It seems that the model for this analytical construction is taken from neoclassical microeconomics, in which well-defined assets are marketable at externally given conditions (which may or may not be perfectly competitive). Even there, the separation between the ownership and nature of property rights is questionable given the ambiguity over the definition of property rights. It is all the more so in the presence of other forms of entitlement.

In short, at the micro level, entitlements are attached to individuals through a generalisation of the exchange economy to include legal individual entitlements but to preclude socially determined entitlements which tend erroneously to be identified with illegality (or is it illegitimacy). Consequently, for Osmani, p. 255:

> The transfer component includes only those transfers to which a person is legally entitled – for example, social security provisions of the state. This leaves out not only illegal transfers (such as stealing and looting), but also non-entitlement transfers, such as charity ... The general point is that entitlement analysis is concerned with legal as distinct from moral entitlement.

Osmani presents this as a matter of *definition*, following logically from the conceptual apparatus employed, p. 256:

> Since the entitlement set is derived by applying E-mapping on the endowment set, it is only through changes in either endowment of E-mapping that any change in entitlement can occur. Note that this is not a theory or a hypothesis, but simply a logical implication of the definitions. It then follows that 'entitlement failure', and thus famine, can occur only through some adverse change in either endowment or E-mapping or both.

However, the simple *causal* structure from endowments and E-mapping to entitlements that results is not as neutral a conceptual framework as Osmani appears to suggest.[30] It pre-empts the socioeconomic processes by which endowments are created and in which entitlements play a causal role – you cannot participate other than passively in the endowment/E-mapping process if you are starving or you may seek to shatter the E-mapping through a (necessarily collective) food riot!

This is not to suggest that entitlement outcomes fail to materialise. Rather, they cannot be understood without confronting the tension between the social and individual specification of the entitlement process, in which the exercise of socially determined power is crucial. Whilst extra-entitlement action and exercise of power might be undertaken by the individually deprived, it is also the source of collective action that renders problematic the dichotomy between entitlement relations and individual entitlements.

Now, Osmani tends to treat contributions breaching the boundaries of the entitlement approach as extending the list of factors to be incorporated, as representing concern with the dynamics of famine, or as lying outside the scope of the approach. Some of these points will be taken up later, but a different interpretation has been offered here. It is that the micro-foundations of the entitlement approach are to be rejected because of their inability to address satisfactorily the social relations and structures through which famines are fundamentally caused.

3.2   Classes, Value and Economic Theory

So far, the tension between micro and macro within the entitlement approach has been addressed in terms of the definition of entitlements. A second form of the tension between micro and macro, already present in Sen's account at the outset, centres around the economic theory to be employed. As previously observed, the technical analytical structure around entitlement draws its inspiration from the microeconomics associated with neoclassical general equilibrium theory. It does examine the conditions under which an *individual* choice set includes an entitlement that avoids starvation. In order to address famine, however, this account is immediately translated into the incidence

---

30   Since famine might be considered as a 'market failure' in distributional and/or Pareto-efficiency terms, there does seem to be a parallel between Osmani's method and the use of an explanation based on market failure. But, unless tautological, this notion is deeply embedded within an explanatory framework in which market success (Pareto-efficient and equitable general equilibrium?) is taken as central even if by way of departure. Despite its logic, many of us would be reluctant to view the world as market failure in the sense of deviation from a perfectly competitive general equilibrium. The point is that an approach is not conceptually nor causally neutral even if it only proceeds as far as definitions.

of entitlement failure within *social* classes. Thus, "the exchange entitlements faced by a person depend, naturally, on his position in the economic class structure as well as the modes of production in the country" (Sen, 1981, p. 4).[31] Here, then, there is a clear marriage between the micro-foundations of choice theory and the macro-foundations of the theory of classes and of modes of production. That this involves a tension does not seem to be recognised nor to be addressed. For, if the macro-analysis organised around classes is to be endowed with analytical priority, it is not apparent why the entitlement apparatus should be the analytical starting point. And, vice-versa, with the entitlement approach as the starting point, their social determinants appear to be exogenously imposed.

There is no doubt that Sen's stance is one in which the social determinants of entitlements are of considerable importance. This is in part reflected in his reference to classes and modes of production, but it is also a consequence of the appeal for a grounding in classical political economy even if on rather different grounds. For, as in Drèze and Sen (1990a, p. 2), the political economy of hunger needs to be addressed not only from economic perspectives but also from those of political, social, and cultural influences on economic matters. This should not, however, blind us to the yawning analytical gap that remains between such social determinants of entitlements and their realisation at the individual level.

The simplest way to bridge that gap is to treat classes as reducible to individual representatives. Then, shifting entitlements can be analysed in terms of changing market opportunities (employment, trade, terms of trade, distribution etc) and re-distributional measures adopted by the state. This is characteristic, for example, of the illustrative models of exchange entitlement given in Appendix B of Sen (1981).[32] What these models have in common is a simple demand analysis on the basis of the class analysis, with equilibrium determined by given (short-run) supply. In the range of studies collected in Drèze and Sen (1989a–c), similar, if more complex, procedures tend to be adopted around supply and demand, with limited direct reliance upon, and without analytical development of, the entitlement approach. Rather, supply- and demand-side factors are worked together to suggest empirical or theoretical outcomes, whether these factors are pitched at the traditional level of microeconomics or, as is more usual, at the institutional or social level.

---

31   See also Sen (1981, p. 170).

32   One is of Malthus on the Poor Laws and the price of corn, and involves two representative classes, and the other is of the Bengali famine with five classes.

It is in this context, that the tension between micro and macro analysis is sharpest in Osmani's account. For he exhibits a profound confusion between the abstract, the general and the level of aggregation. As already seen, the analytical starting point is pitched at the level of individual entitlements. But this is generalised to the representative individual as a proxy for class. Consequently, this has nothing to do with more or less abstract levels of analysis, since it is simply the same level generalised, with greater or lesser empirical accuracy, across more or less similar individuals. Nonetheless, Osmani believes that he has ascended to a higher level of analysis comparable to the Marxist theory of class and its attachment to the concept of mode of production, p. 268. By analogy, it is then argued that "endowment and entitlement may be expressed as single ideas at the *highest level of abstraction*" and then disaggregation to different classes or fractions of classes will represent a lower level once again since they may have different entitlements and "what is a 'single idea' at the highest level of abstraction may need to be differentiated at a lower level".

In a sense, there is only one level of abstraction in Osmani's approach – it is at the level of the individual. This can be generalised to class or whatever as the representative individual but a different level of abstract analysis is hardly created by then disaggregating what has previously been aggregated. In another sense, though, the aggregate analysis can take on a life of its own, as a class analysis, with and at a higher level of abstraction. But this logically requires analytical and causal priority over what has previously been pitched at the level of aggregated individual entitlements. Osmani appears to hop between these positions and, as such, provides an excellent illustration of what is a general feature of the literature – the tension between micro and macro, especially where the micro is taken as starting point as in the entitlement approach.

The point being covered here can be put in another way. Despite its combining the microeconomic formulation of entitlements and the socioeconomic determinants of classical political economy, the entitlement approach does not incorporate an economic theory which would force a compromise or choice between the two levels of analysis. If neoclassical theory were chosen, then the social determinants could simply be taken as exogenous, and outcomes determined by the aggregated behaviour of individuals on the basis of their entitlements.[33] On the other hand, if value theory is selected from classical political economy, the analytical framework is entirely different from a focus upon supply and demand however determined. For Smith, agriculture is subject to rent

---

33   Of course, this does not necessarily imply full and efficient, let alone equitable, employment of resources – but it does require that the social constraints be consistent with the aggregation over individuals.

in part determined by absolute fertility and to accumulation governed by the growing division of labour and the constraints imposed by the extent of the market. For Ricardo, value is determined separately in agriculture and industry, with differential rent arising at the margin of cultivation and rising along with the value of corn and the value of wages, as accumulation leads to the use of ever-worsening land. And, for Marx, value is the outcome of contradictory pressures to increase the production of surplus value and to realise it as productivity decreases values, with rent arising out of the obstacles imposed on capital accumulation, or not, by landed property.[34] Whatever the merits and scope of application of these interpretations of classical political economy, they do serve to illustrate that the resolution of the tension between micro and macro levels in providing a political economy of hunger requires a value theory that goes beyond supply and demand, even if still determining factor incomes, price of food, etc. This is not simply, nor primarily, a means by which to establish the exchange entitlements of individuals, by determining the size and value of their endowments. Rather, value theory, even in its neoclassical version by default, specifies the economic mechanisms by which social determinants give rise to individual or class-based entitlement outcomes.[35]

3.3   *Approach and Method*

To some extent, these observations may have been anticipated by Sen (1981, p. 162) in his claim that, "the entitlement approach provides a general framework for analysing famines rather than one particular hypothesis about their causation". The selection of the term "approach" rather than "theory" appears to be judicious, possibly reflecting tensions in method as much as those around approach versus hypothesis as in Osmani's interpretation. But it has led subsequent commentators to question the extent of causal content

---

34   These drastic summaries are elaborated at greater length in Fine (1982).

35   Osmani, p. 268, appears to propose "a general equilibrium analysis of the various forces affecting the disaggregated entitlement of different social classes". Apart from the previously observed confusion over whether abstraction allows you to have both social classes (except as a rough approximation through representative individuals) and general equilibrium, this would seem to indicate a preference in his case for neoclassical theory. Note also, a point to be taken up briefly later, that the notion of "various forces" has surreptitiously been introduced. This once again represents a tension between the micro and the macro for either they are the aggregated effects of individuals as in most general equilibrium in which case they are derivative and do not determine, or they are logically prior and negate the entitlement's micro foundations. It is also particularly bizarre that the term "equilibrium" should ever be used in the context of famine. This is indicative of a bias towards the micro in Osmani's unresolved tension with the macro.

within entitlement theory. Osmani (1991) suggests that the approach is merely confined to the proximate causes of famine and distinguishes these from the dynamics and longer-term factors, themes taken up in his later contribution. De Waal (1990 and 1991) questions whether proximate causes can be defined and analysed independently of dynamics and how the meaning of famines is defined. He rejects the notion of famine which is confined to short-term and acute deprivation of staple foods, focusing instead upon historical processes leading to vulnerability, the inextricable link between starvation and the disease environment,[36] and the choice of vulnerability to acute hunger as a means to retain assets for preserving a particular way of life (refusal to sell or consume cattle). For Gray and Kevane (1993), famine is not an event, separated from the historical processes that create it. To treat it as such is liable to lead to relief that is both too little and too late. De Waal ultimately either questions the empirical validity of the entitlement approach or the extent to which it provides an explanation at all beyond a descriptive account around a potentially unlimited set of factors determining generalised starvation entitlements.[37] Rangasami (1985) also dismisses the view of famine as an historical episode or aberration, understanding starvation as a long-drawn process, in which socioeconomic and biological factors are integrated with one another.

The issue of micro/macro tension has then emerged in the literature, if indirectly at times. The extent of explanatory content has been addressed through questioning the adequacy of the scope of variables included, as previously discussed, the relationship between longer-term factors and the proximate incidence of famine, especially given limited historical perspectives which structure the conditions which precipitate famine (initial endowments and entitlements, for example), and the connection between under-nutrition, starvation, famine and other factors in morbidity. Inevitably, these considerations tend to put the entitlement approach on the defensive and to limit its analytical claims. For Sen (1981, p. 164), there is only a "very *general* hypothesis underlying the approach, which is subject to empirical testing. It will be violated if starvation in famines is shown to arise not from entitlement failures but either from choice characteristics (e.g. people refusing to eat unfamiliar food which they are in a position to buy, or people refusing to work), or from non-entitlement transfers (e.g. looting)".[38] This is obviously a very weak claim,

---

36   This is acknowledged from within the entitlement approach by Dasgupta and Ray (1990) and Osmani (1990).

37   See also Mitra (1982).

38   This quote does tend to support the extent to which Sen attaches famine to starvation (rather than to the influence of under-nutrition upon morbidity), a focus on exchange

and involves an admission that the approach is not well-suited to analysing the role of violence and war in prompting famine conditions – or looting or whatever in pre-empting them.

In contrast to the thrust, and criticisms, of the theoretical disclaimers attached to the entitlement approach, this Chapter argues that it has considerable analytical content because of the framework that it adopts. This has already been seen in the context of the unresolved tensions between the macro and micro levels. But this can be taken a little bit further, given that even a descriptive account or narrative draws upon some analytical structure both in terms of what it includes and excludes and in terms of the implicit, or even explicit, organisation of the intrinsic content. In particular, for the latter, the entitlement approach recognises the relationship between social causes and their socioeconomic incidence at the level of individual entitlements in a particular way.

For, in contrast to FAD, the entitlement approach is different not only in reaching down to more disaggregated levels than that of food supply as a whole but also in providing some discussion of how the two levels are connected with one another. It is most reasonably argued that there is many a slip twixt cup and lip when it comes to the access to, as opposed to the supply of, food. Hence, the emphasis on the lack of a necessary positive relationship between increasing supply of food and generalised security of entitlements to food. This can be so for three different general reasons. First, increases in the supply of food, for whatever reason, may directly lead to the reduction of entitlements for some groups – should it lead to a decline in exchange entitlements, for example, through changes in terms of trade or access to employment. Thus, an increase in supply might reduce prices and farmer revenues and their capacity to employ landless wage labour. Second, the same factors that cause supply of food to increase might independently cause exchange entitlements to fall for some groups. An economic boom might increase the demand for food, and hence food prices, proportionately more than the incomes of vulnerable groups. Third, the factors that cause food supply to increase might be associated directly with loss of exchange entitlements (although this is a special case of the first reason). Technological change may increase productivity and yields in agriculture, but at the expense of employment, for example.

These possibilities are illustrated in the diagram (Figure 1), although the connections indicated to entitlement do not necessarily have to be via the

---

entitlement, and the relative lack of importance of war and violence (although this does not follow logically from the entitlement approach).

route of changes in supply. Consider other causal factors connected to the level and distribution of entitlements. These might include technological progress, methods of financing and marketing, social provision whether for production (infrastructure, extension services etc) or for consumption (welfare), conditions governing employment and access to land, etc. Each of these factors can be addressed at different levels of disaggregation from within the household "upwards", over shorter or longer periods of time, and with more or less attention to the connections with other variables. Thus, the potential role for an independent media in highlighting famine and acting as a check upon otherwise irresponsible or inactive government does it itself pre-suppose a sufficiently independent relationship between the government and the media. If, government is itself pursuing a policy of repression which induces starvation, it is liable to adopt a correspondingly tight control over the media.

More generally, adopting the same logic as in the penultimate paragraph where the focus was upon food supply, it follows that variables can be ordered according to whether they affect food consumption directly or indirectly and, for the latter, through the intermediate step of entitlement or not. Of course, the entitlement route is necessary if its definition is broadened sufficiently (e.g. to include non-legal mechanisms), and all of the routes can materialise simultaneously. This is in part the attraction of the entitlement approach. For mechanisms that increase food supply (or other factors generally favourable to consumption), and hence overall entitlements in aggregate, may simultaneously undermine them for some sections of the population through shifting terms of trade, access to employment, distribution, social provision, and so forth.

For those who remain staunch defenders of the FAD hypothesis, the counteracting mechanisms must be overlooked or be perceived to be too weak to

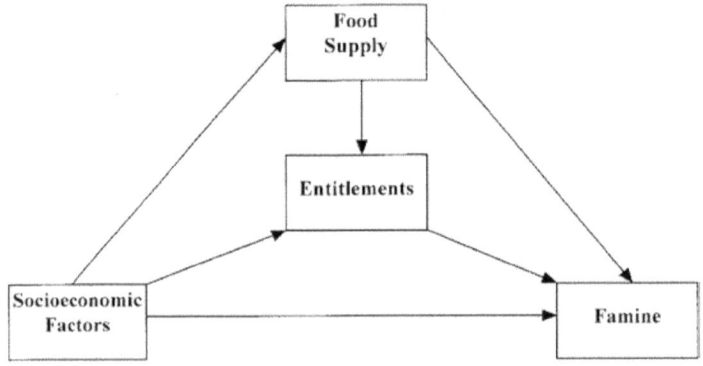

FIGURE 1   Structuring entitlement

dominate the beneficial effects of an increase in food supply. To some extent this is an empirical question but it is indefensible as a general hypothesis. Nonetheless, those adopting a critical stance to the entitlement approach *and* to FAD emphasise that the more common outcome is for the mechanisms raising food supply, at different levels of disaggregation, not to be counteracted by loss of entitlements, especially as increasing food supply, often on the basis of national agricultural development, is to be associated with industrialisation.[39] Whilst such considerations remain consistent with the entitlement approach, the latter is criticised for having, however innocently, discouraged recognition of how important is raising food supply in line with population growth and the dictates of economic development (provision of surplus for urbanisation and industrialisation).

Many of the points covered in this section are recognised by Osmani in distinguishing the FAD and entitlement approaches and hypotheses, and in his supporting the entitlement approach as including the FAD hypothesis as a special case. This overlooks, however, a *methodological* aspect of the FAD approach which, whatever its specific merits, distinguishes it from the entitlement approach. In focusing on food supply in aggregate as the likely cause of famine, FAD potentially addresses the socioeconomic causes at the macro level and is, to that extent, concerned with famine-susceptibility and not with its realisation and incidence. Not surprisingly, by way of contrast, Osmani places heavy emphasis upon the merits of the entitlement approach as against the FAD in confronting the plurality of causes and the asymmetry of disaggregated impact. But the critics of the entitlement approach[40] can be interpreted not only, as in Osmani, as broadening the range of causal factors but also in adopting a different method pitched more at the macro-level which, like FAD, is concerned to discover the causes of famine-susceptibility prior to the proximate events that trigger and distribute its incidence.

A different point concerns the way in which the various socioeconomic mechanisms are analytically organised. At the formal level of individual entitlements, a clear distinction is made between those that arise through the market (exchange-entitlements) and those that do not (the wider network of entitlement relations). This can then lead to a discussion of the adequacy or not of exchange entitlements and how they may be subject to acute failure. Thus, the market mechanism, especially if not working perfectly in the Walrasian sense or if skewing distribution against the impoverished, can generate loss of

---

39   See especially Nolan and Sender (1992) and Nolan (1993).

40   And not all of them or even a majority are supportive of FAD.

entitlements through adverse movements in terms of trade, employment and income redistribution.

The initial separation between exchange and other forms of entitlement is then replicated at the level of outcomes. To some extent, there seems to be a presumption that non-exchange entitlements are liable to be more stable (especially with the exclusion of the illegal, etc). Consequently, at the policy level, in dealing with famine, government or other agencies are required to make up for the deficiencies in exchange entitlements (although not necessarily in the direct provision of food, with some preference for income transfers or, less directly, employment creation).[41]

Thus, the entitlement approach has been based upon a traditional analytical dichotomy between the economic (market-exchange) and the non-economic, and an equally traditional notion that the non-economic should correct for the failures of the economic. This is so even though, unlike orthodox economics, a fuller account is taken of non-economic factors and their interaction with the economic (hence appeals to the traditions of classical political economy). Much of the literature critical of the exchange entitlement approach, but not from a FAD perspective, can be interpreted as having implicitly rejected this dichotomy between exchange and other forms of entitlement, at whatever level of disaggregation they are determined. For the issues of power and class, for example, cut across such divisions. Both the market and the state (and, indeed, the household) are different forms in which economic and political interests are expressed and fought out. It might be more appropriate to identify these underlying interests, and then their political and ideological counterparts, prior to the definition of the different forms of entitlements which are their outcome.

In short, if underlying class and property relations are a cause of famine through entitlement failure, then these relations have to be examined as such rather than as the source of *individual* attachment to entitlements. For otherwise, even if state power only imperfectly reflects underlying socioeconomic interests, it may necessarily reinforce the lack of entitlements, rather than ameliorate them, as a reflection of the system of property relations of which it is itself derivative.

This discussion once again highlights the analytical structure involved in the entitlement approach. It can be interpreted as suggesting that causes of famine, whether proximate or not, are to be filtered through their impact upon entitlements. This demonstrates how an analytical structure of the type

---

41   Direct provision of food may undermine the prices of domestic producers and traders.

represented in the diagram is not causally neutral. It involves the privileging of certain lines of causation even where they are increasingly unsuitable to bear the weight and complexity of causal relations that are thrust upon them. This is so irrespective of where the boundaries are drawn in defining entitlements, with the corresponding causal content or theory left open without being specified. For the entitlement approach explanatory factors are necessarily filtered through the analytical framework provided by the microeconomics of individual entitlements.[42]

Is this all a problem for the entitlement approach? This is exactly the way in which much of the critical commentary previously outlined can be interpreted. Consider, for example, the level of disaggregation. This is already problematic in Sen's account with a compromise usually being made at the level of the household. This leaves open the possibility of delving deeper into intrahousehold distribution but also of aiming at higher levels, such as the nation as in Kanbur (1990). Sen and Drèze (1990a, p. 4) explicitly guard against such an approach, advising:

> The analysis of hunger has to be, ultimately, thoroughly disaggregative, and the food entitlements of regions and countries cannot by themselves tell us whether many people will go hungry and who they will be. But between the extreme aggregation of global food analysis ... and the totally disaggregated picture of the entitlements of families and individuals, there is an important intermediate focal point of regional and country-specific food entitlements.

However, once other factors determining access to food are introduced, it becomes increasingly questionable whether they should be filtered through the appropriately disaggregated level of analysis.

In fact, the level at which to pitch analysis of entitlement has to be determined, and it may shift across time and across classes. Where famine conditions arise, the household unit itself may become endogenous. The same is true of other institutional forms, not least communities and even nation-states or regional entities in times of war and migration. In other words, the very same processes that are intended to provide the underlying determinants of entitlements at the household or other levels may themselves undermine the solidity of these forms of access to food. Further, the ground that has previously been covered in terms of the tension between macro and micro level

---

42   For such filtering, see also Swift (1993).

analysis (together with their constituent components) and the ambiguity over the definitions of endowments and entitlements raise exactly the same issues concerning the appropriate analytical structure both for defining and providing a causal examination of famine.

To some extent, the commentary here would appear to have been anticipated by Von Braun et al. (1993). They argue that, "the study of famine must integrate institutional, political, market, and production spheres, at both macro- and micro-levels", p. 73. The short term must be related to the secular. Further, they suggest that the entitlement approach should be interpreted as belonging to four different layers of analysis, with resources, war, population, etc at the top level, and the fourth, lowest layer, addressing entitlement failure and mortality.[43] The difference between the layers seems to be primarily determined by the extent of non-causal feedback mechanisms as the analytical descent is made. Endogenous are distinguished from exogenous factors, and causes from symptoms. Nonetheless, entitlement discourse can fruitfully be conducted both within levels and between them as linkages are specified between their constituent variables. Essentially, this can be considered to be an elaboration of the diagram offered here, throwing in more and more factors and layers to contain them, and such is provided by von Braun et al. (1993). Moreover, it is even suggested that the unresolved disputes within the literature reflect the lack of dialogue between contributions made at different levels of analysis.

This does not, however, resolve the tensions between micro- and macro-analysis; it merely intensifies them. For the allocation of factors at the different layers of analysis is essentially arbitrary and far from consistent (mortality and population, respectively belong to the lowest *and* highest levels). Why should some factors be endogenous and others exogenous? And, if the approach is attached to the notion of social reproduction, with or without famine, rather than to once and for all outcomes at the level of individual households, then the whole causal structure collapses as the lower levels, in turn, reproduce the higher levels.

---

43   For other approaches to famine and entitlement that proceed in terms of different layers or levels of analysis, see Young (1996), who moves from international to national and the state, to regional and minorities, and to the household, and Watts and Bohle (1993) who throw together a particular distribution of entitlements, how they are defined and won or lost, and the structured political economy of entitlements incorporating distribution, institutions and classes. Both writers see such layering as necessary for confronting the issue of power.

Again, these tensions are well-illustrated by Osmani's synthesis although he unwittingly adds a further dimension. As already seen, the notion of levels of abstraction are rendered chaotic in his account. In addition, he seeks to sustain the entitlement approach not only by broadening the scope of explanatory factors but also by compartmentalising them into backward linkages (history), forward linkages (intertemporal choice or entitlement constraints), and dynamics (contributory factors to mortality other than starvation). This is, however, to overlook the possible intent of those advancing such considerations as criticisms of the entitlement approach. For appeal to history, for example, is not simply to refer to the long run but to identify longstanding socioeconomic processes which *continue* to prevail and render famine-susceptibility. Similarly, choosing to starve in order to preserve social relations is an explicit recognition of how entitlements have and might continue to reproduce endowments rather than vice-versa. The same applies to the dynamics of famine and Osmani's apparent distinction between the dynamics and causes of famine as if the two were mutually exclusive. These are not debating points but demonstrate how the entitlement approach, with its micro roots in individual endowments is in tension with causal relations and dynamics at a macro level which tend to undermine that microeconomic analytical framework.

4   The Specificity of Food

These methodological conundrums are familiar across the social sciences, if less so within orthodox economics, for they concern the relationship between structures, relations, agency and outcomes. In this light, except for those adopting methodological individualism, the analytical privileging of the household in analysing famine appears to be both unusual and not to have been justified. For there are plenty of instances in which household characteristics can be analysed without necessarily descending to the level of the capabilities and choices of the households themselves (although this may be done in empirical investigations). This is true, for example, of demographic characteristics of the population, the nature and extent of democracy, etc. It is possible that a case could be made that food and famine in particular are different and must be understood at a highly disaggregated level. But this seems less plausible the broader the scope of (social) determinants and the longer the period over which causation is construed. The purpose of this section is to highlight a rather different feature of the entitlement literature than the micro/macro tension, the limited extent to which it has actually dealt with food.

Consider, for example, by way of comparison, theories of unemployment. There are some attractive parallels with famine, given that unemployment is endemic but only becomes critical in a deep recession. Of course, unemployment theory can be based on methodological individualism in the context of socioeconomic constraints such as levels of unemployment benefit. But there are healthy traditions within economics, Keynesian or otherwise, which view unemployment as a consequence of the workings of economic forces in the context of specific economic structures. For these, the individual incidence of unemployment is important but secondary. Indeed, as the lowest paid are often the worst hit, the approach based on representative individuals can be highly misleading. By the same token, the entitlement approach is effective in disputing the FAD approach but is not necessarily the appropriate starting point for explaining famine's social determinants.

More generally, the individual/social dichotomy is recognised across a range of socioeconomic phenomena. Durkheim's account of suicide, for example, was specifically designed to uncover population susceptibility as a consequence of the tensions of industrial society.[44] Closer to food issues, the eating disorders and western diseases of affluence – anorexia, bulimia, and obesity, and coronary heart disease, dental caries, and various cancers, etc, respectively – can scarcely be understood on the basis of an entitlement approach even though individual choice and responsibility do represent one ideological response to these conditions. Rather, and this is the form taken by the vast majority of the medical and psychological literature, a focus upon individuals as a starting point in terms of their physical and mental symptoms, is a barrier to developing a proper identification and understanding of the appropriate socioeconomic processes even when these are taken into account.[45]

Now it might be argued that these examples are unfair or inappropriate, even though the latter concerns food, since famine is *sui generis* and involves uniform and severe deprivation of a common character across a significant section of the population. This analytical case has not been made in the literature – that famine is different from other social dysfunctions and *must* be rooted in an entitlement approach. Nor is such an exception for famine notable for its presence in the analytical apparatus employed. As Osmani suggests, "there is also a great potential for applying this framework in the study of long-term endemic hunger", p. 292. By the same token, it could easily be extended to capabilities in general which have, significantly, been the focus of Sen's

---

44   See Turner (1987) for a discussion.

45   For an account of anorexia, see Fine (1995), and Fine (1998d) for eating disorders and western diseases of affluence more generally.

discussion of poverty. Clearly, for food, we could substitute housing, health, etc, and continue to work with the entitlement approach.[46]

This suggests the analysis could equally apply to any other aspect of subsistence. These all have a physiological relationship to one another and to the social relations under which they are constructed. But how they are socioeconomically structured is different from one element of subsistence to another, and this should be addressed since the housing, food and health systems are different from one another in their social characteristics – something which is overlooked by the individualistic element of the entitlement approach which is generalisable across all aspects of consumption. Elsewhere (Fine and Leopold, 1993; Fine, 1994a and b; Fine et al. 1996; and Fine 1998b,[47] it has been argued that the political economy of food is distinctive in that it does tend to be tied to a set of specific and integral structures and processes, which are open to transformation and which are characterised, without degenerating into biological determinism, by a particularly heavy dependence upon the "organic" nature of food. At one extreme in the food chain, it is literally consumed; and, at the other, it is dependent upon the biological processes attached to agriculture.

Each of these activities, and those in between, are structured in relationship to one another, and are governed by socioeconomic processes. Watts (1991) and Watts and Bohle (1993) seem to have gone furthest in recognising this in the entitlement literature,[48] although they gather a whole series of factors together incoherently under the (inconsistent) notion of structural tendencies – the fiscal crisis of the state, civil war, geo-political conflict and, most interestingly, the struggle between the forces of retention (self-provisioning) and the forces of extraction (commoditisation).[49] From the work on the political economy of food, the following set of underlying determinants can be suggested:

(1) Landed property must be addressed in terms of historically and socially specific conditions of access to the land (and not simply as an endowment) together with the associated class relations of production which determine how surplus is appropriated and subject to conflict.

---

46 See Sen (1985) for a more general analysis of capabilities and Gasper (1993) for implicitly observing how the generality of the entitlement approach lends it to be applied in areas other than food, such as the environment.

47 More recently, see Fine (2002a) and Bayliss and Fine (2021).

48 Watts seems to have dropped this approach as evidenced by his debate Watts (1994) with Fine (1994a and b).

49 Patnaik (1991) provides an account along these lines in the context of uneven development within India. See also Teubal (1992) on Argentine. He combines the entitlement approach with regulation theory and analysis of the agro-food system.

(2)   The shifting relationships between agricultural production and the food
        system as a whole must be specified, as these determine the possible
        displacement of surplus through the system (to landlords, usurers, mer-
        chants, food processors, the state, etc) quite apart from the immediate
        source of exchange entitlements in the more direct forms of employ-
        ment and terms of trade.

(3)   Tendencies within the food system must be identified, such as the
        'technological treadmill', which can have contradictory outcomes both
        by cheapening agricultural inputs and raising productivity and also by
        undermining the commercial viability and survival of some producers
        and employees. These processes need to be linked to differentiation and
        restructuring of class relations on the land.

(4)   The role of the state (and of violence), including international agencies
        and trade organisations and agreements, and of developments in inter-
        national commodity markets must also be analysed in terms of under-
        lying economic and political interests as well as the tendencies that
        accompany them (such as the increasing productivity in the supply of
        food grains and their use to source meat for high income consumption,
        and the growth of commercial export crops to feed increasingly varied
        and exotic tastes in the developed world in the face of transformations
        in the forms of retailing, transport and storage, and contracting). These
        factors should not be taken as exogenous.

(5)   The position of food in subsistence more generally needs to be
        addressed, together with the interaction with household formation
        with the latter understood as variable in both type and content.

This cursory list of determinants is not intended to be comprehensive nor is
there an implication that the factors concerned have been overlooked by the
entitlement approach literature. Rather, in the spirit of the approach itself, the
motivation is to uncover the underlying determinants of the levels and quality
of food consumption, even if not necessarily descending to the level of the
individual nor the analytical structure that this implies.

5   Concluding Remarks

Whatever its subsequent analytical content and evolution, the entitlement
approach was initially motivated by an antipathy to the FAD approach and a
wish to identify the proximate causes of famine so that remedial action could
be more readily and effectively adopted. Consequently, the broader scope of
analysis being suggested here might be thought to be an indulgent luxury in

face of the acute increase in death associated with famine. Better to fix than to understand. However, there can be no guarantee that the policies proposed from the entitlement approach will be adopted, implemented and prove effective if the deeper factors underlying the political economy of hunger have not been identified.

What, then, is the analytical role of the entitlement approach, given that some embrace it fully or with modification whilst others cast it aside altogether? Because the approach explicitly directs itself at addressing the proximate causes of famine from which further hypotheses can be developed, this is how it should be understood. It is a mode of *investigation* and, in addition, may prove an effective mode of exposition depending upon the audience and issue to be addressed (e.g. combatting FAD).[50] What it is not is a structured and socially and historically rooted causal analysis. This can only be provided after analytical investigation has been undertaken. Following this, it is unlikely that the individualistic content of the entitlement approach would be retained. This seems to be accepted by Osmani who concludes that, p. 289:

> The search for causes is then directed backwards to identify the *forces* that have led to this (entitlement) failure ... The task of the analyst then reduces to searching for *forces* that might have impinged upon either endowments or entitlement mappings, or both. (emphasis added)

The forces involved have sprung *deus ex machina* from Osmani's text, and there is no presumption that the entitlement analysis is necessary, let alone appropriate, for their exposition.

Perhaps an analogy will help. In undertaking an investigation of the inequalities suffered by women, even in the area of hunger itself, it is almost inevitable that the distinction between men and women will be a starting point, together with an assessment of how men exercise command over women. This, possibly implicit, use of patriarchy theory is a powerful way of discovering and organising a variety of empirical and analytical propositions. However, as has been generally recognised, patriarchy theory is unacceptable as an underlying, transhistorical, causal factor. Consequently, the analytical transformation of investigative into causal analysis will require the modification, and possibly displacement, of the investigative categories. This does not preclude or deny study of male power; it merely rejects it as a causal starting point.[51] By the

---

50   See Solway (1994, p. 482) for the suggestion, following Gasper (1993), that the entitlement approach should be considered as an investigative tool.

51   This argument is made at length in Fine (1992).

same token, the entitlement approach is an investigative analysis that can only suffer by being retained as, or treated as if it were, a causal analysis. And, to the extent that it fails to focus on causal mechanisms, it is liable to be an uncertain guide to policy.

Finally, I return to the theme of the introduction, the place of the entitlement approach in the current colonising revolution in economics. As heavily emphasised, the entitlement approach does incorporate tensions between micro-foundations and macro-relations. But, in doing so from the original contributions of Sen and the endowment mapping, it does not draw upon a model of optimising individuals, with a subsequent creeping incorporation of a fuller range of factors and endogenously induced social institutions. Nor has the balance of the subsequent literature moved to conform more closely to the principles of methodological individualism applied more widely across the social sciences. Whilst the literature on famine, then, has not succumbed to the new revolution in economics, this is no guarantee for the future. Indeed, it is possible to imagine models of famine in which it is endogenously deployed by optimising individuals to gain economic advantage, as a weapon of war, often taken to be the most infertile application of the entitlement approach to its critics. It would be paradoxical for such critics to be answered by a deeper embedding of the entitlement approach within optimising behaviour through, for example, more sophisticated models of household behaviour.[52] To avoid or to combat, if not entirely to pre-empt, such analyses, the entitlement approach cannot remain as it is. Rather, it is essential both that socioeconomic factors be analysed as causally prior and that famine be specifically tied to food rather than to a general theory of access to life's capabilities.

---

52   An analytical route which Sen has also traversed. For a review on the basis of neoclassical economics, not addressing famine directly but opening the way through examining inequality in intrahousehold distribution, see Haddad et al. (1994) for example.

CHAPTER 3

Economics and Ethics: Amartya Sen as Starting Point

Preamble

This piece was published with its own preamble that now follows immediately with a few minor amendments. Then I offer a postscript drafted afresh for this Volume.

This Chapter has an unusual history that may be worth recounting in order to shed some light on the community of scholarship to which we belong. Initially, it was commissioned by the editors of a special issue for a journal to be devoted to the topic of Sen's capability approach. The editors of the special issue made comments and suggestions for revisions that I duly undertook. Then, to our mutual surprise, the editor himself of the journal refused to publish the piece as it had been decided that the special issue was to focus on operationalising the capability approach. Had I known this in advance, I would not have undertaken the commission as my concern had been to bring out some of the tensions in the development and content of Sen's thinking, rather than the strengths and weaknesses in its empirical or policy application.

Consequently, the piece was put aside although it was, and remains, posted on the SOAS web site (Fine, 2002f). Sometime later, I received an email from a World Bank organiser of its annual conference, the Annual Bank Conference on Development Economics, ABCDE, requesting me to suggest a theme for its 2002 conference to be held in Stockholm. Being of a critical, or is that cynical, realist bent of mind, I assumed that this was a general circular doing the rounds in an attempt to circumvent criticism of the putative knowledge bank that it should be more inclusive in its thinking and participants. I decided not to reply to prevent the World Bank from free-riding on my token participation in determining its agenda that I was sure would not be considered seriously.

But, at least in part, I appeared to be wrong. I received another email reinforcing the invitation to suggest a theme. However, my cynicism did not desert me, and I responded to the effect that if they genuinely wanted my suggestions, I would make them but not if this was a general circular. To my surprise, I was informed that I had, indeed, been selected as an individual to make a proposal.

I did so, suggesting that the study of development should be assessed in the context of the relationship between economics and the other social sciences, economics imperialism, a subject on which I was then, and have remained, seriously engaged. My suggestion was declined, and I thought no more of it other than that I had, indeed, been used for legitimising purposes.[1] That is until I began to hear rumours, exaggerated or not, through the grapevine of what lay behind all of this. First, the organising committee for the conference had included some more progressive economists, and this is why I had been suggested to propose a theme. Second, however, it seems my participation had been vetoed from the highest level.

Now, this was a time of concerted and violent protest against globalisation and its agents. Sweden decided not to host the ABCDE, but Norway took its place and gained the right to nominate a theme of its own. As chance would have it, I was invited by the theme organiser to participate in a stream on Economics and Ethics. I explained the history of what had happened so far, that I felt I had no expertise as such on the topic, but that I did have this paper on Sen that could be bent in the direction of the theme if so wished. To my surprise, I found myself attending the ABCDE after all.

It was a surreal experience. There must have been a thousand or so delegates, luxuriously accommodated in a hotel on the hills overlooking Oslo where, down below, protestors demonstrated their opposition. Video links to more or less empty rooms in the developing world signified commitment to wider participation. I attended three workshops; one, naturally, on ethics and economics; one on gender and development; and one on labour standards. Attendance declined, respectively, from about fifteen through little more than double figures until the last session where the presenters, three or four, threatened to outnumber the audience. This would appear to say something about the priorities of participants.

After the conference, I was asked to revise my paper for consideration for publication in the conference volume, and did so taking full and careful consideration of the strict word limit[2] and comments given including those from

---

1 Shortly after this, I searched the whole World Bank web site to see if any of my works were cited as part of its stock of knowledge. I found that the only occurrence of my name was in a document showing that I had proposed a theme for the ABCDE! It was not, by the way, immodesty that prompted the search. On the only occasion that the "World Bank" has engaged me in direct public debate, with Michael Woolcock on social capital, he insisted on each of us providing the other with three questions in advance. One of his was why did I only publish in obscure left-wing journals. Whatever the intent of his question, I presumed – it seems correctly more than I could have anticipated – that the search on the World Bank web site provided some part of a telling response. I have not undertaken a more recent search on heterodox economists more generally nor myself. Others might like to do so.

2 The paper had to be reduced to a third of its original length.

one of the two editors of the conference volume. All to no avail, the paper was not included.

Postscript

On the face of it, this contribution is not really about development. But it is organised around Amartya Sen's work and this has had influence, like his other work, on the development literature even when not focused upon it as such. So, I have opportunistically included it here.[3] It also adds, in the preceding Preamble what might be thought to be a telling vignette over the putative role of the World Bank as an honest broker of knowledge.[4]

Otherwise, the piece is well into the role of economics imperialism, ultimately being published a number of years after my first assault against it (Fine, 1997a). This contrasts to some degree with the earlier piece on famine (Fine, 1997b), in which the tension between micro and macro can be thought of as standing as a proxy for the tension between individualistic economics (whether choice sets/entitlements allow avoidance of starvation as the proximate cause of famine) and attention to the social/historical/structural involving power, conflict and the meanings of food. The piece is also notable for highlighting the tensions between generality/formalism as opposed to specificity/context, an issue that plagues the specification of what are basic/universal needs and the ethics attached to them.

1 Introduction[5]

Economics as a discipline, in teaching, research and policy, is very poor at ethics.[6] There are six inter-related reasons for this. First, whilst the rigid

---

3 For my other work directly related to Sen's contributions, see especially Fine (1975, 2001b and 2018a) and Fine and Mendes Loureiro (2021). I also return to the issue of ethics, and the critique of the mainstream, in Fine (2013c). In passing, Sen's (ed.) (1970) introduction to (old) growth theory offered me a compelling way in which to teach the topic ($s/v = n$ according to how each of s, v and n are determined with corresponding implications for distribution).

4 On which see also Fine (2010b) and the sorry tale of the World Bank and social capital.

5 As indicated in the Preamble, this Chapter, originally published as Fine (2004a), was prepared for the ABCDE, Fine (2002f), by revising and shortening Fine (2001) to a third of its original size. It was then lengthened by half, especially in light of penetrating commentary around the ABCDE from Des Gasper, Desmond McNeill, Mozaffar Qizilbash, Asuncion St. Clair, and Bertil Tungodden. It remains marked by the author's levels of (in)competence. So, it is now about one-half of its original size.

6 See also Fine (2013c).

distinction between positive and normative economics (and theory and fact) has long been recognised in principle to be invalid, the discipline has continued in practice as if nothing were wrong with the separation(s) between the two. Second, economics is negligent of, and backward in, methodology, and so unlikely to interrogate its own ethical or other foundations. Third, economics also neglects its own history as a discipline, and so its own shifting ethical approaches and content. Fourth, economics has been isolated from the other social sciences so that their contribution to ethical questions has been ignored. Fifth, mainstream economics has always been and is now almost absolutely intolerant of heterodox alternatives with which ethical differences might be teased out, and from which ethical lessons might be learnt and incorporated. Sixth, in sum, with method, methodology, history of economic thought, interdisciplinarity and heterodoxy sidelined to marginal status, this has all meant that economics is extraordinarily lacking in circumspection around the (ethical) meaning and implications of its standard concepts such as production, consumption, utility and the market, let alone development itself. It stumbles among these as if partially sighted, a lack of vision that is compounded in turning to development where the urge to prescribe is rarely matched by attention to context.

For reasons laid out later to do with the latest phase of economics imperialism,[7] some of these features are liable to change in the near future. Of course, little, or none of these faults applies to those working concertedly on ethics of economics itself, for which the body of literature is sophisticated, scholarly, and grounded in full understandings of both disciplines in ways that preclude the criticisms of the previous paragraph (Qizilbash, 2002). The problem is that this work, like methodology, history of economic thought, and alternatives to orthodoxy, lies outside even the casual acquaintance of most economists in all of their practices as much as by design as by default. This applies almost as much to those economists who stray in and out of the ethical. Such occasional forays into the subject matter are exceptions that prove the rule. Stiglitz's (2002) contribution, for example, is more interesting for his feeling the need to say what he has to say rather than what he actually says. His opening gambit might be thought to portray a certain naiveté (and eccentricity) on the part of those who regularly deal in the subject matter:

---

7 Note this, and elsewhere, refers to the second, market imperfection new phase, and not the current latest, newer phase based on market imperfections plus whatever other consideration are fancied.

> There are five concepts, in particular, on which I will focus: honesty, fairness, social justice (including a concern for the poor), externalities, and responsibility ... the meaning of most these terms should be self-evident.

Against such (weakness of) competition,[8] over the past few decades it is hardly surprising that the issue of ethics and economics, especially in the context of development and in exerting influence upon economists, has been dominated by Amartya Sen, almost to the extent of being a one-man show with supporting acts. No doubt, this is a consequence in part of his commanding an established and, as such, unrivalled position in both fields of economics and philosophy simultaneously. He has not, however, been capable of fully compensating for many of the lacunae outlined in the opening paragraphs. The key issue now is how his contributions will be taken forward. This paper argues that the evolution of his work, from social choice to development as freedom, has brought us to an appropriate starting point for further work. For Sen can be interpreted as negotiating a number of tensions, not simply nor primarily those of interdisciplinary endeavour. In this paper, the focus will be on two tensions, between micro and macro, or the individual and the social; and also between generality/formalism as opposed to specificity/context. Sen can be seen as moving both from micro/individual to macro/social and from general/formal to specificity/context. By critically tracing the trajectory of his work, the case is made to begin where his journey now ends.

2   From Social Choice to Development as Freedom

Social choice theory (from the classic Sen, 1970/2017, to his Nobel acceptance Sen, 1999b),[9] has remained at the heart of his thinking. In retrospect, two central issues have been raised and resolved. First, supposing the value of alternative states of the world to different agents could be quantified, then interpersonal comparisons come to the fore – how much should *one person's* welfare count against *another's*? Second, a dual problem, is the intensity of one *individual's* preferences – how much weight should be given to *one* individual's welfare in moving from one *alternative* to *another* of different utility?

---

8 Despite casual reference to Kant and Rawls, there is no citation of any work on ethics in Stiglitz's piece, let alone to Sen.

9 For an appreciation in light of his Nobel Award, see Fine (2001). His initial 1970 book was reproduced in 2017 with updating and more informal parallel chapters. See also Fine (2018).

Crucially, for each of these issues, much analysis has been purely formalistic, with both ethical and substantive issues on the backburner. We have little or no idea who are the individuals, (poor, rich, men, women, ...), nor the alternatives over which they have preferences (food, arms, ...). In addition, society itself is absent – beyond somehow offering individuals unexamined choices, and being the outcome, in principle, of individual choices. The framework is one of deriving the social from the individual, with no feedback in the other direction. Sen (1995, p. 3) himself simply but devastatingly puts it:

> Another issue, related to individual behavior and rationality, concerns the role of social interactions in the development of values, and also the connection between value formation and the decision-making processes. Social choice theory has tended to avoid this issue.

One way of interpreting Sen's subsequent work is in rendering social choice less individualistic and formal. As Sen (1999b, p. 350) suggests:

> Also, some investigations, while not directly a part of social theory, have been helped by the understanding generated by the study of group decisions (such as the causation and prevention of *famines and hunger*, or the forms and consequences of *gender inequality*, or the demands of *individual freedom* seen as a 'social commitment'). The reach and relevance of social choice theory can be very extensive indeed.

Inequality is the first step. Over and above the general if not universally valid claim that more income is better, ethical considerations can be introduced concerning income distribution. Alternative states of the world are simply specified as different numerical distributions of income. These are ranked according to (I) how each person's own changes in income are valued and (II) how one person's income is measured against another's.

Formally, for (I), Atkinson (1970) suggests the use of a parameter ε to measure inequality aversion. This is misleading because inequality is not addressed directly by the parameter ε as it pertains only to changes in income for a *single* person. It is attached to a measurement of inequality only by adding up ε-adjusted incomes across individuals. To gain a measure of inequality, interpersonal comparisons, (II), must also be made. Atkinson implicitly does this by treating all individuals equally subject to ε-adjusted incomes. As Fine (1985) shows, rather than setting the parameters of interpersonal comparison, b_i all equal to 1 (weight all people the same as does Atkinson) and varying ε (more or less inequality-averse), the b_i can vary with ε fixed. Raising the b_i for those on lower income represents a greater 'bias' against inequality. So, varying ε and the b_i are essentially equivalent to one another from a formal point of view. The less you rank more income for an individual, the more you favour the poor against the rich in interpersonal comparisons and vice-versa.[10]

This result highlights the formalism of the inequality literature and its limitations. For, whilst the two approaches to inequality are mathematically equivalent, they are far from ethically equivalent. Comparison of given incomes between people is entirely different from comparison of different incomes for a single person. Further, the ethics can only be engaged meaningfully at some level of detail concerning the nature of the people and the uses to which income is or can be put. In this respect, Sen's (1987b) *On Ethics and Economics* is notable not only for charging economists with the need to debate ethics but also for his own questioning of the ethical content of human motivation.[11] This leads to a corresponding rejection of simple utilitarianism in the form of targeting the greatest aggregate happiness/welfare. For Sen (1995, p. 8), "To try to make social welfare judgements *without* using any interpersonal comparison of utilities, and *without* using any nonutility information, is not a fruitful enterprise".

The shift in Sen's focus from inequality and poverty to a renewal of interest in famine can be viewed in these terms. Food and starving are concrete applications. Sen counterposes the entitlement approach, EA, to supply-side explanations, food availability decline, FAD. Two features stand out from EA, marking continuities with Sen's previous work. First, the formal analytics of EA are derived from set-theoretic microeconomics, with generalisation through access to non-market-related entitlements. What can I get from what I have, given the conditions for transforming one to the other? Consequently, EA is individualistic in methodology. Second, as is immediate, the formal analytics of EA are not food-specific. They could apply equally to anything – whether basic needs or luxuries.

This is not to suggest that EA, as deployed in practice, is purely micro-based, and never macro, and fails to be food-specific. Nor that it is ethically neutral (and hence biased given lack of equality in the world) despite its analytical origins and affinities with neoclassical economics. Despite this, Sen has been driven by major humanitarian issues and the ethical values that they raise rather than succumbing to mindless application of the nostrums and

---

10   I have returned to such work around the measurement of inequality in recent times. See
      Fine (2019a) and Fine and Mendes Loureiro (2020 and 2021).
11   Note that Becker (1996, pp. 16–18) rejects Sen's distinction between ethical and personal
      preferences on the grounds that the one is reducible to the other.

techniques of neoclassical orthodoxy. So Sen (1999a, p. 170) argues, famine is dependent upon "the exercise of power and authority ... the alienation of the rulers from those ruled ... the social and political distance between the governors and the governed". Such considerations, however, tend to enter separately from the micro-analytics of entitlements. In part, macro references to food and famine arise directly out of empirical applications rather than from the theory. The macro-social also enters more obliquely through the incorporation of *social* relations, structures and processes. But these are superimposed, not built, upon the micro-foundations. An obvious example is the *class* of *landless* labourers. Unable to produce for own consumption or to command sufficient (wage) revenue or payment in kind to gain sustenance, they are potentially subject to famine irrespective of overall aggregate supply of food. Yet, such arguments presuppose social relations on the land, between landlords and labourers, and in the distribution of food. None of these is reducible to the individualistic micro-analytics of EA.

My own assessment of EA was motivated less by famine than by earlier research on food that drew upon a broader study of the determinants of consumption (Fine, 1997b). The organising theme was to hypothesise that commodities serving consumption are attached to distinct, integral "systems of provision" – structurally integrated along the chain of activities from production to consumption itself, as in the clothing, energy and food systems for example (Fine, 2002a most recently).[12] As a result, I was acutely sensitive to the limited extent to which EA had in theoretical principle, if less guilty in empirical practice, addressed the specificity of food and of food systems as the latter vary by crop, time and place. In a nutshell, given its transparent conceptual and technical origins in the mainstream microeconomics of feasibility sets, EA is profoundly neutral with respect both to underlying social relations and historical specificity (except in defining endowments and their potential transformation into outcomes) and to the specificity of food itself in both material and cultural terms.

At this time, I was already concerned with developments in or, more exactly, around economics, see website http://www2.soas.ac.uk/Economics/econ imp/econimp1.html [no longer running but see Fine (2024a–c)]. In brief, my argument is that economics has been colonising the other social sciences as never before. This is a consequence of its new micro-foundations with informational asymmetries to the fore. On this basis, economics purports to explain the economic and the non-economic as the rational, path-dependent response

---

12   But, more recently, see Bayliss and Fine (2021).

to market imperfections. This includes economic and social structures, institutions, customs, culture and so on. Previously, in the older form of "economics imperialism", the non-market was addressed as if it were akin to a perfect
market, most notably in the work of Gary Becker. Now there is a corresponding reductionism of the economic and the social to market, especially, informational *im*perfections. It has given rise to a whole set of "new" fields within
economics – the new microfoundations of macroeconomics, the new trade
theory, the new financial, the new development, the new institutional, the new
labour economics – as well as new fields outside economics or influence upon
the old – the new political economy, economic geography, economic sociology,
and so on. I have parodied such initiatives by the formula ss=e=mi^2.[13] First all
economics is reduced to market imperfections, mi, and methodological individualism, mi, (in the form of imperfectly informed rational economic agents).
Then, all social science is reduced to such economics.

These perspectives informed my assessment of EA. I suggested an unresolved tension in Sen's own work – between the micro-foundations of the entitlement analytics and the broader recognition of famine as irreducibly macro,
not least because famine is more than the sum of its individual parts – not
merely personal starvation for the many. Is famine the choice to starve by self
or other on your behalf, a replicated but rational response to market imperfections? Sen commendably refrains from attaching the EA to the new micro-
foundations despite his micro-analytics (and emphasis on the informational
role to be played by a free press). Nor have I come across any sympathy for
such an approach in his work, hardly surprising in view of his uncompromising
stance on "rationality" (Sen, 1977).[14]

Further, when he addresses the macro, it is from a perspective independent
of the micro – as in the role of the free press and democracy in guarding against
famine, although classes are at times perceived to have entitlements. Further,
I argued that the same micro-macro tension is to be found in EA debate. Those
adopting a critical stance towards EA have not so much been engaging with it
as an alternative to FAD as questioning whether their macro-interpretations of
famine had been or could be accommodated within EA – issues of the nature
of property, violence, culture and custom, all heavy with ethical content.

This is an appropriate point to move on to well-being, capabilities, development and freedom, with (Sen 1985) as stepping stone. This constitutes more
than a generalisation and concretisation of what has come before, as in the

---

13   I was proud of this jokey formula with its affinities to Einstein's, e=mc^2 but it never
      caught on.
14   See Desai (2001) for an account of Sen's antipathy to neoclassical economics.

shift from inequality to famine. For, in the light of economics imperialism, there are other tensions than those attached to micro-macro. The marginalist revolution is recognised to have taken the social out of economics in two senses. It represented a shift to methodological individualism *and* the construction of the non-market as separate from the market. Information-theoretic economics claims to bring the social back in, on its own terms – of optimisation subject to informational constraints. Similarly, the path followed by mainstream economics initially separates out material and cultural analyses and sets the latter aside. Yet, once again in its own inimitable style, the current phase of economics imperialism is reintroducing the cultural (trust, customs, norms, etc) as an informational calculus.

Although Sen's work too has increasingly embraced the social and the cultural, once again, there is no evidence that he has been seduced by the unsubtle charms of economics imperialism. Indeed, if anything, there is a shift, at least discursively, away from the micro-analytic technicalities of EA. The practice was established in the context of famine and can, subsequently, float freely to serve intermediate or macro levels of analysis across capabilities more generally. In short, Sen (1999a, p. xii) sees a "deep complementarity between individual freedom and social arrangements". As in EA debate, commentators have questioned whether the macro, the social and the cultural have been or can be appropriately addressed on the basis of Sen's approach. Gasper and Cameron (2000), for example, edit a collection that explicitly assesses in order to extend Sen's work. Gasper (2000, p. 999), under the rubric of freedoms, achievements and meanings, raises the issue of, "whether to have more options is valuable depends on the meaning the options have for the actor and her audience". Giri (2000) is concerned with well-being as involving mental self-development and personal transformation towards sharing with others, Cameron (2000) with Sen's neglect of opulence or upper end of capabilities, and Carmen (2000) with "capacitation".

These all sit uncomfortably within an individualistic and formalistic methodology. The social and contextual are imperative. Thus, the new welfare economics proceeds on the basis of informationally imperfect contracts between state and citizen. But, by extension of the earlier argument around the specificity of food (and other basic needs), it is essential to attach public as well as private contributions to capabilities to specific systems of provision (Fine, 2002b). To ask not only "How is each of health, education, housing and welfare differentially created, distributed and used" but also how are these interactive with, and constitutive of, corresponding cultures, ideologies and political practices, each with their own ethical content.

Whether for food or other capabilities, Sen's analysis does not appear to engage sufficiently with these issues to the extent that it remains formalistic/ individualistic. In arguing, controversially, that famine (dire under-provision for the many) is liable to be avoided by the presence of a free press and democracy, what exactly is the analytical content of such an observation? Is it specific to food, or does the same apply to housing and education (and excessive mortality of female children)? What are the mechanisms through which the free press and democracy work (or not)? Are they the same or different across different capabilities, entitlements and freedoms? My presumption is that they are different both for the nature, forms, levels and incidence of provision and their mode of functioning. By the same token, the nature and consequences of the ethics of provision are diverse according to what is provided, by and for whom, and how.

With respect to Sen himself, I suspect that these comments may be pushing against an open door not least in view of his longstanding empirical work that does engage with context and specificity, from Drèze and Sen (1989) to Drèze and Sen (2002). This is simply to support the organising principle of this Chapter – that the evolution of Sen's work has brought us to an appropriate starting point, with the social, the specific and the contextual to the fore rather than, if not to the exclusion of, more formal and general treatments. My concern is that Sen should not be appropriated, and his achievements reversed, by the new phase of economics imperialism. One result would be to block progress in what are already weaknesses, if not absences, in his work – the attention to ethnographic (contextual meaning) and to processual (capacitation) issues.[15]

Lest this warning be considered unnecessary, consider the treatment of ethics by those economists who dally in notions such as trust, norms and values. These always come in stripped down versions, as in Dasgupta (1993 and 2001), and Stiglitz (2002a) whose ethics are drawn in exemplary fashion from the new economics imperialism:[16]

---

15 See Gasper (2002) for a wide-ranging assessment along these and other lines.
16 Equally, as pointed out by Adam Smith, there is an equally powerful argument in favour of unethical behaviour through pursuit of self-interest or other motives. Also, in light of the infinite flexibility of game theory, unethical rather than ethical behaviour may lead to more ethically satisfactory outcomes, a means-ends conundrum, with Stiglitz confessing he "faced a similar dilemma as Chief economist at the World Bank", ultimately choosing to speak out against the IMF.

In simplistic models, individual self-interest leads to efficient outcomes; individuals act, and are expected to act, in their own self-interest. But in modern theories in which information imperfections and incomplete markets play an important role, self-interested behavior in general does not yield efficient outcomes. Equilibria based on trust can yield better outcomes than those in which trust is absent ... There is thus an *instrumental* argument for ethical behavior.

I suspect that many working seriously in economics and ethics will willingly accept the limited analytical content of such prognostications and proceed with more sophisticated and challenging ideas. Whilst to do so is liable to be more intellectually rewarding in the field of ethics, the danger is in conceding ground on the economics underlying the assault on ethics from economics imperialism. For, with little prospect of the discipline of economics being contested from within, given its intolerance of alternatives, debate about the economy and economics can only primarily take place at the boundaries of the discipline around which ethics must engage as well as politics, sociology, history, and so on.

3   Conclusion

The lessons drawn from reviewing Sen's passage from social choice to freedom are:
- The social, contextual and empirical should be the starting point for discussion of economics and ethics as opposed to the individual, the formal and the a priori.
- It is as important, if not more so, to examine how ethics are created as it is to target what they should be.
- The connection between economics and ethics varies according to the specific entitlements, capabilities, developments and freedoms involved.
- Last, controversially and not previously argued, the study of the political economy of capitalism is the key to progress on these and related issues.

The case can begun to be made by reference to the dictum of Brecht, "first grub, then ethics". This is open to at least three different interpretations cutting across priorities, epistemology and ontology.[17] First, you have to eat to be able

---

17   Cited by Sen (1989, p. 769) who essentially only uses the first interpretation to follow – in order to argue the importance of reverse priority and causality as well.

to engage in the luxury of ethics (as unwittingly revealed by Marie Antoinette). Second, each food and way of providing food generates its own corresponding ethics (from vegetarianism to cannibalism).[18] Third, the nature of ethics depends upon the nature of food and eating (you are what and how you eat as in conviviality, national cuisines, and the Sunday roast).[19] Whether for food or other capabilities, the issues raised by each of these interpretations rests on an understanding of the political economy of capitalism in economic, cultural and ethical terms.

18 See Lestringant's (1997) explicit reference to Brecht in these terms.
19 Consider Marx's eleventh thesis on Feuerbach not only as a moral imperative but also as a way of inducing philosophers to understand the world in a different way and through different practices. Such praxis is the target of Carmen's (2000) *prima mangiare, poi filosofare*.

CHAPTER 4

Economics Imperialism and the New Development Economics as Kuhnian Paradigm Shift

Postscript as Personal Preamble

I remember in the early 1970s, a time when radical political economy remained strong in the wake of student radicalism of the sixties, Keynesianism was in disarray, and monetarism (and the New Classical Economics as its extreme version) were in their hegemonic infancy, that there was enormous excitement over the application of Kuhn's notion of scientific revolution to economics. Both left and right could claim it for their own. For the left, mainstream normal science was in crisis and radical political economy of whatever variety offered the prospects for a new paradigm. For the right, or orthodoxy, mainstream economics was understood to be an exceptionally robust and longstanding normal science.

As a result, some thirty years later, it is hardly surprising that I should turn to the Kuhnian paradigm of scientific revolution to shed light on what I was dubbing a revolution in economic thought, marked by the rise of market (information) imperfection economics within the discipline and its associated application to, the colonisation of, the other social sciences (and non-economic topics) – something for which I then adopted the moniker of economics imperialism. I was fortunate to be offered a two-year, full-time fellowship to study economics imperialism, which straddled the turn of the millennium.

This allowed me to study economics imperialism in depth and breadth, adding to what were already a number of themes informing my understanding of economics imperialism. The most important were, and remain, the nature of market imperfection economics and the extent to which, and how, it diverges from market perfection economics; how this informs the relationships between the economic and the non-economic and economics and other social sciences; and how these factors materialise within economics imperialism in different ways across different disciplines and topics. Given the huge presence of Stiglitz across both market imperfection economics and development (as Chief Economist at the World Bank and the source of the Post-Washington Consensus), it is hardly surprising that I should both look to development economics as an example of economics imperialism and to assess it through the lens of Kuhnian revolution.[1] As a result, whilst my initial treatment of economics imperialism through, and in critique of, a Kuhnian lens was wide-ranging and lengthy across numerous examples (Fine, 2001c), a shorter, more focused version on development was teased out for the publication that follows.

At the time, and even more so in retrospect, it is apparent that the Kuhnian moment in economics had been extremely short-lived. Its life and influence more generally have been marginally greater but it has been eclipsed by the rise and fall (or evolution) of, and from, postmodernism. Interestingly, in this context, in the Chapter, I introduce the notion of the dual retreat across the social sciences from the excesses of both the culturalist turn attached to postmodernism and the market fundamentalism (in thought if not practice)[2] of neoliberalism. I am anticipating a return to the material and the real as academia increasingly gets to grips with the consequences of everything from the neoliberalisation of everyday life to the emergence of, and conditions attached to, the Global Financial Crisis, environmental crises and, most recently, the pandemic. In this act of foresight, I suspect I have been proven correct, although the current intellectual environment is marked by considerable variation across how the material turn (and cultural analyses), in reaction against postmodernism and neoliberalism, has evolved. In part, this reflects the strength of (development) economics as a discipline as it launches its assault on the other social sciences and associated (non-economic) topics, but also its weaknesses and vulnerability to criticism from the methodologies, theories, and conceptualisations associated with other disciplines as it exposes itself to them. And economics imperialism, in its newer, third phase, (alongside its progeny in the newest development economics, especially as promoted by the World Bank)[3] remains strong, generally unrecognised as such,[4] and highly supportive of the third phase of neoliberalism.[5]

The original abstract for the published paper puts it well and is reproduced by way of conclusion to this preamble (even if with some repetition with the next paragraph).

---

1 A further major influence on my thinking at this time was an almost obsessive attention to criticising the social capital paradigm (Fine, 2001a, 2010b and, most recently, 2023a, for example).

2 See Fine and Saad-Filho (2016) and Bayliss et al. (2024).

3 See following Volume, Fine (2025).

4 See especially Fine (2024b and c) for watershed drop in the acknowledgement of economics imperialism.

5 See Chapter 1.

This paper addresses the evolving relationship between economics and other social sciences. It sets the present intellectual scene as one in which economics imperialism is rampaging across other disciplines. The designs of economics upon development studies are examined in terms of the Kuhnian notion of paradigm shift. Thereby the conclusion is drawn of the potential prospect of open debate around the economy and development, not least outside economics itself. But there is danger of economics imperialism, in the form of the Post-Washington Consensus, foreclosing the analytical agenda at the expense of approaches based on the political economy of capitalism.

1   Introduction[6]

This Chapter addresses the evolving relationship between economics and the other social sciences with some special attention to development studies. It begins in section 2 by setting the present intellectual scene as one in which economics imperialism is on the rampage across the other social sciences even as these are in turn on retreat from the cultural turn associated with postmodernism and the market turn of neoliberalism. Section 3 examines the designs of economics upon development economics and development studies in terms of the Kuhnian framework of paradigm shift. Section 4 concludes by suggesting the potential prospect of open debate around the economy and development, not least outside of economics itself. There is, though, a danger that economics imperialism, in the form of the Post-Washington Consensus, will set and foreclose the analytical agenda at the expense of the political economy of capitalism.

2   Neoliberalism, Postmodernism and Economics Imperialism

The contributions to the symposium on "The Case for Cross-Disciplinary Approaches in International Development", *World Development*, vol 30, no 3,

---

6   Originally appearing as Fine (2002e), this Chapter is heavily shortened and revised from Fine (2001c). The research was primarily undertaken whilst in receipt of a Research Fellowship from the UK Economic and Social Research Council (ESRC) under award number R000271046 to study "The New Revolution in Economics and Its Impact upon Social Sciences". For an account, see http://www2.soas.ac.uk/Economics/econimp/econimp1.html (no longer up and running). Thanks to many for comments on earlier drafts.

2002, are to be welcomed for the variety of insights that they demonstrate is to be found by introducing the content of other disciplines to economics. But, across each of the papers, and taking them as a whole, there is a serious omission. It might be best summed up by a lack of broader context, readily posited in terms of a sequence of questions. Why is this issue being posed now? Why has it not been settled in the past? Is it perennial, and nagging, re-emerging from time to time like a bad conscience or is the issue different now than in the past? If so, is it the world that has changed, economics or the other social sciences? In short, these papers might reflect the intellectual times in which they are situated but they do not reflect upon them.

To some extent, this is a consequence of the ground rules under which the papers appear to have been solicited. As Jackson (2002) reveals, the authors were instructed to address the strengths of other disciplines rather than to dwell upon well-known weaknesses of economics. At one level, this is disturbing. If economics has well-known weaknesses, why have they not been put right? There is no shortage of literature exposing where economics has gone and continues to be wrong (Ormerod, 1994; Hodgson, 2001; and Lawson, 1997, for a mixed sample), but its influence is at most fleeting and marginal. Perhaps the exception that partially proves the rule is McCloskey (1986), and the notion of economics as rhetoric. Significantly, McCloskey's work otherwise remains strongly committed to orthodoxy in content.

In addition, apart from economics failing to address, let alone rectify, its faults at home, if other disciplines have strengths, why have they not already been recognised and incorporated? At a deeper level, this places us into the sociology of knowledge, and the history of disciplines and their boundaries – precisely the wider context that has been overlooked by the symposium. Further, without wishing to exaggerate the influence of the symposium, its authors are surely concerned to enrich the presence of other disciplines within economics. But is the effort not liable to be futile, given the uncorrected weaknesses of economics and the continuing neglect of the strengths of other disciplines? Indeed, as argued here, the problem should be seen not so much as strengthening economics by incorporating the insights of other social sciences but as the need to question an unyielding and intolerant orthodoxy within economics itself. Putting it polemically, mainstream economics is caught in a paradox. If it is the only truly rigorous and scientific discipline within the social sciences, not least because of its notion of human rationality and reason, why do the other social sciences persist rather than succumbing to the fatal charms of the dismal science? And what explains their own paths and the rhythm of their interactions with economics? Are other social scientists simply irrational?[7]

These opening remarks would be little more than idle chatter if the symposium simply reflected another minor skirmish around economics and the other social sciences. But I consider this is not the case and, inadvertently or otherwise, it has caught a swing in intellectual mood that needs to be identified. In particular, the relationships within and between the social sciences are currently undergoing major changes. These are uneven and diverse in content but, at the general level, two broad trends are discernible. For, around the turn of the millennium, the social sciences have been marked by the dual retreat from the excesses of both neoliberalism and postmodernism. For the first, peddling the idea of leaving everything to the market and making as much activity as possible subject to market forces has begun to exceed its sell-by date. As a result, the debate around market versus the state has given way to the exploration of their complementary roles. Further, the influence of postmodernism has also been on the wane, especially its preoccupations with discourse, meaning, the subjective and identity. It has increasingly been recognised that such concerns need to be wedded to the material processes that make them possible as well as the constructions that are placed upon them. In case of consumption, for example, possibly the focus of postmodernism par excellence, it is now a matter of how objects are received in every sense and not just how they are interpreted (Fine, 2002a for a discussion of the literature and its shifts in emphases over the past decade).

The declining influence of neoliberalism and postmodernism is indicative of a more general wish to get to grips with what might be termed the realities of contemporary capitalism as opposed to the creation of a "virtual world" of free and pervasive markets (Carrier and Miller, eds, 1998). Accordingly, the social sciences are marked through the 1990s by the successive emergence of two key concepts. The first is globalisation. It is notable for the way in which it began as the quintessential consequence of neoliberalism promising, both for left and right, the erosion of national barriers to the market and the death of the state. Across the social sciences, it has now become the opposite – in recognising the global only to counterpose it with the "local". In particular, death of the nation-state is deemed to be premature, with the "glocal" ranging over finance, knowledge, communications and the media, culture, technology, oligopolies, and so on (Fine, 2002b for an overview).

---

7 For a critique along the lines of this paradox of Lazear's (2000) claims for the favourable prospects for economics imperialism, see Fine (2002d).

Following hard upon the idea of globalisation has been social capital. Whilst pitched at the level of the nation-state or below, this notion has been motivated by the wish to address the role of culture, custom, associations, networks, etc as *real* factors in economic and social outcomes (with the discursive occupying a distinctly rearguard position).[8] The point here is not so much to appraise the emergence and use of these concepts but to suggest that they provide evidence of the dual retreat from neoliberalism and postmodernism in the attempt to come to grips with how the world is at the turn of the millennium.

Development studies has participated in, and promoted, the use of these concepts. But the picture around (development) economics is much less clear-cut. For a start, economics never participated in postmodernism and has had, therefore, neither reason nor potential to retreat from it. Amariglio and Ruccio (1998, p. 237) implicitly see this as a methodological advantage:

> If postmodernism as critique has exhausted itself in cultural and literary circles, this result stands in sharp contrast to the situation within contemporary economics. The destabilizing effects of postmodernism are only beginning to be noticed in the area of economics, and the resistance of philosophers and historians of economic thought to the critical currents of postmodern theory is precisely because they have understood (correctly, we think) the mostly nihilistic implications of adopting epistemologically "relativist" antiscientific stances.

This is, however, of little relevance to your bog standard economist (as opposed to philosophers or historians) who still remain ignorant of such methodological issues.

The retreat from neoliberalism, however, is a different story as far as economics is concerned, although commitment to the market remains strong.[9] Indeed, I have argued that something akin to a revolution is taking place in or, more exactly, around economics as a result of its emphasis upon market *im*perfections.[10] Consideration of the latter has given rise to a *new* phase of

---

8   For a comprehensive critical account of social capital, see Fine (2001a and 2002c). See also Harriss (2001), and Bebbington et al. (2004) for a revealing account of how social capital came to the World Bank and for an attempt to rationalise its use as part of a strategy to reform World Bank economists.

9   See Deraniyagala and Fine (2001) on the tension between new trade theory and new trade policy, for example.

10   Initially in Fine (1997a) and, most recently, in Fine (2002d) with reference to other contributions.

what has been termed economics imperialism, the colonisation of the other social sciences by economics. The *old* phase, notably represented in the work of Gary Becker, proceeded on understanding the economic and the social as far as possible as if they were ground out by the optimising behavior of individuals as if in the presence of a perfect market. In terms of colonising other social sciences, Becker's "economic approach" achieved some telling successes, not least with human capital and the new household economics.[11] But it has had, from the perspective of other social sciences, the distinct disadvantage of denying the social other than as aggregation over individuals or as externally given and unexplained. In contrast to Becker, the present and more virulent form of economics imperialism is based upon the idea of market imperfections. These, as such, are far from new to 'traditional' neoclassical economics (with implicit rationale for state intervention) since they have long been recognised, especially but not exclusively within partial equilibrium, alongside transaction cost, say, as an influence on the organisation of firms and other institutions. What is more fundamentally innovative within the new microeconomics of informational asymmetry is its ability to examine social structure, institutions and customs, albeit on the continuing basis of the peculiar form taken by methodological individualism. Utility maximisation is the ultimate rationale for both economic (and market) and non-economic (and non-market) behaviour, with equilibrium, reproduction or evolution of the social on the basis of aggregate individual behaviour. Relative to the old, the new approach adds market imperfections in the form of informational asymmetries but, on this basis alone, it also extends the scope of the analysis more or less indefinitely across the social sciences.

It does so, without going into details, through the use of informational imperfections to explain why markets might be inefficient, might not clear (supply and demand remain out of equilibrium), or might not emerge at all. As a result, whilst still drawing upon a methodology of optimising individuals, it is able to suggest why economic *structures* might arise – as, for example, in the division between the employed and unemployed when the labour market does not clear. Such developments are reflected in the proliferation of "new" fields of economics – the new institutional economics, the new economic sociology,

---

11   Becker's Nobel Prize was in part awarded for economics imperialism, an explicit criterion (Lindbeck, 2000). For his own claims, see Becker (1990) and also Tommasi and Ierulli (eds) (1995) and Febrero and Schwartz (eds) (1995). See also Frey (1999), who attracts praise from Nobel Laureates Becker, Stigler and Buchanan, and Olson and Kähkönen (2000), who prefer the telling metaphor of economics as metropolis and other social science as the suburbs.

the new political economy, the new growth theory, the new labour economics, the new economic geography, the new financial economics, the new development economics, and so on. In this vein, Stiglitz (1994, p. 5) feels able to claim that a new approach to economics has been established. It diverges from the old mainstream, enhances the understanding of how markets work, and is applicable across a wide range of subject matter:

> During the past fifteen years, a new paradigm, sometimes referred to as the information-theoretic approach to economics ... has developed ... This paradigm has already provided us with insights into development economics and macroeconomics. It has provided us with a new welfare economics, a new theory of the firm, and a new understanding of the role and functioning of financial markets.

Whilst significant for developments *within* mainstream economics, even more important in some respects are the implications for other social sciences. For non-economic or non-market behaviour is now understood as the rational, i.e. individual optimising behaviour, response to market imperfections. It is appropriate in face of informational, and hence market, imperfections to form social structures, as reflected in collectives, institutions and the state, and to engage in what would otherwise appear to be non-rational behaviour, as in customs, trust and norms.

Such simple analytical advances considerably expand the capacity of economics to colonise the other social sciences, not least because of the formal and abstract nature of the models employed within economics – they apply in principle to any imperfect (non-)market situation. Accordingly, the principles involved have no historical nor social roots other than in the language deployed. For, in content, they rely entirely upon categories such as utility, production, inputs and informational asymmetries, quite apart from the timeless and rootless optimising of individuals, themselves located in history and society only by virtue of the preceding optimising of their ancestors. Thus, the new, like the old, approach is characterised in its starting point by excising social and historical content in anything other than name. Consequently, such content can be (re)introduced formally as multiple equilibria or path dependence in some form but also informally on the basis of the continuing traditions and concerns of the colonised disciplines and topics. The social is the non-market response to market imperfections. Further, such incursions do tend to be informal, adopting the language rather than the models of economics, as previously in use of human capital in any number of applications and rent-seeking and collective action when discussing institutions. Now customs, culture, trust, identity, etc come within the compass of economics.[12]

The emergence of this new phase of economics imperialism has been felt in diverse ways and depths across the social sciences. It is almost impossible to give an overview in empirical terms so widespread, uneven, mixed and changing are the outcomes. Apart from the "new" fields listed previously, evidence is to be found in my own work on social capital and economic history, for example.[13] More informally, the personal response experienced in response to the hypothesis of a new virulent phase of economics imperialism is often an initial scepticism followed, after a short lag, by the proffering of examples![14] Further, the point is not to deny the presence of resistance, and even impermeability in some instances, to the encroaches of economics. Rather it is to emphasise that a shifting relationship between economics and the other social sciences is currently being renegotiated with, as yet, uncertain outcomes by topic and discipline.

Development economics, and development studies more generally, is no exception. To a large extent the process is symbolised by the transition from Washington to Post-Washington Consensus,[15] and through the weight of Stiglitz's influence and contributions. In launching the Post-Washington Consensus, he soon referred "to providing the foundations of an alternative paradigm, especially one relevant to the least developing country. It is based on a broad conception of development". Further, "I shall explain why not only the Washington Consensus, but earlier development paradigms failed: they viewed development too narrowly" (Stiglitz, 1998a, 57/8).[16]

---

12   Of course, it is also possible for formal economic models to be directly applied theoretically and empirically to other disciplines or non-economic topics without such informalities, as in the new growth theory in which any social variable can be incorporated in a model and regressions. For a critique of the new growth theory on these and more general scores, see Fine (2000) and Kenny and Williams (2001).

13   For details, see website cited in opening footnote.

14   One referee collapses the lag by both asking for more details of incursions by economists into non-economics and also pointing to the renewed assaults on economic anthropology, not least through a more or less unwitting renewal of the formalist versus substantivist debate. Reference was also made to Moore's (1999) critique of economics on political science, which is particularly harsh on Americanisation.

15   For critical presentation of the post Washington Consensus, see Fine et al. (eds) (2001), Hildyard (1998) and Standing (2000) for example.

16   Hence Stiglitz's citation for "being one of the founders of modern development economics" (Nobel, 2001, p. 10).

3   Post-Washington Consensus as Kuhnian Revolution?

These are extremely clear, if excessively grand, claims. Nor is it clear, through frequent appeal to the notion of paradigm, whether the resonance with Kuhn's notion of scientific revolution is intended or simply accidental and unconscious. Either way it is worth considering the new paradigm from a Kuhnian perspective because of the light it sheds on the questions raised at the outset over the contribution that other disciplines can make to the economics of development. It is now forty years since Thomas Kuhn laid out his theory of scientific revolution. Kuhn was initially concerned to explain how science changes, drawing a distinction between normal, smoothly evolving science within a given paradigm and revolutionary science that blazes a shorter, if not short, sharp shift between paradigms. As a result, Kuhn's language, especially the notion of a paradigm for example, has become commonplace even as substantive understanding of his contribution, and criticism of it, has declined. Further, in the scholarly literature, more than enough time has passed for his approach to have been fully traversed, if not forgotten, territory in understanding the sources and nature of intellectual change. For those economists who participated, even if merely as an audience, in the Kuhnian revolution, it ought in retrospect to stand out as a remarkably rare period of self-examination of a discipline that is notoriously unaware of, and uninterested in, its own history and methodological underpinnings.[17] Whilst primarily concerned with the history of science, Kuhnian notions were readily transposed to the social sciences without economics standing on the sidelines as an exception, as has been so for other intellectual fashions such as postmodernism in the more recent period.[18]

But what exactly is the Kuhnian approach to scientific revolution. A useful summary is provided by Suppe (1977) on which I draw freely.[19] Central to Kuhn is the notion of paradigm, with science proceeding through discontinuous

---

17   De Vroey (1975) observes, for example, correct from my own memory, how influential Kuhn had become in discussion of history of economic thought. In preparing this paper, however, I have been struck by how little Kuhn's influence has been reflected in practice in journal publications in economics.

18   For Kuhn applied across the social sciences, see Gutting (ed.) (1980). Khalil (1987) reviews the application of Kuhn to economics but see also Gordon (1965), Coats (1969), Bronfenbrenner (1971), Kunin and Weaver (1971), Karsten (1973), Ward (1972), Stanfield (1974), De Vroey (1975), Blaug (1975), Chase (1983), Dow (1985), and Argyrous (1992 and 1994) in debate with Dow (1994).

19   Page references are to him but see also Barbour (1980) for an excellent précis of Kuhn and the debate that he prompted.

breaks between them rather than through a continuous evolution, as is high-lighted by Toulmin (1972) in critique of Kuhn. A paradigm is multi-faceted, rang-ing from exemplars (or standard applications) to disciplinary matrix (or world view), "but according to Kuhn the scientist obtains his disciplinary matrix from the study of exemplars, and they in large part determine that matrix", p. 139. For Kuhn, the matrix is not acquired "through the study of explicitly formu-lated methodological rules ... and a theory always is advanced in conjunction with various exemplars which are presented as archetypal applications of the theory to phenomena", p. 140. Further, generalisations are not explicitly and formally specified but proceed through implicitly acquired skill in interpreta-tion. So, there is a need for apprentices both to learn exemplars and the skill to extend them. "It follows that two scientific communities whose symbolic generalizations are the same or employ some of the same theoretical terms, but possess significantly different exemplars, will attach different meanings to the theoretical terms and thereby interpret their generalizations differ-ently", p. 141. Suppe cites Kuhn to the effect that, exemplars "are achievements sufficiently unprecedented to attract an enduring group of adherents away from competing modes of scientific activity [which are] ... sufficiently open-ended to leave all sorts of problems for the redefined group of practitioners to resolve", p. 143. This all occurs in response to mounting theoretical or empirical anomalies produced, often unintentionally, within previous paradigms. The weight of anomalies leads to cumulative switch to other exemplars and, ulti-mately, to logical incompatibility between disciplinary matrices, differences in prediction, differences in vocabulary, and to "an argument over competing world views and competing ways of doing science". With a division into com-peting camps, without common assumptions, persuasion rather than logic becomes decisive in commitment to one or other paradigm. The new matrix has "changed meanings attached to theoretical terms" possibly with the old as approximation, p. 147.

In short, as the highly cited Masterman (1970) has observed, although Kuhn's notion of paradigm has been attached to 21 different interpretations, these can be boiled down to three. First is as exemplar, second is as world vision, and third is as a body of professionals. Irrespective of the validity of the Kuhnian framework for addressing intellectual change, or the sociology of knowledge, each of these core elements of a paradigm is useful in shedding light on cur-rent developments within and around (development) economics.

For paradigm as exemplar, the distinctive character of the new phase of economics imperialism is clearly delineated. Masterman (1970, p. 70) under-stands a "construct paradigm" as an "artefact", and "only with an artefact can you solve puzzles". With the creation and solving of problems within a paradigm as normal science, it is not difficult to identify the artefact involved. It is the notion of asymmetric information and the consequences this has for market and non-market outcomes. Indeed, the founding artefact is an exemplary exemplar – the market for "lemons", or second-hand cars, as laid out by Akerlof (1970).[20] It solves a number of puzzles – why the market might not work perfectly despite optimising individuals and no exogenous impediments to market-clearing. As observed, there are three possible outcomes – markets clear but Pareto-inefficiently (there are buyers and sellers who would like to exchange at some other price), they do not clear (those on the short side of the market do not have incentive to change price in their favour), or there is no market at all (undermined by presence of moral hazard or adverse selection for example).

Following Akerlof, information-theoretic economics has proceeded by accumulating different types of informational asymmetries and applying them across an equally diverse range of markets. Although with the physical sciences in mind, Masterman (1970, p. 70) astonishingly and unwittingly anticipates recent developments within economics, as economists have searched out applications for asymmetric information:

A normal-scientific puzzle always has a solution which is guaranteed by the paradigm, but which it takes ingenuity and resourcefulness to find.

Further, as Chase (1983, p. 816) observes, a paradigm fills out a new analytical terrain:

---

20   More generally, see Akerlof (1984 and 1990), and Fine (2001a, Chapter 3) for comparison
      of Akerlof and Becker as economic imperialists, revolutionary and non-revolutionary,
      respectively, although Becker has become more revolutionary, and in the vanguard, with
      his adoption of social capital (Becker, 1996). Note that Kanbur (2002) favourably refer-
      ences Akerlof and Kranton (2000) for its having addressed the question of identity. But
      it does so in the crudest reductionist fashion, as an element in a utility function, and as a
      asocial and ahistorical factor (archetypically without substance as reds and greens), prior
      to moving to consider the substance of gender, race, etc. Akerlof and Kranton do draw
      upon a limited range of the vast quantity of work in social science that has examined
      identity. But they do so as if postmodernism never existed (how is identity socially con-
      structed with meaning) despite this being the theme of much of the work that they cite
      (with authors liable to be appalled at the way in which they have been interpreted). Note
      though that Akerlof's work tends to bring the (reinterpreted) insights of the other social
      sciences to economic problems (not vice-versa). This, however, smooths the way for colo-
      nisation in the opposite direction. On a personal note, the interpretation by Akerlof and
      Kranton (2000) of Sen's Paretian Liberals as attached to interdependent and/or game-
      playing preferences was first put forward in Fine (1975).

> The acceptance of a new exemplary paradigm by a community of sci-
> entists will often require a redefinition of the corresponding science
> ... some old problems may be relegated to another science or declared
> entirely 'unscientific', while others that were previously nonexistent or
> trivial may ... become the very archetypes of scientific achievement.

In case of economics imperialism, a wider definition of economic science is involved since it is not simply a matter of explaining market imperfections but also of incorporating the non-market responses to them, thereby establishing a presence within the other social sciences. Masterman suggests that a paradigm is established by taking an exemplar, A, and finding other applications for it, B, by analogy whereby B becomes A-like. This is precisely what has been characteristic of economics imperialism – for economic and social analyses have been reduced, respectively, to market imperfections and the non-market responses to them. From lemons or the market for second hand cars, the entire terrain of economic and social theory is opened up!

Interestingly, Masterman (1970) considers that the exemplar attached to a paradigm is more important than its world view, and this seems to be borne out by the "disciplinary matrix" attached to information-theoretic economics. How does the new information-theoretic economics differ from what went before? It takes as its point of departure the model of perfectly competitive equilibrium. In its place is posited an imperfectly competitive world, with imperfect markets and imperfect information, leading both to inefficiencies and to non-market responses to them (whether these correct market imperfections or not). In other words, the world vision of the new approach is its micro-foundations writ large. In case of development economics, for example, Stiglitz and Hoff (1999) argue that:[21]

> In leaving out history, institutions, and distributional considerations, neo-
> classical economics was leaving out the heart of development econom-
> ics. Modern economic theory argues that the fundamentals [resources,
> technology, and preferences] are not the only ... determinants of eco-
> nomic outcomes ... even without government failures, market failures are
> pervasive, especially in less developed countries.

---

21   The approach was previously aired in Stiglitz (1989). Note how both economic history and
     development studies more generally come within the analytical orbit.

Further, with casual reference to the Black Plague, as an illustrative accident of history (like AIDS today?), and multiple equilibria, an explanation is provided for the fundamental problem of why "developed and less developed countries are on different production functions":

> We emphasize that accidents of history matter ... partly because of perva-sive complementarities among agents ... and partly because even a set of dysfunctional institutions and behaviors in the past can constitute a Nash equilibrium from which an economy need not be inevitably dislodged.

Apart from specifying exactly what is meant by a "broader vision" of develop-ment, Stiglitz (1998b, p. 58), this appears to be an ideal illustration of Kuhn's (1970) own understanding of how paradigms are generated by, and trans-formed into, an evolving disciplinary matrix. There are symbolic generalisa-tions, of which production functions and Nash equilibria are archetypal. The metaphysical content of "modern economic theory" is one of "failures" – mar-ket, government or otherwise – as opposed to the ideal, perfectly competitive, world of "neoclassical economics". Values within a paradigm are of two types – those concerning predictions and puzzle formulation, and those attached to overall consistency, simplicity and plausibility. For the new approach, there is a common reliance with the old both upon econometrics and upon a method of optimising individuals, but the puzzles are about how the market understand-ably works imperfectly rather than how it diverges from perfection because of externally imposed constraints.

The third broad category of meaning of paradigm identified by Masterman (1970) is the sociological as opposed to the metaphysical (world view) or the construct (exemplar). This refers to the community of scientists and their common practices which, in retrospect, Kuhn (1970) confesses he would have preferred to have taken as his analytical and expositional starting point. Paradoxically, although the new approach appropriately presents itself as less dogmatic than the model of perfect competition that it has sought to replace, it has prospered in an intellectual climate in which economics as a discipline has itself become even more intolerant of alternatives. Radical political econ-omy has been considerably depleted and, even where it has not, the model-ling and statistical techniques of the orthodoxy are increasingly imperative as a condition of entry to the profession, to the exclusion of almost all else. Blaug (1998a, p. 12) reports from John Hey, previously managing editor of the *Economic Journal*, that there is a 'journal game', based on use of irrelevant material, the stylised facts observed by an author, and designed to demonstrate cleverness rather than address crucial economic problems. Blaug (1998b, p. 45) himself opines:

> I am very pessimistic about whether we can actually pull out of this. I think we have created a locomotive. This is the sociology of the economics profession. We have created a monster that is very difficult to stop.

Blaug (1998a, p. 11) also reports from a survey of a lack of interest in the real world on the part of elite graduate economics students as opposed to honing their skills in the latest econometrics and mathematical economics.[22]

Particularly striking is the degree of "Americanisation" of economics.[23] This is not simply excessive and irrelevant use of mathematics, statistics, methodological individualism of a special type, and obsessive pre-occupation with equilibrium and efficiency. It is marked by the excessive command of journals, textbooks, appointments, doctoral training, even Nobel Prizes, by a limited range of institutions and individuals. Significantly, whilst the number of doctoral students in economics is increasing in the United States, the number of US origin is in decline, revealing the export and adoption of its economics at the top of the profession throughout the world.[24]

But perhaps the most rhetorically persuasive and satisfying evidence for the Americanisation of economics is provided by the leading proponent of the new paradigm.[25] For Stiglitz (2001, p. 6), "the question is, how can we *institutionally* facilitate the replacement of the old [neoliberal, competitive equilibrium] paradigm with the new perspectives?". The answer is through networking and

---

22   See also Khalil (1987, p. 126) who, in drawing upon Leijonhufvud, observes, "Isolating practitioners in an ivory tower allows the aesthetic criterion to play a role in theoretical endeavours ... (with) beauty and elegance rather than empirical corroboration as the basis of theory selection."

23   On this and related issues and for what follows, see Coats (ed.) (1996), Hodgson and Rothman (1999), Bernstein (1999), Siegfried and Stock (1999), and Lee and Harley (1998), for example.

24   Thus, whilst there are traditions that lie outside the Anglo-Saxon, these are subject to erosion, most symbolically reflected in the emergence of the acronym, ATKE, for American-trained Korean economists. The same story, with or without acronym, could be told for most, if not all, countries, not least China, transitional societies, and the developing world more generally.

25   Note the apparently unwitting deployment of new Kuhnian paradigm as exemplar and vision, p. 5, "There is no single, overarching model to replace the competitive equilibrium model: the world is too complex. But there are a set of tools and perspectives (such as those that derive from models of imperfect information and incomplete markets) that can be used."

PhD programmes, to be sponsored by foundations. But tenured jobs are hard to find as these depend upon publications but, "many journals are not as open to alternative perspectives as they should be", p. 6. So new journals will also be necessary. Yet, this is the view of a Nobel Laureate, a former |Chief Economist to the US President and to the World Bank. His contribution ten years ago on the (negative) prospects for socialism, Stiglitz (1994), contained over one hundred citations to his own work, predominantly published in the major journals. Thus, whilst Stiglitz is correct to point to the strength of neoliberal thinking, and the stranglehold of (American) orthodoxy on the economics profession, it is not a monopoly either at his expense or of the (equally American) approach that he would seek to foist upon us all.

To some extent, of course, whilst Stiglitz presents himself as against neo-classical orthodoxy,[26] his approach incorporates considerable continuities with it. Consider methodology. The current phase of economics imperialism has primarily reverted to the image of the discipline as engaging in falsifying activity and posing and testing hypotheses. According to Lazear (2000, p. 102/3), for example, whose article and title celebrate economics imperialism:[27]

> The power of economics lies in its rigor. Economics is scientific; it follows the scientific method of stating a formal refutable theory, testing the theory, and revising the theory based on the evidence. Economics succeeds where other social sciences fail because economists are willing to abstract. The old joke about a stranded, starving economist assuming a can opener to open a can of food pokes fun at our willingness to assume away what we believe to be unimportant or difficult details. Economists are used to posing the counterfactual question to do an analysis. What would one expect in the absence of the hypothesized effect? What would be observed? Do the data allow us to choose between various hypotheses? Economists are not alone among social scientists in following this method, but this form of enquiry has become standard for economic research.

---

26   Hardly surprising in view of his earlier definition of it as, "the perfect competition, perfect market model in all of its representations" (Stiglitz, 1991, p. 135). This piece, looking forward to another century of economics science, is also remarkable, in light of later prognostications, for its pessimism over development economics, the "one important area in which I am less sanguine about the future success of our profession", p. 140.

27   Note that his assertions about what economists do have long been known to be a false image of themselves. See Blaug (1980), McCloskey (1986) and Lawson (1997), for example.

In this light, the impact of Kuhn on economic methodology within the discipline has even been perverse. Initially, to the extent that there was a response to Kuhn, it was a shift towards recognising the difficulties in principle and in practice of holding to positivism or the less stringent Popperian standards of falsifiability. Paradoxically, Kuhn thereby had the effect of justifying an unchanged practice of proceeding as if on the falsifiability track whatever its deficiencies, on the grounds that this constituted normal science. In short, what, from the perspective of critical realism, Lawson (1997) dubs the deductivist method characteristic of mainstream economics has, if anything, strengthened since Kuhn.[28] Consequently, a shift in methodology does not mark the current phase of economics imperialism. It is more of the same on, if anything, an even shallower basis, with less likelihood of critical self-reflection.[29]

On a more mundane level, to what extent has economics imperialism been associated with a shift from the orthodoxy in "habit-governed, puzzle-solving activity"? On the face of it, very little has changed. Whatever its methodological deficiencies, mainstream economics has remained firmly committed to an unchanging method – one attached to methodological individualism of a special type, utility maximisation, to equilibrium as an organising concept, and to considerations of efficiency, the three distinctive scientific elements emphasised by Lazear (2000). In addition, the technical apparatus and the barrage of associated techniques has at most become a little more sophisticated and extensive – with the fundamentals in terms of production and utility functions being instantly recognisable, albeit supplemented by the incidence and sources of (market and government) failure.

Thus, as a profession, there can be little doubt, as Garnett (1999) observes, that mainstream economics continually and dogmatically reasserts its scientific status and superiority relative to other forms of economic discourse, thereby creating boundaries for definition of the profession, entry conditions, and associated benefits in employment, prestige, financial support and intellectual independence. But, why as a discipline should it seek to extend its supposedly superior form of science to other disciplines, over and above its

---

28   This leads Lawson to the conclusion that methodology is the Achilles' heel of mainstream economists. For an alternative view, see Fine (2004c).

29   Boylan and O'Gorman (1995, p. 27 fwd) refer to a post-positivism phase as prevailing in economic methodology over the last quarter of a century, characterised by a desperate but unsuccessful attempt to rescue falsifiability from its inescapable fallacies. Yet, economists as such have rarely been aware of, let alone participated in, the futile quest, preferring to proceed as if it had already succeeded.

enhanced capacity to do so in light of the new information-theoretic economics?[30] It is possible to posit a certain maturing in the current dynamic of the discipline and its disciples. First, observe that the conditions of entry to the intellectual vanguard of the profession are extremely technically demanding. As the degree of mathematical and statistical sophistication has been ratcheted up, so existing professionals who do not conform have found themselves marginalised to a greater or lesser extent. On the other hand, the newly trained academic economists have been highly tuned in the techniques and are growing in numbers. On casual observation, and discussion with colleagues, there is now no shortage of "American-trained" economists, searching out careers.

Second, in a world in which publish or perish and a doctorate are not enough, the new recruits need outlets for their abilities, satisfied to some extent by the emergence of new journals. But a crucial intellectual factor is involved here. This is that the analytical and technical *principles* underlying the new information-theoretic approach are demanding but, once commanded, are limited in scope and economic application. It is simply one market imperfection after another. Whether by virtue of intellectual boredom of those who are already well-established – one more market, one more twist on a technique – or the search for new avenues by those who have yet to establish themselves, the other social sciences provide a virgin terrain on which to play out those skills that would otherwise exhibit rapidly declining marginal productivity! In effect, neoliberalism is the death of economics because, if the market works perfectly, there is no need to study it. By contrast, the market imperfection, information-theoretic approach keeps the discipline alive but only at the expense of intensifying technical virtuosity, relying upon ever more esoteric models and, most important in reserves of potential, by their extension to non-market applications.

Third, academia in general increasingly depends upon external research funding. Compared to their colleagues in business, accounting, marketing and finance, academic economists are generally unsuited to serving the needs of the private sector. Where they are able to oblige, the rewards they can command by being within the private sector itself heavily outweigh those of remaining within academia. On the other hand, economists have also been less than willing and attractive participants in more publicly-minded research,

---

30   I do not seek to provide a full sociology of knowledge in explaining the new phase of economics imperialism, failing to link it more fully both to changing interests and to material developments outside of intellectual endeavour itself. In part, this is because I do not consider that the world of ideas follows so closely and crudely upon its objects of study.

not least because of being unworldly. As Balakrishnan and Grown (1999, p. 135) reveal in their study of foundation support for economic research:

> When the Ford Foundation funded multidisciplinary graduate pro-
> grams in social science and health, for example, it found it impossible
> to convince economists to join the effort. Similarly, when the MacArthur
> Foundation sponsored a competition for multidisciplinary research on
> the human dimensions of global environmental change, economists
> were generally absent from the teams of investigators.

However, in deploring this absence of economics, Balakrishnan and Grown are heartened by "recent developments in economics and philanthropy [that] provide new openings to reexamine and renegotiate this relationship". They refer specifically to, "lively interest in the economics of information and incentive problems due to asymmetric information in settings as varied as the provision of public services, labour markets, credit markets, insurance markets, and Third World agriculture", p. 124/5. Thus, intellectual, professional and personal imperatives have been conducive to the outward thrust of economics imperialism, consolidating a paradigm of market imperfections extended to non-market outcomes, despite internally unexamined analytical weaknesses from the perspectives of other social sciences. In short, economics imperialism allows for intellectual complacency (if not arrogance and ignorance), (competition for) jobs, publications and research grants!

Last, bringing these other factors together in cementing a core community of development economists, is the World Bank. Previously, throughout the 1980s and into the 1990s, it occupied a hegemonic position in setting the developmental agenda of market versus state. It did so through its own research, that commissioned from others, and through its more general rhetoric in support of structural adjustment and stabilisation. Whilst the World Bank and IMF set the terms of debate through the Washington Consensus, and leaned exclusively to one side, it could not prevent the emergence of the increasingly influential stances of its opponents. Key in this respect have been the ideas of adjustment with a human face and the significant historical and prospective role of developmental states.

The position of the Post-Washington Consensus, whilst more temperate in its attitude towards the virtues of the market, is otherwise more disturbing. For it not only seeks to set the analytical agenda as being confined to uncovering and addressing the incidence and consequences of market and non-market imperfections, it also claims that this exhausts the problems of development. Hence the previously quoted claims by Stiglitz for a broader approach to development than previously, and the idea that the new information-theoretic approach breaks with, rather than, promotes mainstream neoclassical economics. In this and other respects, a considerable rewriting of the history of development economics is underway with two disturbing elements. On the one hand, development as a process as well as a field of study is reduced to market and non-market imperfections. On the other hand, it is as if the critique of the Washington Consensus only began with the Post-Washington Consensus, and with the World Bank's (1993) *East Asian Miracle* perceived as a watershed. Subsequently, all earlier contributions to development are filtered through the information-theoretic or market imperfection approach, as the post-war classics are rediscovered, brushed down and reinterpreted as no longer anomalous through the prism of the new paradigm.[31]

4   The Prospect Ahead by Way of Conclusion

By bouncing current advances in economics in general against Kuhnian notions of paradigm shift, it has been argued that development economics and studies in particular are both under assault from economics imperialism. But the discussion so far has almost entirely been restricted to the "supply-side", with the design of economics on other disciplines. What about the demand-side, how these are ventures being received? Not surprisingly, the reception is mixed in depth and content. It is undoubtedly warmest where rational choice methodology has already prevailed. But social science has primarily been concerned with the social and not the individual. In case of sociology, for example, Velthuis (1999) has shown how it was distinguished from economics in the eyes of Talcott Parsons, the leading functionalist of the discipline, by its method rather than by its subject matter – dealing in the social independent of the individual. Consequently, mainstream economics is liable to remain alien to the other social sciences to the extent that its analytical roots are recognised and quite apart from its intimidating technical virtuosity and statistical methods. Further, in retreating from the excesses of postmodernism, a continued emphasis upon the cultural, the customary, the institutional, etc as involving

---

31   The most stunning illustration is provided by Paul Krugman. His "The Fall and Rise of Development Economics", https://web.mit.edu/krugman/www/dishpan.html, offers a reconstruction of the lost development economics of the 1940s and 1950s in general and of Albert Hirschman in particular but opens by confessing that "My acquaintance with Hirschman's works is very limited"!

the social construction of meaning will not be abandoned but, rather, be wedded to understanding of the material forces upon which they depend.

In this respect, however, the presence of an understanding of the economic across the social sciences is extremely weak, in part reflecting the previous "cultural turn" and in part explaining the rapid rise to prominence of analytical surrogates such as globalisation and social capital. Exaggerating, these serve as simple fixes in place of economics. But each does so in a different way. Globalisation takes pure financial markets as an extreme exemplar, timeless and boundaryless. It has the effect of incorporating systemic analysis, and the corresponding presence of process, power and conflict beyond the bounds of individual agents. Not surprisingly, globalisation rarely appears in mainstream economics, at most serving piecemeal as an umbrella for liberalisation of trade, finance and investment in disaggregated fashion.[32]

By contrast, social capital is more, if not entirely, acceptable to mainstream economics, and it has been heavily promoted by the World Bank. It has increasingly become a way of examining the social that is entirely compatible with the new phase of economics imperialism. Associations, networks, customs, culture, etc can all be understood as the rational, time-dependent response to market imperfections. Conflicts, power and the systemic in any other sense simply fade into the background. In polemical terms, globalisation leads to protests at Seattle, social capital does not.

The broader implication is that cross-disciplinary endeavour that includes economics is liable to be caught on the horns of a dilemma, how to incorporate the economic without economics. If the analysis remains truly social in the sense of the systemic distinct from aggregating over individuals, then mainstream economics has very little, if not nothing to offer. For it is silent over the social relations, structures, power, conflicts and meanings that have traditionally been the pre-occupation of the social sciences. This is especially important for development studies. Significantly, as Connell (1997) has shown, the initial impetus to sociology was given by confrontation with those other worlds revealed in practice by imperialist expansion, raising the issue of what characterised the modernity of the colonising powers by way of contrast to the colonised or primitive. Only after such concerns had been safely set aside, not least with the horrors of civilisation associated with interwar fascism, could the enduring classics of sociology – Marx, Weber, Durkheim, etc – be sanitised

---

32   See, for example, the almost total absence of globalisation in Chang's (2001) collection of
       Stiglitz's papers, although we do get *Globalization and Its Discontents* from him in 2002,
       with over one million copies sold (Stiglitz, 2002b).

and canonised as dealing exclusively with the social relations, structures and even conflicts of modernity. Meanwhile anthropology emerged as a separate discipline to deal, primarily ethnographically with the intellectually initiating world that had been abandoned by sociology. Thus, running the insights of these disciplines through economics for the purposes of studying development would complete rather than remedy the substantive damage done in splitting them apart in the first place!

In short, the task that faces us is not the asset-stripping of the social sciences in order to improve economics. Many social scientists recognise, and some welcome, the export of ideas from other disciplines to economics, judging it to render a civilising influence, even a reverse imperialism. In practice, whatever the intentions of those pursuing this route, the net effect will be to consolidate and promote economics imperialism. For the Panglossian perspective overlooks that a warm embrace is only offered to such incursions as long as they are consistent with an unchanging methodology and method; and it is stretching credibility to imagine that mere social theorists will transform a discipline that has effectively outlawed any dissent from within. Rather than bringing social science to economics, it is necessary that economics be brought to the social sciences where it will find an increasingly welcome reception. But it cannot be mainstream economics nor, unhappily, derive primarily from the contemporary discipline of economics more broadly. For heterodoxy and political economy have been more or less systematically squeezed out of contention by the intolerant intellectual policing wielded against other schools of thought for their supposed lack of rigour and science.

With the retreats from neoliberalism and postmodernism, then, there is liable to emerge a debate around the economic that remains, as yet, remarkably open. Economics imperialism in general, and the Post-Washington Consensus in particular, are attempting to occupy that space. If they succeed, a great opportunity will have been lost to have promoted the political economy of capitalism and development. And much more than the world of ideas is at stake. For, as is sharply apparent in case of the resignations of both Stiglitz and Kanbur, there is considerable disharmony between the scholarship and the rhetoric and ideology of the World Bank, let alone the policies that do (or do not) flow from them.[33] Significantly, the Post-Washington Consensus is a paler, micro-, contingent version of the welfarism/modernisation/Keynesianism

33 See Wade (2001) for an account of the resignations and their implications, although unreasonably forcing a distinction between the two on the grounds that one does and one does not reflect US hegemony over the Bank.

of the McNamara era with which it is more usefully (and unfavourably) contrasted than with the Washington Consensus. Its vision of development, and how to achieve it, is weaker and confronts less conducive circumstances. It must not prevail whether for the health of development studies, political economy, or economies themselves.

CHAPTER 5

New Trade Theory Versus Old Trade Policy: A Continuing Enigma

Postscript as Personal Preamble

In the mid-1990s, I was requested by the Congress of South African of Trade Unions (COSATU) to prepare a number of policy documents in critique of ANC Government policy and as a way of opening up alternatives. One of these (Fine, 1997c) covered the dos and don'ts of industrial policy, with trade policy as one aspect.[1] For the latter, in order to meet GATT (now WTO) conditionalities, government policy perversely targeted the reduction of tariffs on what were the most black labour-intensive industries, and essential for industrialisation and economic development, despite the high levels of black unemployment and extensive disadvantage within labour markets where employment could be found. The rationale underlying such trade policy was drawn from Washington Consensus arguments that so-called effective rates of protection should be reduced both to increase static efficiency and to reduce the scope for rent-seeking.

In order to offer alternatives, I undertook a review of the (mainstream) effective protection literature and, in short summary, found that to be able to define effective protection, to measure it and to draw the conclusion that it should be reduced to enhance performance requires an extraordinary set of assumptions, such as no unemployment, only two sectors (so no non-traded goods), perfect competition in input and output markets, no economies of scale and scope (or externalities across sectors), no intra-firm trading, perfect capital markets, and no technical change other than through switch to already available more or less capital-intensive methods of production. In a sense, let us eliminate all the factors that might make protection effective for

---

1   The others addressed privatisation and the steel industry (Fine, 1997d and e, respectively), although the latter was originally requested jointly from the steel-using employees' union and the employers' association that used steel due to their mutual concerns over discriminatory pricing against the domestic steel-using industry by domestic steel suppliers – as the story goes, they were paying more for the steel to make fridges than the domestic price of South Korean imported fridges that were being made with South African steel being dumped on international markets.

economic development, and we find that is ineffective.[2] As discussed in much more detail in Chapter 7, there are two positive aspects, or corollaries, to these results – that trade policy needs to take these decisive factors into consideration, and that it cannot be legitimately constructed in the absence of other aspects of (industrial) policy, such as competition, technology, employment, financial and equity policies (and meeting basic needs), as well as policies towards multinational corporations.

From these beginnings on effective protection, I joined forces with my colleague Sonali Deraniyagala to offer a more wide-ranging theoretical and empirical take on trade policy, especially in light of the new trade policy that emphasises the virtues of free trade in stimulating productivity increase. This Chapter was the result alongside Deraniyagala and Fine (2006), drawing conclusions from both theoretical and empirical literatures that dispute the conventional wisdom. Perversely, unlike the minimum wage debate over its (non-negative) impact on unemployment that was turned upside-down by empirical work and developments,[3] mainstream faith in the virtues of free trade remains extremely strong despite the historical record, and the kicking away of the ladder for developing by developed countries(Chang, 2002), as well as the bringing into account those factors that go far beyond the impact of trade restrictions on static efficiencies.[4]

1   Introduction[5]

As reported in Prasch (1996), support for free trade amongst academic economists in the United States is astonishingly high at 97%! It has enabled Anne Krueger (1997),[6] Chief Economist at the World Bank during the 1980s and chief promoter of the neoliberal Washington Consensus, to engage in a history of

---

2   I undertook a similar exercise for Mozambique in critique of World Bank policy proposals to reduce effective protection and even though its own policy document acknowledged that smuggling imposed an entirely uncertain impact of tariffs on trade, and hence, economic performance.

3   See Konopelko (2023).

4   See Murphy (2013) for plus ça change, toujours la même chose as far as new trade theories are concerned.

5   Originally appearing as Deraniyagala and Fine (2001), completed whilst I was in receipt of a Research Fellowship from the UK Economic and Social Research Council (ESRC) under award number R000271046 to study "The New Revolution in Economics and Its Impact upon Social Sciences". It draws upon Fine (1997c) and see also Fine (1996b).

6   See also Krueger (1998) and response from Ocampo and Taylor (1998).

economic thought in which the central question becomes one of explaining why economists should have resisted the charms of free trade for so long given both its virtues in practice and its centrality within standard theory of comparative advantage. Her answer essentially boils down to the idea that otherwise idle theorists have made mischief by deploying models of market imperfections without due regard to the stylised facts. In short, for her, if the stylised (neoclassical) theory does not support the stylised policies, it's time to get real. However, as will be shown in much of the discussion that follows, the recent trade literature has, within the confines of an evolving neoclassical theory of market imperfections, made great attempts to address at least some of the realities of trade. By doing so, from the perspective of neoliberalism, it has been extremely mischievous, if not troublesome in view of the extent to which its conclusions have been over-ruled by the forward march of support for trade liberalisation.

This Chapter critically examines the theoretical and empirical grounds for trade liberalisation. We note that many of the conventional arguments relating to the static and dynamic gains from liberalisation are based on fragile theoretical grounds. We also show that although new trade theory takes account of some of the complexities of international trade and although the analytical thrust of many models justify intervention, such policy conclusions are rejected even by those at the forefront of these theories on the grounds of political economy arguments which do not stand up to careful scrutiny. Finally, we show that arguments favouring trade liberalisation are not supported by existing empirical research which generally fails to capture the complex and ambiguous effects of liberalisation and openness.

Section 2 examines conventional theoretical arguments relating to trade liberalisation and it also reviews recent developments in new trade theory. Section 3 examines the empirical research relating to liberalisation dealing with both cross-country research and industry and firm-level studies. We close with a pithy summary.

2   Conventional Arguments for Trade Liberalisation

The literature on trade liberalisation differentiates between the static and dynamic gains from trade policy reform. Whilst the economic arguments relating to static gains are straightforward it is also generally acknowledged that the magnitude of these gains is fairly low. Static, once-and-for-all gains arise as the misallocation of resources under protection and import substitution is corrected, and resources shift from inefficient to efficient sectors, activities and firms. The gains take the form of the well-known Harberger welfare triangles. However, empirical estimates of the welfare costs of these relative-price distortions rarely exceed two or three percentage points of GDP (Bhagwati, 1993; and Pursell, 1990). The response of mainstream theorists to these negligible welfare gains has been to extend these welfare triangles by emphasising the dynamic, long-term gains from liberalisation. Whilst a range of arguments relating to long-term benefits has been produced, closer scrutiny shows them to hinge on fairly arbitrary assumptions, thus lacking both theoretical consistency and empirical validity.

One way of inflating welfare triangles has been to incorporate rent-seeking, with the focus being on the calculation of welfare losses from government trade interventions, especially the introduction of import quotas. It has been argued that the resource costs of trade interventions are multiplied several-fold by the existence of rent-seeking. Empirical estimates have shown the magnitudes of the costs to be large (de Melo and Robinson, 1982; Gallagher, 1991; and Tarr 1992). As Ocampo and Taylor (1998) note, however, it is difficult to accept these estimates at face value; if quotas cover only a fraction of imports and if imports are only a fraction of GDP, rents and rent-seeking outlays cannot be significant. It is also interesting to note that there has been little empirical research on whether rents have actually declined following liberalisation. This is especially so of institutions such as the research department of the World Bank which has undertaken large multi-country studies to establish the gains from liberalisation. Onis (1991) is a notable exception, showing that Turkish policy moves towards export-orientation gave rise to a new type of rent-seeking directed at obtaining export quotas.

Another argument relating to the dynamic gains from liberalisation centres around X-efficiency and entrepreneurial effort. By reducing competition and increasing relative prices in import-competing sectors, protection encourages entrepreneurial slack. Formal representations of this argument have revealed its fragility (Tybout, 1992). It only holds when the entrepreneurial labour supply curve is upward sloping in the relevant range and when changes in work incentives operate in the same direction for both exporters and import-substituting producers. As we show in Section 3, the empirical evidence relating to trade policy and efficiency also fails to provide conclusive support for this argument.

Increasing returns to scale (IRS) are frequently cited as an important source of dynamic gains from liberalisation. Firms in more open trade can supposedly operate at lower costs due to higher levels of output, available through participating in world markets. This argument, however, is based on the assumption that liberalisation necessarily expands IRS activities. If scale economies are mainly concentrated in protected sectors which decline following trade reform, this type of dynamic gain will not materialise. As Rodrik (1994, p. 159) notes, "whether scale effects add or subtract from resource allocation effects depend on a variety of factors with no clear-cut presumption either way". Another variant of this argument is that protection increases profitability and leads to the co-existence of too many firms producing at below minimum efficient scale. Liberalisation, therefore, leads to industry rationalisation and allows firms to benefit from scale effects and produce at lower average costs. Again, this argument is also questionable as it assumes easy and frictionless entry and exit into markets.

Long-term productivity gains are also seen to ensue from the correction of the anti-competition, anti-export bias of protection which will have discouraged cost-cutting technological change. In much of the policy literature on developing countries, the precise mechanism by which trade reform has promoted technological dynamism has never been fully spelt out (e.g. Balassa, 1988). Increased levels of competition are taken as sufficient to generate increased innovative activity and productivity gains across all sectors. The fact that relative-price distortions such as tariffs may adversely affect learning and technology development in some sectors but not in others and the possibility that various instruments of trade intervention may have differential consequences for innovative activity, has not always been considered. More importantly, the simplistic notion that high levels of competition unambiguously promote technological change ignores the well-established body of research on market structure and innovation, which indicates that this is not necessarily true (Evenson and Westphal, 1995). Such assertions about the beneficial effects of trade-related competition on innovation are also found in recent analyses which otherwise claim to question the mainstream approach to trade policy adopted by the World Bank and the International Monetary Fund (IMF), in forming a new Post-Washington Consensus (Stiglitz, 1998a).

Overall, a general feature of conventional arguments relating to the dynamic effects of trade liberalisation is that they are not located within a coherent theory of industrial performance. In recent years, considerable attention has been focused on technology-related factors in influencing firm and industry-level productivity and the fact that technology development is the outcome of a complex interaction of supply-side and demand-side factors. That these are highly sector- and country-specific (such as technological skills and institutions, scientific and technological paradigms, relative price and demand changes and so on) has been emphasised (Evenson and Westphal, 1995). The adaptive and incremental types of below-the-frontier type of technological activity typically undertaken by developing country firms have also been shown to be the outcome of such processes (Bell and Pavitt, 1992). In this context, to expect productivity improvement to be largely determined by trade liberalisation and international competition alone is naïve. As we show below, such notions of industrial performance are evident both in recent trade models which incorporate increasing returns, imperfect competition and technology spillovers and empirical analyses of liberalisation.

3   New Trade Theory

New trade theory is now entering its middle-age, having been established in the 1980s (Ethier, 1982; Krugman, 1984, 1986 and 1989; Brander and Spencer, 1985; Eaton and Grossman, 1986; Grossman and Horn, 1988; and Grossman and Helpman, 1991). In general, its models attempt to address the shortcomings of standard trade theory by dealing with some of the realities of trade in a more complex and sophisticated manner by incorporating a fuller range of factors. However, they provide few, if any, unambiguous conclusions.

New trade models incorporate four innovations within neoclassical economics: market imperfections; strategic behaviour and the new industrial economics; new growth theory; and political economy arguments. Many of the models based on market imperfections and strategic behaviour justify interventionist trade policy. Whilst much of the literature linking trade and new growth theory favours trade liberalisation (mainly on the grounds of knowledge spillovers), here too the possibility that free trade may be detrimental to economic growth is allowed for. Overall, however, interventionist trade policies are rejected even by those at the forefront of these theories, mainly on the grounds of political economy arguments (such as rent seeking). Below, we examine the fragility of these political economy arguments when we discuss the four innovations linked to new trade theory in detail.

3.1   *Market Imperfections and Strategic Behaviour*
The increasing returns to scale (and infant industry) conventionally used to justify protection has been complemented by a range of other market imperfections. These include informational asymmetries and imperfections which inform so much of recent innovation within mainstream microeconomics which is itself usually seamlessly transformed into understandings of the economy as a whole. Secondly, new trade theory also draws upon the new industrial economics with models incorporating the strategic behaviour of all agents, firms as well as governments. This involves game theory, intertemporal optimisation, and issues of time-consistency especially for government policy (the possibility of changing policy commitments after the private sector

has invested of which the latter can be aware).[7] We will address the literature around these two sets of innovations together.

Informational asymmetries and adjustment costs are dealt with in models which consider optimal technology choice over time. Ohyama and Jones (1995) allow for one country deliberately to fall behind another so that, with adjustment costs, leaping ahead in the future becomes less expensive. It becomes possible to explain both falling behind, catch-up and leapfrogging. Leahy and Neary (1996) consider such issues in the context of R&D rivalry, although Durkin (1997) shows that pursuit of comparative advantage in producing technological progress itself can lead to inefficiency (home county may be better at producing innovation in the factor-rich sector of the other country!).

In models involving strategic behaviour, results differ depending upon stylised assumptions. Various assumptions about the sorts of competition and oligopolistic behaviour considered are made. Thus, Bhattacharjea (1995) finds that both strategic industrial policy (on entry/exit) and tariffs are necessary under imperfect competition at home and abroad and endogenous market structure. Fuerst and Kim (1997) and van Long and Soubeyran (1997) take account of heterogeneity in cost functions with trade policy affecting the distribution of production across (more or less efficient) firms within countries as well as across countries. The effect of vertical integration is modelled by Bernhofen (1997), Ziss (1997), Holm (1997), Jie-A-Joen (1997). Pal and White (1998) incorporate considerations of privatisation (the removal of a firm that acts strategically to maximise domestic welfare rather than profit), and Devereux and Lee (1999) address interaction with internationalisation of financial markets and extent of trading in productive assets across countries.

Strategic trade models also involve consideration of the policy instruments that governments are allowed to deploy and the sequencing of decision-making. Sleuwaegen et al. (1998) examine the issue of cascading protection – to what extent and in what circumstances is protection passed on and how are its costs and benefits distributed. Karp and Perloff (1995) find differential effects of protection when policy instruments are targeted at investment as opposed to output (not affecting or affecting long-term outcomes, respectively).

The relevance of these new trade models to developing countries has been debated (Lucas, 1988; Bardhan, 1995; and Ruttan, 1998). Whilst some strategic models with oligopolistic players dominating world markets may be of limited relevance to low-income developing countries (Stewart, 1991), arguments for

---

7 See McKay and Milner (1997) for problems in the design of policy so that ex post outcomes coincide with ex ante intent.

intervention based on scale economies and imperfect competition are widespread in developing countries, rendering these theories especially relevant for them (Helleiner, 1992). Empirical evidence indicates that imperfect competition is indeed rampant (Lee, 1992), although the evidence on scale economies is much more limited.

Thus, models based on strategic behaviour are highly diverse given the underlying factors and assumptions over which they range. But, what they all tend to share in common is the result that strategic trade policy is justified and, in addition, that it should be complemented by other forms of policy (or take a variety of forms). Such a conclusion should not come as a surprise. For, it is presumably only by accident that free trade will be optimal in the presence of market imperfections and, further, the more the imperfections the more the instruments we need to deal with them. Further, given the diversity of the models, it also follows that interventions will need to be selective and country/ sector specific depending upon the type and strength of market imperfections involved.

Of course, the standard neoliberal response to these models is to claim that government has neither the knowledge nor the ability to be selective in its policy interventions. The supposedly large informational requirements are one reason why the analytical thrust of trade theory in justifying interventionist trade policy has been rejected even by those at the forefront of the theory. Yet, the literature is itself well suited to handle such issues since it has drawn upon the economics of imperfect and asymmetric information. If governments are less well-informed than the private sector (and less able), does it follow they should do nothing? The answer is resoundingly in the negative and should not come as a surprise. For the implication is that we should leave the generals and the military industrial complex to make defence policy since they know more about waging war and the true costs and capabilities of weapons.[8]

Clearly, as in any principal-agent problem, there is a trade-off between (lesser) knowledge and (others') motives. Brainard and Martimort (1997) address the issue directly as suggested by the title of their paper.[9] Their conclusion is striking, p. 56:

> Attainment of the informationally constrained social optimum requires a complicated menu of contracts combining per-unit subsidies and lump-sum transfers.

---

8 Alternatively, to be topical, chemical companies should be allowed to make policy on genetic engineering.

9 See also Wong and Chow (1997) and Wright (1998).

Even more remarkable is the conclusion reached by Creane (1998) to the effect that policymakers may be better off, and justified in using trade policy, the less information that they have. It is not, however, necessary to engage in trade theory to see why this conclusion arises in the context of imperfect competition. For, consider a monopolist who wishes to exercise product discrimination. To do so, customers (including countries contemplating trade policy) must have the knowledge to discriminate products (as is recognised in practice by advertising irrespective of whether 'genuine' differences are created). Without this, monopolists may be forced to rely upon a more Pareto-efficient but less profitable strategy and be unable to exploit product discrimination. Nor is this some esoteric point in the context of development where, both for welfare and growth, economies may be better served by supplying a cheap mass market than in targeting a more profitable elite.

3.2   Links with New Growth Theory

Apart from strategic behaviour and market imperfections, the new trade theory is integrated with the new growth theory which is also essentially based upon market imperfections (translated into variable growth rates rather than deadweight loss).[10] In endogenous growth theory the long-run growth rate can be improved by government policy to induce a higher saving rate and/or to incorporate externalities. Models linking trade and endogenous growth have examined the various channels through which trade can influence growth, but provide few generalisable conclusions.

Technology and knowledge spillovers are key mechanisms which link international trade and endogenous growth.[11] In their classic work, Grossman and Helpman (1991) show how international trade can boost a country's Research and Development (R&D) sector (which is the sector which drives economic growth) by transmitting technological information, increasing competition and entrepreneurial effort and expanding the size of the market in which innovative firms operate. But trade can also have negative effects on the R&D sector by displacing innovative activities, making the overall effects of trade openness ambiguous.

Other technology-based models emphasise the positive effects of openness by focusing on the role of capital goods imports in promoting economic growth (Coe et al. 1995; Lee, 1995; and Pissarides, 1997). In these models, technology spillovers are generally proportional to capital goods imports. Imported capital

---

10   For a critical account, see Fine (2000).
11   For an overview of trade, growth and knowledge, see Zhang (1994).

goods embody information about new technologies, and producers who are exposed to this information are seen as more likely to innovate. Romer (1992) describes this as "using ideas" (as opposed to "producing ideas"), and Pack (1992) sees them essentially as a free dividend for being a latecomer. Many of these models imply that increased amounts of resources will be devoted to R&D following trade liberalisation.

The positive conclusions about openness in these models are largely dependent on specific assumptions about the nature of technology and technology transfer and can be reversed when the definition of technology is refined. Most models assume that technology can be perfectly codified and easily transferred. If, however, we acknowledge that learning by importing capital goods is partly dependent on the absorptive capacity of countries, the gains from trade (especially for poorer countries) may be more limited. Keller (1996) presents a model which differentiates between technology embodied in capital goods and capabilities (or 'absorptive capacity'). Using a Rivera-Batiz and Romer (1991) type endogenous growth model, he shows that the productivity and growth effects of increased access to foreign capital goods will be short-lived unless absorptive capacity increases at a more rapid rate than during the period prior to trade reform. In the long run, the rate of growth of output is forced down to the rate of human capital growth. Similarly, van de Klundert and Smulders (1996) allow for technology spillovers between North and South, but the latter's low level of high-tech production limits learning by doing.[12] In the light of recent evidence that increased openness leads to less investment in human capital at the secondary and tertiary levels (Wood and Ridao-Cano, 1999), this all implies that the gains for poor countries from access to technology imports can be limited.

A negative conclusion about the effects of openness is also reached by a few recent endogenous trade models which revisit infant industry arguments by explicitly dealing with the role of learning under protection in countries with low levels of industrialisation. In these models, poor countries are shown to specialise in low technology products if free trade were allowed, but trade restrictions allow them to develop complex industries (Reddy, 1999).

These ambiguous results of endogenous growth/trade models are complicated further by the fact that growth-enhancing trade policies do not always improve welfare. Thus, Westerhout (1995) focuses on consumer variety and allows firms to exit and enter. With trade liberalisation, consumer prices and

---

12   See also Walde (1996) who suggests that, with perfect international technical spill-over, convergence will depend upon conditions of competition.

costs of production are lower but so can be product variety, as domestic producers are eliminated, and this can outweigh the other effects on consumer welfare. For a small open economy, Osang and Pereira (1996) find that all tariffs are damaging to long-run growth but there can be increases in welfare in the short run.[13] In addition, there is no reason to presume that tariffs should be uniform across goods in maximising intertemporal welfare.

Models linking growth and trade also deal with the issue of convergence. Again, they provide few robust conclusions, with convergence or divergence depending upon how openly competitive is international trade. Boileau's (1996) model allows for international externalities, but with non-traded and non-market production within countries. He is able to generate growth and cycles in which, contrary to most models and in conformity to received wisdom, cross-country correlations on output exceed those of consumption and productivity. Lau and Wan (1994) argue that trade is necessary but not sufficient for poorer countries to converge. For middle-income countries will be able to accrue the benefits of catch-up since the costs of doing so declines with growth, whereas the poorest countries will experience a widening income gap. A complex model is provided by Fischer and Serra (1996) in which the domestic economy grows faster the greater the level of equality because of higher incentives and returns to investment in human capital.[14] As growth rises, unskilled labour may be rewarded more as it becomes scarcer but inequality may also increase as the wealthier invest more in human capital. With a world economy of rich and poor countries, free trade is in part disadvantageous for the former in raising inequality at once (skilled labour is immediately worth more in opening up to trade) and over time, and in lowering the growth rate as poorer countries converge. Poor countries unambiguously gain from each of these effects. The implication is free trade for poor countries and subsidised education for the worse-off in rich countries.

3.3   Political Economy Arguments

In short, the marriage between new trade and growth theories serves to render each more complex. In addition, they also tend to share a particularly underdeveloped notion of what constitutes a nation. Indeed, in conformity with longstanding traditions in trade theory, the nation is simply a special individual, usually with both benevolent goals (social welfare) and special

---

13   See also Kaneda (1995) who shows in presence of increasing returns that the one country of two with lower time preference is liable to industrialise first.

14   See also Gould and Ruffin (1995) for the case that human capital is crucial to growth and trade.

powers (policy).[15] A simple step is taken to progress beyond such simplicity once account is taken of internal influences upon government policy, thereby incorporating a fourth factor in new trade theory, that of political economy in general and rent-seeking in particular. Rodrik and Fouroutan (1998), for example, debate whether trade liberalisation has stalled in Africa because of a combination of distributional and informational problems (who knows consequences and who gets compensated for them).[16] Fung (1995) examines the redistribution between capital and labour as rents are shifted and shared with change in trade policy in the presence of oligopoly. In a model of electoral competition, Riezman and Wilson (1997) find that limits on number of donors and amounts of donations by interest groups can lead to inefficiency in the making of trade policy.

Most important, though, in the political economy of trade policy have been the rent-seeking arguments. It is as if all of more narrower 'economic' analysis above can be set aside since, for to act upon their prescriptions is to solicit unproductive rent-seeking through trade policy. Here, however, there is a major problem. If there are underlying economic and political interests in favour of trade policy, why would they allow trade liberalisation to proceed? And, if they do not have the option of this form of rent-seeking, might they not engage in even more costly forms of pursuing their advantage? This is exactly what is perceived to have happened, if not anticipated, in the wake of the Uruguay Round, with trade policy pursued by other means and, most notably, through antidumping measures which have become the new form of (privatised) trade policy in the WTO era.[17]

4   Empirical Evidence

Empirical research has examined the effects of trade liberalisation on growth, productivity and efficiency at cross-country, industry and firm-level. Below, we discuss each of them in turn.

---

15   Hence the capacity for the theory to move effortlessly between lower and higher levels than the nation. See Krugman and Elizondo (1996) for the idea that third world cities are too large because of economies of linkages accruing out of ISI. See also Lall (1998). For new trade theory and regional integration (and the idea that this can even intensify internal protection), see Bilal (1998).

16   See also Edwards (1997).

17   This is the subject of a separate paper in preparation. But for a comprehensive empirical overview, see Miranda et al. (1998). Note that the paper in preparation never progressed to standalone. But see Fine (2011).

4.1   Cross-country Research

The country-level research on liberalisation and growth consists of cross-section 'before and after' studies (Greenaway et al. 1997), and 'with and without' studies (Mosley et al. 1991; and World Bank, 1990) as well as of country-specific time-series analysis (Papageorgiou et al. 1991; Greenaway and Sapsford, 1994; and Onafowora et al. 1996). In general, many of these studies suggest that the effects of liberalisation on growth are ambiguous and complex; whilst some groups of countries show an improvement in growth (as well as other indicators such as investment), others show a marked deterioration. Here again, however, the alternative models provide very different estimates of the long-run effects on growth (with the pay-off ranging from 2% to 46%!), indicating the limitations of capturing complicated growth effects using cross-country single equation growth regressions which are discussed below.

At best, most of the literature seeking to investigate the effects of shifts in trade policy (towards liberalisation) develops a model from which a reduced form is estimated. At worst, simple regressions are run on some index of economic performance against some index of openness (although the best and worst often coincide in practice). Here, we leave aside perennial problems (like much of the literature!) concerning the data, and how we measure openness,[18] the value for an individual country's development over time for what are often cross-section studies, the fallacy of composition (if all liberalise, export prices may fall),[19] and the direction of causation between variables.

Consider, however, two problems that are generally overlooked. The first is that only a single equation tends to be estimated rather than a model. However, even if a significant and desired result is obtained, this is not a proper test of the theory. For, within the model, there will implicit mechanisms through which trade policy has affected trade performance. These include both shifts in composition of output and in capital-labour ratios as well as shifts in domestic prices, factor rewards and composition of consumption. These usually

---

18   See Greenaway et al. (1998) for a discussion. Note that the problems in measuring openness are recognised theoretically by the wish to construct sensible indices, as in the notion of a uniform-tariff welfare-equivalent to any existing level of protection. See Anderson (1995 and 1998) and Anderson and Neary (1996). These measures, however, depend upon genuine equilibrium comparative statics and cannot eliminate the problem of perverse prices, that increases in a tariff may be equivalent to a decrease in (effective) protection. In addition, in the absence of perfect competition, as is well-known, export subsidies and tariff reductions (or other trade measures) are not equivalent to one another for a variety of reasons for both partial and general equilibrium. See Chen and Devereux (1997) and Okawa (1997) for example.

19   See Bandyopadhyay (1996).

remain unexamined. If, as is to be expected,[20] such empirical regularities do not hold, to what extent is the theory properly tested? To be more concrete, if trade liberalisation in a labour-rich economy is associated with growth in capital-intensive exports, there will be an apparent connection between trade reform and export growth but not for the reasons posited.

The second point is a more developed form of the first and is to be learned from the more sophisticated treatments of the endogenous growth literature.[21] The models involved in the new trade theory, even with a few factors, are extremely complicated in terms of their outcomes – potentially generating multiple equilibria and complex patterns of adjustment to, or around, them. For a single economy, this raises issues of what exactly are we estimating – comparison of static equilibria or paths between equilibria. For a cross-section of economies, trade performances cannot be taken to be independent of one another. Countries serve the same world market, one country's exports are another's imports, and economic variables are not independent of one another given flows of capital, labour and technology, quite apart from strategic behaviour of firms and governments, etc.

Ideally, of course, the dynamics of trade performance would be properly modelled, and models fully estimated across panel data. The literature generally falls far short. Even so, it is far from supportive of the trade liberalisation hypothesis. Neatly illustrating some of these observations is the study of Greenaway et al. (1998) who use panel data across liberalisers and non-liberalisers (with/without and before/after) to come to a negative conclusion on the effect of trade reform on growth but then suggest this may be due to a shorter-run J-curve impact of liberalisation.

4.2   *Industry and Firm-Level Studies*

A substantial body of empirical literature has focused on the dynamic effects of trade liberalisation and has investigated the effects of trade policy and openness on total factor productivity and efficiency at the industry level. Evidence from these studies, however, is inconclusive. Some early empirical exercises found a negative (but weak) correlation between import substitution and productivity growth (Nishimuzu and Robinson, 1984), others showed TFP growth rates to be high in highly protected industrial sectors (Waverman and Murphy, 1992), whilst continued and accelerating TFP growth rates in both periods of high and low protection have also been reported (Aswichayono et al. 1996).

---

20   Not least from the theory itself in view of the discussion above!

21   These points are discussed at length in Fine (2000) and carry over, if less observed in the literature, from statistical investigation of growth to trade performance.

High levels of import penetration have also been found to be associated with low rates of productivity growth (Nishimuzu and Page, 1991). Given the varying country coverage of these studies, the different industrial sectors included, and the varying definitions of liberalisation and openness used, attempting to provide a rigorous net balance of the evidence would serve little purpose. Some key weaknesses of these industry-level studies, however, must be noted. None of them discriminates between the effects of trade policy and macro policy choices and it is, therefore, difficult to attribute causality to trade policy itself. Many of them also fail adequately to control for other influences on productivity growth. In particular, the failure to control for industry effects is especially problematic.

The firm-level literature circumvents the need to control for industry effects, but still fails to establish a direct causal link between trade liberalisation and improved economic performance. Much of this literature examines the link between trade liberalisation, openness and firm-level efficiency estimated using frontier-production-functions. Some studies find support for the conjecture that efficiency levels are highest among industries experiencing the largest declines in protection (Tybout et al. 1991). The firm-level literature also examines the relationship between export-orientation and productivity/efficiency, although the link between trade liberalisation and exporting is not empirically investigated. Several studies have found exporting firms to be more efficient than their domestically oriented counterparts (Chen and Tang, 1987; Haddad, 1993; Aw and Hwang 1995; Tybout and Westbrook, 1995; and Aw and Batra, 1998), and have attributed this result to the positive learning effects which accrue from contact with foreign buyers.

There are three major weaknesses with this firm-level literature. Firstly, most studies examine one-time changes in the *level* of efficiency and their findings are consistent with the claim that trade liberalisation generates static gains. They do not however, provide conclusive evidence relating to long-term, dynamic improvements in firm-level efficiency. Secondly, the indicator of firm performance used by many of the studies, total factor productivity, is characterised by theoretical inconsistencies and estimation problems (with Nelson, 1981 providing a critical discussion of these issues). Thirdly, they fail to establish the causal links between trade policy, export-orientation and efficiency. For instance, the literature on exporting generally does not ask whether the direction of causality runs from exporting to efficiency or vice-versa. The latter is a strong possibility as more efficient firms are more likely to be competitive in export markets. A study of exporters in Colombia and Morocco attempted to address the causality issue by plotting long-term cost and productivity trajectories (Clerides et al. 1998). It found that entry into export markets does not significantly shift the cost and productivity functions of firms and concludes that the association between exporting and efficiency is most plausibly explained by low-cost producers choosing to become exporters.

Finally, much of the firm-level research fails to shed light on the various channels through which trade liberalisation might affect productivity and efficiency in changing populations of heterogeneous firms. A few studies have attempted to do so, focusing on the effects of trade policy on industry rationalisation and entry and exit patterns and cost-price ratios (Tybout, 1992; and Roberts and Tybout, 1991). Overall, however, no strong conclusions emerge. There is little evidence of an association between import penetration and entry and exit patterns, contrary to predictions that import liberalisation is likely to result in the exit of inefficient firms and the entry of low-cost ones. There is also little support for the argument that liberalisation allows firms to benefit from scale economies. Positive firm-level effects of liberalisation are reported by Steel and Webster (1992) in their study of small firms in Ghana; they found new firms (i.e. those entering after liberalisation) to have faster growth rates than older firms and concluded that this demonstrated that liberalisation brings forth dynamic new entrants. This, however, is highly misleading as the negative relationship between the age of a firm and growth is a well-established empirically (McPherson, 1995), having little to do with trade policy.

The dynamic gains from liberalisation are supposed to accrue largely from technology upgrading but few empirical studies have directly examined the technological response to liberalisation at the firm-level. One group of studies has examined the relationship between technology imports and domestic technology development. Both Basant (1993) and Fikkert (1993) found that domestic R&D and foreign technology were substitutes in the case of India. Braga and Wilmore (1991) and Katrak (1997) examine whether improved access to imports increased the extent of R&D at the firm-level. They report a positive but weak association between measures of technology imports and R&D. In general, the evidence indicates that the extent to which foreign technology can stimulate R&D depends on factors such as availability of necessary skills and expertise (Evenson and Westphal, 1995).

In the context of developing countries, informal technological effort (mainly to modify and adapt foreign technologies) is more relevant than formal R&D, but the links between trade policy and such informal technological activity have rarely been explicitly examined. Some exceptions are Deraniyagala and Semboja (1999) and Latsch and Robinson (1999), who examine the technological response to liberalisation in Sub-Saharan African countries. They find very little evidence of widespread technology development following import liberalisation, with most firms being hesitant or unable to invest in new technologies in the face of very intense import competition. Well-known qualitative studies of interventionist trade and industrial policies in East Asia have demonstrated in detail their impact on technology strategies, learning effects, entry and exit dynamics and micro-level aspects of industrial performance and have highlighted the point that these effects vary considerably according to the type of trade policy and according to the specificities of industrial sectors (Amsden 1989; and Wade 1990). It is important that empirical research on the effects of trade liberalisation also examines such factors and provides an in-depth analysis of the manner in which various policy instruments impact upon aspects of performance in specific sectors and in countries at specific levels of development.

In general terms, then, the existing empirical research on trade liberalisation allows us to make the following observations. First, there is little to suggest that trade policy is itself an important determinant of industrial performance and, even so, a positive role will derive from export expansion (through export performance requirements, for example) rather than from import liberalisation.[22] As Helleiner (ed.) (1994, p. 31) concludes:

> On the basis of currently available evidence, it is difficult to escape the conclusion that trade policy has *not* been the major influence on productivity growth in manufacturing that many analysts have said that it should be. Such associations as there have been between productivity growth and trade phenomena relate to the probable positive role of manufactured export expansion, and *not* to import liberalization.

Second, at least as important as trade policy have been the other elements of industrial policy, such as research and development, and the impact of technology transfer and the scale and growth of domestic markets. Also important has been the macroeconomic environment, especially the level and stability of the exchange rate, the level of domestic demand and real wage restraint. At a more detailed level of targeting, favourable access to credit can be used

---

22 See also the review provided by Edwards (1993, p. 1389) who concludes on the mixed results in favour of trade liberalisation, "Much of the cross-country regression based studies have been plagued by empirical and conceptual shortcomings. The theoretical frameworks used have been increasingly simplistic, failing to address important questions such as the exact mechanism through which export expansion affects GDP growth, and ignoring important potential determinants of growth such as educational attainment. All of this has resulted ... in unconvincing results whose fragility has been exposed by subsequent work."

to promote exports, especially to complement low levels of domestic demand relative to scale economies. Given the significance of stability in the macroeconomic environment and the structure of incentives to industry, it is hardly surprising that liberalisation beyond trade, to capital markets, has not been favourable to industrial performance. The impact of speculative movements of capital can discourage long-term investment; and attempts to stabilise capital movements and the exchange rate can lead to high interest rates further discouraging domestic economic activity.

Third, trade policy involves a very wide variety of complex instruments with an equally varied set of outcomes depending upon how the trade policies interact with other policies and factors in the specific economic conditions in which they operate. Consequently, trade policy should not be seen in isolation from other policies and as a bias in one direction or another. Rather, it needs to be situated carefully in a sectoral context (for example, Agosin and Ffrench-Davis, 1995 for Latin America; and Soludo, 1998 for Africa). But, even more important, the process of restructuring industries, both vertically and horizontally, needs to range far beyond considerations of trade policy alone and to recognise how the structure and functioning of sectors are very different from one another – by virtue of technology, markets, sources of finance and ownership, vertical integration with other sectors as well as established historical patterns.

In short, the factors underlying appropriate trade policy are not only varied and complex but require trade-offs to be made. Macroeconomic conservatism, for example, in order to provide stability for potential investors and exporters, could prove to be a self-defeating exercise if the level of domestic demand is insufficient to support scale economies. Certainly, however, there is no rationale for accepting the general case in favour of trade liberalisation, and the merits of trade policy need to be examined at a detailed and specific level. Given infant industry considerations, the sequencing as well as the content of policy is crucial, especially as trade, macroeconomic or other policy could kill off infants or even adolescents before they have the opportunity to attain maturity.

5   Concluding Remarks

A number of conclusions follow from our review. First, free or freer trade is heavily favoured by the economics profession and is gathering momentum under the WTO regime. Second, the thrust of theoretical and empirical literature is far from supportive of such postures.[23] Third, it is totally inappropriate to address trade theory and policy separately from other aspects of industrial policy and performance and macroeconomic considerations. Fourth, crude dichotomies such as those between free trade and protection should be rejected and the need recognised for sophisticated, sector- and country-specific trade and industrial policy. Fifth, in this respect, to the extent that the neoliberal consensus has promoted trade liberalisation, it has done a double disservice both by undermining interventionist trade policy and its integration with other policy areas.

---

23   This is despite Krueger's (1998, p. 1517/8) claim that the traditional infant industry argument of dynamic gains outweighing static losses has now been overturned.

CHAPTER 6

A Formal Note on New Theories of International Trade and Development

Postscript as Personal Preamble

This Chapter has a peculiar genesis. By the mid-1990s, I had been working on the systems of provision approach (SoP) to consumption for a decade or so (see especially Fine and Leopold, 1993; Fine, 2002a; and Bayliss and Fine, 2021, for subsequent staging points in the evolution of the SoP approach). Having developed the approach and applied it to some degree to the ownership of (putatively gendered, labour-saving) consumer durables (and its impact on female labour market participation), a second research project targeted close theoretical and empirical application of the approach to food systems as part of an ESRC research programme on the Nation's Diet, and why it was so bad (Fine et al. 1996; and Fine, 1998b). I became interested in all things food, especially in determining aspects of food provisioning located away from, but informing, its consumption. Necessarily, I took an interest in Sutton's (1991) book as it was focused on the impact of competitive processes on industrial structure, with examples drawn from the food sectors.

In the event, this interest took on a life of its own, focusing on theories of competition and monopoly, on which I already had form (Fine and Murfin, 1984a and b). Sutton, with developments from Schmalensee (1992),[1] was primarily concerned with modelling the ways in which competition within a sector – how firm's decisions in pricing, costing, advertising, and investing, etc affect its profits both directly and indirectly through the responses of other firms to its actions – dovetail with competition between sectors – entry for new firms and/or exit of the old, for which there would be fixed costs to be borne. Significantly, he focused on the tensions between these two forms of competition. The more competitive within a sector through whatever mechanisms, the less likely competition through entry since the resulting profits were

---

1 Schmalensee is an extremely prominent industrial economist. From a position of being primarily anti-monopolist, he found it possible to interpret the evidence in a diametrically opposed way, not least upon becoming a witness for Microsoft in its anti-trust cases. See Fine (2024c) in context of path dependency and discussion below of competition appearing as its opposite.

more likely to be harmed through more intensive post-entry competitiveness. So, things like high entry costs, or high elasticity of sales to increased output, are more likely to discourage entry. But high monopoly profits due to small numbers of firms is an invitation to entry.

Sutton's motivation in developing these models was grounded entirely within mainstream concerns. Given the two forms of competition (intra- and inter-) can pull in opposite directions, what sort of equilibrium emerges (in terms of number of firms) and with what efficiency properties. In particular, given his models involve increasing returns to scale because of fixed costs, does the equilibrium number of firms tend to increase with market size (good for competitiveness but bad for replicated fixed costs) or does a relatively small number of firms result (the consequences of competition within the sector are more than enough to discourage the number of firms to increase indefinitely with market size).

I studied and developed Sutton's models with gusto, the (derivation of the) results of which are reported elsewhere (Fine, 1999)[2] and are simply drawn upon in what follows in this Chapter. But my motivation was different, as well as critical of, Sutton's. First, I had no interest in equilibrium as such as a way to understand industrial development and competition.

Second, as part of a more general strategy of bringing out the full implications of the mainstream in order to expose its limitations and move on, I sought to show exactly how the mainstream's methodology ultimately means that its theoretical results depend upon taking certain vital factors to be fixed (as parameters, literally fixed costs in some instances, but also demand responsiveness, market size, etc). As a result, although these parameters can themselves be made into variables, competition can always be taken one step further than the model in hand because competitive outcomes (overall and for individual firms) depend upon the parameters that determine equilibrium. It is a simple step, then, to insist that these become the object of competition, leading to an infinite regression from one parameter to the next (as well as need to take into account the mutual determination of the parameters as they become variable).

Third, in a sense, this observation fulfils the initial goal of stepping back and saying we need to start over and examine sectoral developments in the round and in their broader context, voilà the SoP approach. In addition, it suggests the need to look beyond the parameters attached to the sector, to the economic

---

2 Note that it took much longer to get the 1999 piece published than the one reproduced as this Chapter even though the latter draws upon the former.

and social forces that might influence those 'parameters'. For example, capacity to enter depends heavily upon the financial sector, and whether, for example, it is able and willing to invest in entry; even more telling, just taking into account the potential for competition through mergers and acquisitions, undermines the logic of seeing competition in the confined terms of corporate (new) entry and (old) exit. And, take one step further, and there is the question of the role of state intervention (competition policy, regulation, or even state ownership) that will or will not be induced in response to the inefficiencies that are built into Sutton's world – better to have two railways competing with one another but doubling fixed costs, or just the one with monopoly. Or should we even ban excessive advertising to gain market shares if this contributes to replicated fixed costs that add nothing to the quality of the product (other than in consumers' manipulated minds).

Fourth, although a temporary digression, Sutton's results with higher competition leading to fewer firms is perverse from the mainstream's usual notion of perfect competition as the more the firms the merrier, not least arising out of dependence on increasing returns (fixed capital plus unit costs) for which the model of perfect competition cannot apply. This has resonances with Marx's famous observation that, under competition, appearances within the capitalist economy can be the opposite of the reality. This is appealing to those with a Marxist bent in terms of dialectics and the contradictions between reality and appearance (and most obviously that free and perfect markets are the basis of capitalist exploitation not its negation). But, in this case, no such methodological acrobatics are required. More competition, fewer firms; and there are other examples of such perverse outcomes. Monopoly, for example, would lead to faster extraction of natural resources (deemed to be in fixed supply), boosting supply in the present, because present value of resources now is greater than in the future. Similarly, monopolistic markets can lead to excessive, not deficient, innovation and product variety as each firm seeks to accrue its competitive advantage through technological lead.

Leaving this digression aside for the moment, see below, fifth, I have finally got there, or here – the ultimate rationale for this Chapter. As apparent from the previous Chapter, I was at the time heavily engaged in arguments against free trade in a developmental context, basically for reasons of infant industry protection, written large and wide. There is a long tradition in trade theory, especially with comparative advantage, Edgeworth Boxes, and the like, to treat the nation in trade inappropriately as if an individual. I opportunistically did the same translating Sutton's theory of competition between firms to one of competition between nations. As a result, light is shed on whether developing countries should enter a sector given the first-comer advantages of the developed as incumbents already appropriating markets. The rest, as it were, is history or, more exactly, what follows in this Chapter. Protection for development can be justified not only to accrue static and dynamic economies of scale and scope but also to escape to some degree from the monopolistic provision from those who have already developed. As the abstract puts it:

> Drawing upon the long-run solutions to a number of models in which there are economies of scale and differing degrees of intra-sectoral competition, conditions are found under which an industry's development will spread to further countries and under which the domestic industry should be supported by state intervention.

This is hardly rocket science irrespective of the mathematical sophistication within the models.

Matters did not finish here, though, as my work in this area had an afterlife in two ways. First is in teaching (Fine, 2016b and 2018b). The community of heterodox scholars is in general obliged to teach mainstream methods and applications and to pick away at it as best it can. My view has always been that microeconomics as applied to supply is of more interest and potential than demand given the latter's predominantly unyielding dependence upon a fixed set of consumers with fixed preferences. In contrast, the microeconomics of competition allows for considerably more 'endogeneity' – how many firms there are and the strategies for how they go about their business. The models derived from Sutton offer an important means by which to teach the orthodoxy, in an interesting way, that sheds light on many competitive processes (fixed costs, advertising, entry and exit, price, cost, productivity and quality) as well as the potential to suggest alternatives in light of what is omitted or treated poorly. Second, as both a mathematician by early training and heterodox economist by later choice, I felt caught between acknowledging the deficiencies of a mainstream economics that deemed itself to be scientific in light of its exclusive dependence upon mathematical modelling, and the uses I had found myself in these methods in this and other work. In short, mathematical methods can clarify, and aid presentation of, the substance of our own and the work of others, bringing out implications that might otherwise be overlooked (not least if 'perverse'), as well as offering insight into some economic processes, partially conceived and addressed, without situating them within broader economic and social aspects of which they are a part and through which they need to be framed and (re)constructed (Fine, 2023b).

1   Introduction[3]

In a recent review article, Schmalensee (1992, p. 125) advises that, "every serious student of industrial economics should read John Sutton's *Sunk Costs
and Market Structure: Price Competition, Advertising, and the Evolution of
Concentration*". The purpose of this Chapter is to draw upon Schmalensee's
formalisation of the Sutton theory to shed light on the relatively new theories of international trade, especially in the context of developing countries
and whether they do or do not have the potential to become newcomers in
particular industries. As is well-known, these theories, by drawing upon the
presence of economies of scale and scope, externalities or imperfect competition, seek to explain why more than one country might produce and trade
in the same good, incurring transport and other costs, and violating classical
theories concerning specialisation.[4] Moreover, it can be posited that national
policy to support the emergence of such internationally competing industries
can be justified.

Sutton's work is of relevance, although it does not address issues of trade
and policy, because it is primarily concerned with long-run solutions to domestic industrial structure in the presence of market imperfections. Specifically,
industries are characterised by economies of scale, so that the Pareto-efficient
outcome would only allow for one producer.[5] But different long-run (equilibrium) outcomes are possible contingent upon the different intensities of
market competition within the industries, not least where there is assumed
perfect ease of entry into the industry in the long run. The last condition guarantees that long-run equilibrium is given by zero (excess) profit for each firm,
otherwise there would be new entrants. However, reflection on the intensity
of intra-sectoral competition gives rise to counter-intuitive results. For, the
greater is competition within an industry, the less likely is entry, since potential
new firms are subject to lower post-entry levels of profitability. This contrasts
with the ideal of perfect competition for which large numbers of firms and
ease of entry are presumed.

---

3   Originally published as Fine (1996b). Thanks to anonymous referees for helpful comments
    and suggestions. Note that this was published long before the earlier drafted Fine (1999) on
    which it heavily draws for its simple models.
4   See Baldwin (1992), Dornbusch (1992), Rodrik (1992), Ocampo (1986), Pack and Westphal
    (1986), and Greenaway (1991).
5   This is unless there are genuine welfare improvements from product differentiation in the
    models in which this is the form taken by competition.

The Sutton approach is concerned with how many firms emerge in such long-run equilibria and whether, as the ratio of market size to fixed costs (S/σ) increases (an implicit, negative measure of the cost of entry), the equilibrium number of firms increases indefinitely. What is the relevance of this to new theories of international trade and development? Essentially, reflecting a long run tradition in trade theory, differences between countries are collapsed into differences between firms (or, as in Edgeworth boxes, differences between consumers). Consequently, what was previously a focus upon the equilibrium number of firms within a domestic industry can be interpreted as the equilibrium number of countries that enter an industry. Increases in the ratio S/σ can be interpreted as whether industrialisation (or the spread of different industries) increases as the world market grows. Finally, where a distinction is drawn between a firm and a country, it is generally in the greater capability of the latter to adopt policies that enhance welfare even if at the cost of profit maximisation which is the distinct and sole objective of the firm. In this context, policy can be understood in terms of whether it is worthwhile for a firm/ country to support an industry and, in particular, to reserve the domestic market for itself – thereby running against the ideological and material pressures for liberalising trade. Before running through the particular models involved, it is crucial to emphasise that they are based upon highly restrictive assumptions, a point taken up in the concluding remarks.

2   Model of Type I

Schmalensee proposes a simple model to capture Sutton-type features. In Type I models, there are economies of scale as a result of exogenously imposed fixed costs. Assume that unit variable costs, c, are fixed but that there is competition between firms through product and price-differentiation. For the purposes here, in pure form, the price differences are all that distinguishes the products whose differentiation is otherwise nominal. For perfect competition, the lowest price would command the whole market; assume, instead, that market share is inversely-related to own-price.[6] Schmalensee proposes the following as the ith firm's profit function:

---

6   The first model in the next section allows for 'genuine' product differentiation, with quality, and demand, potentially depending upon costs.

$$\prod_i = (p_i - c) S \left[p_i^{-e} / \left\{ \sum_{j=1}^{N} p_j^{-e} \right\} \right] - \sigma$$

where N is the number of firms. The expression in square brackets gives market share as a negative function of own and positive function of other prices according to the parameter e. The higher (lower) is e, the more (less) competitive is the industry, as own market share changes more (less) for own-price movement relative to others. Here the firm's choice variable is taken as p_i, presuming other firms' prices are kept constant – a Cournot-Nash solution to Bertrand oligopoly.

Differentiating the profit function for p_i and setting it equal to zero, and using symmetry so that $p_i = p_j = p$, results after some manipulation in the equation:

$$(N - 1)e(p - c) = Np$$

In the long-run, perfect entry guarantees a zero profit condition:

$$(p - c)S = N\sigma$$

It follows that:

$$N = (cS/\sigma + e)/(e - 1)$$

In this case, the number of firms increases indefinitely with the ratio S/σ and, as e increases, N falls since price competition is tougher (sales more price-responsive) for higher values of e, and entry is deterred.

Sutton interprets N as an upper bound on the number of firms that are liable to be found in the industry over time. Other factors, especially those influencing the competitive process, may prevent that bound from being realised – a monopoly over a patent, for example, or other forms of entry deterrence. Setting this aside, and presuming that S grows over time relative to σ as a reflection of world development, then the number of firms should grow over time. Of course, more than one of these may be attached to a single country, thereby demonstrating the advantages of being first-movers or incumbents. However, if there are locational advantages for domestic production (less transport costs, more sensitivity to local markets), the implication is that industries should become more widely spread over time.

Should government intervene to encourage this? The obvious policy variable is to reserve the domestic market for the home producer. This is worthwhile if domestic costs of production are lower than market price. The former is given by $c+\sigma/mS$, where m is the country's market share (which would include any exports that could be captured). Now $p=c+\sigma N/S$, so that it is worth reserving the domestic market and promoting the industry as long as $m>1/N$. Once a country's consumption exceeds the output of a typical (long-run equilibrium) firm, infant industry protection is justified. Note that this is more likely as N increases which, as previously observed, occurs as S/σ increases and e falls. These are all appealing intuitively. The greater the world market (as a proxy for potential market for own output), the lower are fixed costs, or the less competitive is the industry internally, the more a domestic industry should be encouraged. This can also be seen from the solution for p which, after simple manipulation, is given by:[7]

$$[1+1/(e-1)][c+\sigma/S]$$

p decreases with e and σ/S. If the industry is highly competitive, as e goes to infinity, the price falls to $c+\sigma/S$ and N falls to 1, yielding the Pareto-efficient outcome for which, of course, there is no incentive for another country/firm to replicate fixed costs. If the single firm attempted to exploit its monopoly, this would lead to competitive entry in the long run, as in perfect contestability.

3   Type II Models

Characteristic of the previous model is that all costs are exogenously given and there is solely price-competition, apart from entry and exit, for a standardised product. For Sutton, Type II models are ones in which there are also other forms of competition. Schmalensee ingeniously constructs a model of this sort. Suppose price is now given but that unit costs can be varied to influence the actual or perceived quality of the product. Profit is now given by:

$$\prod_i = (p-c_i)S\left[c_i^e / \left\{\sum_{j=1}^{N} c_j^e\right\}\right] - \sigma$$

---

7   Note that N and p-c both increase with c, so that the higher are unit variable costs relative to S and σ, the greater the incentive to adopt policies to enter the market.

Here firms can enhance product quality by increasing unit costs, and they increase market share by doing so in competition with other firms to a degree of intensity given by the parameter e. The higher (lower) is e, the more (less) responsive is market share to product-enhancing unit costs.[8] The condition for profit maximisation, together with symmetry, yields:

$$(p - c)e(N - 1) = Nc$$

which together with the long-run zero profit condition for equilibrium, the same as previously, gives:

$$N = (pS/\sigma + e)/(1 + e)$$

The properties, not surprisingly, are as before with price competition. N falls to one as e increases and increases indefinitely with S/σ and p. For e=0, the number of firms is given by pS/σ. Firms get no response from cost competition and so set c=0. They enter until the pure profit out of the fixed price, p, is whittled away by the fixed costs that need to be covered.

Should a country intervene to enter the market in these circumstances? The answer depends once again on the price-cost margin exceeding the unit fixed costs of the reserved share of the market, m. It is worth supporting the industry if:

$$p\text{-}c > \sigma/mS$$

which, as before, is equivalent to m>1/N. It is possible to add a further twist by examining the case at the opposite extreme to the one considered so far, for which additional endogenous costs are necessary to achieve market share. If, at the other extreme, these costs are perceived to be entirely spurious and need not be incurred if the domestic market is reserved, then the condition for intervening is simply that $m>\sigma/Sp$ – more likely the higher are S and p and the lower is σ (although domestic consumers have to be given no choice or be convinced that the domestic product is as good as 'the real thing'). This is also equivalent to the case where e=0.[9]

---

8   One way of interpreting the given price, p, is as normal costs and profits, with c as the extra costs attached to product enhancement, whether 'real' (packaging or advertising, etc) or not.

9   Note that $\sigma<Sp$, otherwise, even with one firm, it is impossible to cover fixed costs even with c=0. The equilibrium value of c is given by $(p-\sigma/S)e/(1+e)$ which is positive for this condition.

A third model considered by Schmalensee allows fixed costs to vary by A over and above exogenous fixed costs given by σ. This might represent advertising expenditure (interpreted here as spurious) or research and development (interpreted as product and economy enhancing). Market share is increased through this expenditure, with both price and unit costs now also taken as given. Suppose ith firm maximises:

$$(p-c)S\left[A_i^e / \left\{\sum_{j=1}^{N} A_j^e\right\}\right] - A_i - \sigma$$

With symmetry, this ultimately gives:[10]

$$(p - c)eS(N - 1) = AN^2$$

Together with the zero long-run profit condition:

$$(p - c)S = AN + \sigma N$$

This leads to a quadratic in N:

$$(\sigma/S)N^2 - (p - c)(1 - e)N - (p - c)e = 0$$

This gives relatively complicated solutions for N, but it is possible to examine what happens as S/σ increases indefinitely. For e < 1, N increases indefinitely.[11] But, for e > 1, as (σ/S) tends to zero, and the quadratic term can be set aside,[12] so N tends to $e/(e - 1)$. This does lead to an upper bound on the number of firms. In other words, for 2>e>1, fixed cost competition is so tough that the number of firms cannot rise above 1 + 1/(e-1) however large the market size grows relative to exogenous fixed costs. This is unlike the previous cases, where N increases indefinitely with S/σ so that m>1/N ultimately. Instead, for 2>e>1, N cannot exceed e/(e-1). If m<(e-1)/e, i.e. m<1-1/e, then it will not be worth entering the sector, no matter how large the world market, or even the price-cost difference, p-c. The reason is that the internal competition through endogenous fixed costs is so great that profitability is gobbled up however advantageous are these parameters.

---

10   e must lie between 0 and 2 for second order conditions to hold.

11   This is most readily seen by rewriting the quadratic in 1/N.

12   As long, as is the case for e > 1, the positive solution for N does not increase indefinitely.

This seems to capture very well and very simply the notion of a technological or product lead. Number of firms will be very low for highly responsive market share either to advertising expenditure (as in coke) or to research and development (electronics) – or some combination of the two (as in electronic games). For the first case, it might be possible to avoid the endogenous fixed costs or, in the second case, write them off as developmental gains. Then, the domestic market should be supported if m>σ/(p-c)S – a much less stringent condition, as endogenous fixed costs, A, do not have to be covered, and which is automatically satisfied as S/σ increases.

4   Concluding Remarks

The purpose of this note has been to formalise, as simply as possible, theories of trade and development in the presence of market imperfections, especially less than perfect competition and economies of scale. No claim is made for the realism of the models presented – they are much too simplistic. But, using S as a proxy for world development, and σ as a proxy for economies of scale, etc, it has been shown that development will spread as S increases. This is more so the higher the ratio of S/σ and the less competitive are industries internally (for this increases long-run equilibrium number of producers). Moreover, it will be worthwhile to intervene to protect domestic market share and to capture a share of world trade, the more firms there already are in the industry.

There is, however, an exception when competition through fixed costs is especially fierce. This might prove a barrier to the long-run number of firms, and other countries might not enter production no matter how large the world or their own domestic market. In this case, if the fixed costs need not be incurred as they represent attempts to shift demand without real product enhancement, or if they can be written off socially as contributing to developmental goals, as for R&D etc, then support to domestic production may become attractive once more as market size grows.

These are, of course, extremely powerful results, readily realised in terms of a few parameters such as S, σ, and e. The power and simplicity of the analysis are a source of strength and weakness. The strength derives from the ease with which *laissez-faire* nostrums of emphasising the benefits of free trade are overturned. This can be done by incorporating the impact of scale economies and market imperfections.

The weakness follows from the lack of realism in the assumptions which render the theory, rather than the strategic outlook it permits, inoperable as an immediate guide to policy. Technology cannot be so simply specified in terms of overhead and unit costs, and nor can demand by the parameters, S and e. Oligopolistic behaviour is notoriously difficult to model unless one aspect of behaviour, Bertrand pricing as here for example, is treated in isolation from others. And, even then, outcomes are contingent upon game-theoretic specification of entrepreneurial behaviour which is open to doubt and variability.

The analysis is also confined to a single sector, a partial equilibrium in which the externality effects with other sectors are precluded. Support for one industry might be at the expense of another with potentially higher gains for the same resource costs – although intervention here is based upon the idea that unit domestic resource costs of production may be able to better imperfectly competitive world prices. It is also possible that inter-sectoral dynamics could be positively promoted. But these are matters that lie outside the scope of the models.

In this context, it is worth recognising that the weaknesses for the purposes adopted here are no less than for those for Sutton's own areas of application. On the basis of such models, he feels able to engage in extensive quantitative analysis of a wide range of food industries, across numerous countries and for long periods of time. The formal discussion is complemented by more specific commentary around a wide set of other influences on intra- and inter-sectoral competition. There is no reason why similar exercises should not be employed in the formulation of industrial policy, whether in a developing country context or not. The results will be as good as the original assumptions underlying the model, together with the acumen employed in the more qualitative understanding.

Elsewhere (Fine, 1999), it has been shown that extensions to introduce further factors on terms set by the model (other forms of competition, for example), have the effect, not surprisingly, of modifying the results without fundamentally altering them. It is as if S, σ, and e take on different values according to the presence of other parameters representing the additional factors. Of more concern is the nature of the models themselves which tend to suffer both from being organised around equilibrium and around the 'horizontal' competition of intra-sectoral relations. For the meaningfulness of equilibrium within the models at least presupposes that it be attained before the parameters shift on which the equilibrium is based. This is dubious in practice given the dynamism of industrial development. The latter, or industrialisation by entry into new sectors, involves the frequent growth and restructuring of vertically (dis)integrated factors – from production, technology, finance, distribution, management and training and functioning of the labour market through to consumption.[13] Traditional and even new industrial economics seems ill-equipped to incorporate all of these factors satisfactorily although, where they do, the case for industrial policy is strengthened.

---

13   For the need to analyse sectoral developments in these terms, see Fine and Leopold (1993).

CHAPTER 7

Beyond the Developmental State

Postscript as Personal Preamble

This is a unique contribution to this series of Volumes because it is the text of a lecture and so, with one exception around my continuing work on the developmental state, contains neither (prolific) footnotes nor references (except for the insertion of those for the quotes that were used). It is also situated in a South African context although a separate, prospective Volume is intended for this purpose. The text of the lecture was polished up and published as Fine (2013). I chose to include this as a Chapter, rather than one of a number of other alternative contributions on the developmental state, because it reduces overlap with the coverage of the developmental state in the following Chapter. Hopefully, it makes for a more informal style for a change as well as focusing upon a particular case study.

As will be apparent, I was very cynical about South Africa declaring itself a developmental state. That it continues to do so, if in a more muted and less prominent fashion, is testimony to how correct was my analysis (and cynicism) even if the tragedy of failing to be a developmental state (however valid is the concept for analytical purposes) has now descended into farce, with Zuma, state capture, coalition government and beyond. Further, what I term the developmental state paradigm (DSP) has not only declined in prominence more generally, even with, or because of, the (form taken by) the contemporary renewal of industrial policy (see next Chapter), but it has also become diluted from the goals of economic and social transformation to whatever can be deemed to be a successful state intervention. In other words, the DSP has been neoliberalised in conceptualisation and reduced in practice to the more or less direct imperatives of financialisation (Fine and Pollen, 2018 for my latest contribution on the topic; and Fine, 2018 for application to South Africa once more).[1] By way of exception that proves the rule, I can claim to having been in

---

1 See also de Moraes (2023, p. 833) for a different reconceptualisation, "However, the concept of the Developmental State – as formulated by academics in the 1980s and 1990s – is outdated as a theoretical-analytical research tool. With the expansion and intensification of the Technological-Scientific-Informational Revolution, consequently, of Globalization, the concept of Developmental State remains elementary, but it has become more complex, intricate, aggregated and dynamic." For an opportunistic attempt to (re)define the developmental

there at the beginning of asking where is China if we are talking developmental states. But, perhaps my main and early contributions to the literature were to point to the distinction between the DSP's economic and political schools and its dependence upon the duality between state and market, just like the Washington Consensus that is taken as its critical point of departure.

On a personal note, the reason why this text exists is because I used to have an informal guide of one page of brief notes for an hour's lecture. But, as I got older, I became less confident in being able to deliver on this basis, other than for well-worn or mathematical material, and so much so that I tended to write up lectures fully before delivering them, accepting reluctantly to the extent that speaking from a fuller, written text reduces informality of delivery and palatability of reception. I have always had five abiding fears in my lecturing: that I will be too difficult and no one will understand; too easy, and I will be considered an idiot; I will run out of time; I will finish long before time; and, most important, the audience will not laugh at my jokes and other antics to retain attention and wakefulness.

1   The Lecture[2]

My topic is the developmental state or, more exactly, beyond the developmental state. But "beyond" in what sense? For those economies that have been dubbed developmental states, in Latin America and most prominently, East Asia, the "beyond" has tarnished their record, at least relative to the economic performance that got them there. This is especially true of Japan that has stagnated over the past two decades. On the other hand, for those yet to attain the status or fruits of a Developmental State, which might include South Africa,

---

state, from a bringing the state back in perspective, as integrating capabilities with endogenous growth theory, see Evans (2014).

2   This Chapter is a slightly revised text of a talk given on May 5th, 2011, for Aporde, African Programme on Rethinking Development Economics (https://www.aporde.co.za), jointly hosted with the National Union of Metalworkers of South Africa (NUMSA). It draws and builds upon longstanding work on both the developmental state and the South African economy. Previous contributions include the following (Ashman and Fine 2013; Ashman et al. 2010a and b and 2011; Fine, 2003, 2006b, 2007, 2008a and b, 2010c and d, 2011, 2012a and b; Fine and Rustomjee, 1996; and Fine and Stoneman, 1996, with Fine et al., eds, 2013 offering more recent perspectives on the developmental state). Note also critical commentary on both the National Development Plan and the New Growth Path (Fine, 2012a and b). And some may wish to consult MERG (1994), for a set of alternative economic policies put forward in 1993, and now available online.

the beyond is too far away to contemplate. Primarily, today, though, I will talk about beyond the developmental state in terms of its strength and weaknesses analytically.

My own relationship with the developmental state goes back 25 years, to the mid-1980s. I was familiar with it as an economist in a casual way but a deeper attachment was inspired by exploring whether what I shall call the developmental state paradigm, DSP, could be used to understand the nature and potential of the South African economy, especially in responding to requests by the ANC to assist in formulating policy for the post-apartheid period. My answer was NO, with an alternative dedicated concept developed to characterise the South African economy as the Minerals-Energy complex, MEC. This notion critically departed from the DSP, and I will explain how and why later.

First, though, I am mindful of why I have been asked to lecture on the DSP. Whilst my own relationship with it, like a bad marriage, has been a combination of love and hate, the developmental state in South Africa has been, at least initially, more like an end of the summer romance or even fling, in which past President Mbeki and his coterie desperately sought to revitalise appeal to the masses through promises of better times ahead. As we now know, though, this attempt at saving a marriage with the people failed miserably, not least as there was little faith that the erstwhile President would be able to hold together a marriage based on two different partners, neoliberalism and the developmental state. On the other hand, the new President may be more accomplished at satisfying the competing if not incompatible demands of forging an alliance between neoliberalism and the developmental state, even though these have traditionally been seen as impossible bedfellows. Nor is this as fanciful as it might sound for, South Korea has, in the wake of the crisis of 1997/98 and the most recent, been understood as a *neoliberal* developmental state. This is so for broader reasons to which I will return.

What of the DSP itself? Whilst it can be traced back in all but name at least as far as the eighteenth century and US protectionism, the nineteenth century and German protectionism, through Japan and Latin American import-substituting industrialisation, the DSP has been most prominent as a way both of explaining the success of East Asian NICs and vehemently and intellectually successfully opposing the neoliberal Washington Consensus and its antipathy to the state that emerged so strongly and rapidly in the 1980s. But, although not to be underestimated in terms of its narratives of successful state intervention and refutation of neoliberal dogma, this prominence and success was achieved at some cost or, more exactly, at the expense of unresolved tensions and limitations of the paradigm that went unnoticed at the time and which primarily continue to be overlooked.

First and foremost, the DSP has been pre-occupied with *successful, late-comer or catch up, industrialisation*, with each of these emphasised terms of some significance.

Second, then, the DSP has offered limited attention, despite a universal framework of analysis to which I will return, to *failures*. This is especially important for Africa for, with minor exceptions such as Botswana and Mauritius, the DSP has proceeded as if the dark continent does not exist.

Third, accepting that development does go through stages, the DSP has little to say about *earlier* and *later stages*. How do we get from agrarian to industrial society so we can even begin latecomer catch up? And getting to the frontier is one thing, getting ahead of it is another as those you are catching can hardly be expected to stand still or, possibly, offer you a helping hand as opposed to kicking away the ladder.

Fourth, then, there is the neglect of other aspects of development apart from industry. What about the role of agriculture, health, education and welfare, democracy and labour (other than in provision of skills). There are also other neglected areas or issues, such as macro-policy, the functioning of the financial system (other than in directing finance to industrialists), and the role of globalisation. To some extent, these absences (and I will also refer to technology again later) reflect, conscious or otherwise, an implicit and complicit acknowledgement of the weaknesses and limitations of the DSP in its mission to discredit the Washington Consensus from a progressive, interventionist stance. It would not help to raise questions of welfare, democracy and trade union rights, organisation and action (and the presumption, to some degree false, that these were minimal in the East Asian NICs and destroyed the developmental states of Latin America). And, despite globalisation, there is a presumption that all can become national developmental states as long as the right policies are adopted, whereas convergence of economies has been notably absent over the past three decades.

Fifth, this belief in the capacity for global capitalism to allow all nation-states to be developmental is a mirror-image to the neoliberal dogma that it is a fait accompli so long as everything is left to the market. In part, within the DSP, this reflects two further weaknesses. One is that the DSP literature has primarily been divided between two separate schools, the *economic* and *political* schools. For the economic school, the focus is on those (economic) policies, often narrowly drawn and conceived, that are necessary for an economy to achieve development. Drawing primarily on the idea that markets do not work perfectly and, correspondingly, upon (imperfect market) economics as a discipline, the state is required to accrue, for example, the economies of scale and scope, to coordinate investments within and across sectors, to harness positive and eliminate negative externalities, and so on. For the economic school, then, it is a matter of identifying the appropriate policies, with the presumption that they will be implemented by a developmental state because they ought and/ or need to be.

By contrast, and completely complementary, the political school with its own disciplinary origins predominantly from within political science (and certainly separate from economics), is remarkably aloof from consideration of the economy itself and the nature of the policies required to bring about development. Rather, the political school is concerned with the nature of the state itself and whether it has the potential in general, and the independence in particular, to adopt the necessary policies more or less irrespective of what these might be. Here emphasis is placed upon the necessity for the developmental state to be free of capture by particular interests, and so to be able to adopt developmental policies.

Taken together, the economic and political schools address what policies are to be adopted and what allows them to be adopted. Successful cases of development in practice can be interpreted through this dual prism, and such is a major methodological thrust of both schools. For each has been highly inductive in practice, examining the role of economic policy in bringing about development and the nature of the states adopting such policies. This is not to suggest, however, that the developmental state literature has been without theory or analytical content. The economic school, for example, strongly emphasises the significance of market imperfections and the role of a developmental state in addressing, if not necessarily correcting them. In highlighting the departure from neoliberalism, Alice Amsden famously declared that it was a matter of "getting relative prices wrong", of not conforming to the dictates of the market.

Similarly, the political school has tried to identify empirically what characterises the nature of the states, and the societies containing them, in which development has proven possible. Posing this in terms of the independence of the state from economic or other interests has itself presumed an analytical approach in which society is structured along the lines of the state as opposed to the market, with the addition of civil society to fill out the remaining economic, political and ideological space. In this way, not only is the (developmental) state seen as potentially independent, the term favoured is autonomous, it is also perceived to evolve interests of its own that prevail over those of the market and civil society, especially where these conflict with developmentalism. This approach of the political school is admirably captured in the notion of "Bringing the State back in" as an agent of development in its own right, at times autonomous from interests, at other times embedded with them as long as this allows it to be developmental.

Across both economic and political schools, then, there is a predilection to set up an opposition between state and market which is the source of another analytical weakness. For the economic school, the state overrules the market and so is able to improve upon it. Class does not tend to appear at all for it is simply a matter of identifying the right policies and not whether they have sufficient support to be implemented, and on whose behalf or to whose benefit. For the political school, the state needs to stand aloof from the market, and the economic interests found within it. It is not that class or more general economic interests are absent but it is important that the state has the capacity to neutralise if not to override them. The result has been to downplay the role of class in the DSP, a skewed neglect rather than an absolute absence. The DSP has tended to focus on state-(industrial) capital relations at the expense of the way in which class relations, and more general economic, political and ideological relations are formed, expressed and evolve through the state and the market (not their opposition). So, class relations should, in contrast to the DSP, be taken as analytically prior to the state-market duality which is shared with the Washington Consensus, albeit on a considerably more favourable stance towards the state.

And, as mentioned, of overwhelming importance if so much taken to be granted as more or less to remain unstated, there is a total pre-occupation with the nation-state and its capacity to bring about development irrespective of the impact of international or global factors. This does not mean that the global is absent, only that it is only incorporated as a positive (availability of catch-up technology, for example) or as a negative (competition from imports or imposition of wrong policies) influence in the policies to be adopted or the attainment of independence in policymaking.

On this basis, let me now turn to the rhythm of the DSP, its shifting profile and content over time. As already indicated, it was at its height from the mid-1980s for a decade, in opposition to the Washington Consensus and drawing upon a systemic, inductive understanding of what brings about successful latecomer, catch up industrialisation and pointing to the irreducible role of the state. From the mid-1990s, though, even before the Asian crisis of 1997/98, the DSP was going into decline the reason being that it was thought to be its own gravedigger, to coin a phrase, a victim of its own success. In South Korea, for example, having created large, powerful conglomerates, the chaebol, that dominated the economy, these could no longer be controlled let alone coordinated by the state. And development also brought strengthened demands for democracy, trade unions and higher wages and benefits. On top of this, both before and after the Asian crisis, some began to deny there had ever been a (developmental state) miracle, and the Washington Consensus gave way to the Post-Washington Consensus which is both more state-friendly, at least in principle if not so much in practice, and yet never mentions the DSP which, consequently, became squeezed on all sides.

Just for the record, the South African Government of National Unity came to power in 1994 just as the DSP was at its height, international solidarity could not have been stronger, internal forces were well organised, the country was not beholden to the IMF or the World Bank and, in any case, the Washington Consensus was in disarray after two lost decades for development. South Africa seemed set to pioneer, and could have pioneered, a developmental strategy led by the state as a beacon for others as well as for itself. But the RDP gave way to GEAR and the Freedom Charter to neoliberalism, properly understood, and it has reigned supreme subsequently.

Over the past few years, though, the DSP has enjoyed something of a limited revival. With tongue in cheek, let me begin to explain why and how by stating two laws of economics, not of the economy. The first will be well-known and is that monetarism flourishes whenever there is inflation. The second is that the DSP flourishes wherever there is development. And, of course, there has been development, especially across the BRIC, if not the BRICS. So, China in particular has been understood as a developmental state. But the DSP has changed to become a failed buzzword.

What do I mean? A buzzword in development is something that is used indiscriminately and incoherently across a wide range of applications. Today, the DSP is used whenever there is any piecemeal example of developmental success involving the state without necessarily referencing development itself as systemic transformation. It could be, for example, biological instruments produced in Singapore or the reconstruction of the Tema port in Ghana. This is what the DSP has become. So, anything good involving the state makes it developmental (and everything else can be carefully or casually forgotten).

This is why and how the DSP has become a buzz. But so much is development discourse dominated by the World Bank that it now effectively decides what is, and what is not, a buzzword. Typically, buzzwords are poverty reduction, social protection, globalisation, participation, citizenship, empowerment, social capital, gender, sustainability, rights, NGOs, social movements, country ownership, transparency, accountability, corruption, governance, fragile states, and knowledge. The state is notably absent, as of necessity is the DSP, since the World Bank remains staunchly opposed to interventionism on a systemic scale and sees its role as supporting the neutrally conceived market as opposed to development itself other than through market means.

This explains why DSP can create a buzz in South Africa, with the added irony of its being a developmental state in the making. By the way, South Korea did not even know it was or had been a developmental state until it was told so by western economists and political scientists after which it trained its own economists, primarily in America, the so-called ATKE, and collapsed into crisis once their numbers reached a critical point. There may be another law here, of economists, the more you have and the more influential they are, the worse is the performance of the economy. Significantly, though, South Africa does the South Korean story backwards, claiming to be a developmental state in advance of achievement!

But, before returning to South Africa once more, I want to take a digression on China as it is illustrative of many of the issues I have raised today, irrespective of the value of the DSP as a policy frame. The value of discussing China arises out of the example it provides (although hard to emulate – get a population of one billion or, as has been pointed out for South Korea, get yourself invaded by Japan to destroy the landed aristocracy and then supported by US aid in the Cold War). And China is also significant simply because of its impact and diversity.

Let me offer here, a few simple assertions. First, Chinese economic development has been primarily based on rapidly expanding *domestic* markets. This has been accompanied by relatively rapid growth in labour productivity, contingent upon very high levels of investment and has given rise to increasing real wages and the emergence even of shortages for skilled labour.

Second, export growth has been of increasing importance more recently, with corresponding widening of China's trade surplus, but this has been more associated with lower levels of wages, for employment in sectors attached to foreign direct investment, particularly geared towards the processing trade. Whilst this has been large enough at least to account for China's total trade surplus, its contribution to value added is no more than 5% of Chinese GDP, more or less conforming to an enclave-type economy, typically found across multinational corporation activity across the world within export-processing zones, etc. But this should not be taken as typical of, nor predominant in, the Chinese economy and its success.

Third, the dependence of China upon banks for finance for industrial investment is staggering. It is proportionately roughly four times higher than for the United States, and at least double that of most other countries. This is, however, paradoxically, indicative of the *limited* extent of financialisation, properly understood, of the Chinese economy, since finance has derived primarily from state-owned banks that have been policy driven. Of course, this does not guarantee developmental success in the absence of other conditions but these are precisely what have been present in China where, nonetheless, development is fraught by the tensions associated with sustaining international competitiveness and domestic economic and social stability.

Fourth, this is indicative of the much more extensive reliance of China upon policies that have totally broken from the Washington Consensus in general and those for transition economies in particular, where the outcomes by comparison with Eastern Europe are salient. Significantly, for a short period, China did succumb to Washington Consensus style policies in the mid-1990s but, as a matter of pragmatism in wake of the crisis this induced, it immediately abandoned them for policies of Keynesian-style expansionism led by welfare provision, a renewal of the role of the state sector, and reversal of foreign sector liberalisation.

Fifth, in this light, it is hardly surprising that a very wide spectrum of opinion from across different positions regarding the sources of China's success and its responsibility, or not, for prompting, aggravating or ameliorating the current crisis, have some common positions on how it should proceed – by expanding domestic production to serve both higher wages and higher levels of social provision, and reducing the overall level of domestic investment as a proportion of GDP. Indeed, such postures are in line with those being adopted by China itself.

Nonetheless, sixth, myths do prevail concerning China and its role in the world economy. These tend to originate from an ethos of blame by either incorrectly specifying factors or their causal roles in response to problems that derive other than from China itself. These include the idea of a global savings glut, unreasonable trade surplus and competitiveness from too low an exchange rate, and China's export growth at the expense of its domestic consumption. In contrast, it should be emphasised that China's success or impact in these terms, properly interpreted, can only be of considerable benefit to the world economy (as well as its own) although the incidence of such benefits are uneven and possibly negative for some. Failure to realise these benefits is no fault of China and that they do not accrue for other, unrelated reasons, of which global and national financialisation elsewhere is clearly culpable, is no reason to displace blame onto China.

In short, the lessons to be learned from China for national developmentalism are, broadly and overgeneralising, in contemporary conditions, especially in the wake of the current crisis, that a corresponding positive role for the state depends upon: insulating the mobilisation and allocation of finance from financialisation in all of its forms; the promotion of secure domestic provision of goods for domestic consumption especially as far as the meeting of basic needs and poverty alleviation are concerned; and a strong commitment to state provision of social and economic infrastructure attached to a developmental welfare state, and targeted industrial (and other) strategies designed to expand investment, employment and productivity in line with corresponding increases in wages.

This does, however, in light of previous remarks, need to be situated in relation to global factors. I want to address this in two ways – in relation to production, especially in relation to technology, and in relation to finance both of which have been less prominent in the DSP than trade (getting prices wrong, and import substitution versus export promotion as elements of a developmental state).

As mentioned, the DSP has tended to neglect technology in terms of close examination of where it comes from and how it improves. The exception in this respect is the 'flying geese' approach. This has two aspects. On the one hand are the dynamic linkages from one sector to another with potentially increasing degree of technical sophistication and value added as we move through the flock. On the other hand, 'flying geese' serves to highlight the shifting international division of labour between, or across, national economies as those at lower levels of development and wages and skills take on the relocated manufacturing roles of those already upgrading or upgraded to higher stages of industrialisation. The classic case is Japan's investment strategy into the Asia-Pacific Rim in the last decades of the twentieth century although China currently presents a more complex picture as it both leads the geese of follower nations *and* competes with them through its vast reserves of (internal migrant) labour. This and closer examination of historical experience in terms of, or increasingly at the expense of the metaphor adopted of flying geese, suggests questioning whether geese fly in a two-dimensional V-shaped pattern or formation alone, and might not other birds or creatures either join the flock and even challenge hierarchy within it. Otherwise is to suggest a limited form of technological determinism that strains both the evidence and the potential for policies that breach with, or progress beyond, confinement to latecomer catch-up that preserves the existing order in the international division of labour, ones that have indeed been broken by the East Asian NICs in the past, with China possibly ready to repeat the exercise in its own fashion.

More specifically, as far as China might serve as an enabling factor in the promotion of developmental states elsewhere, its size and diversity give rise to a complex mix of complementary opportunities *and* sources of competition. Inevitably, these are variously spread across different countries, at different stages of development, across different sectors, technological capabilities and levels of value-added, and corresponding position within global value chains/ networks. Across the literature more generally, the levels of uncertainty and unevenness involved is conducive to appeal to metaphor as China is variously understood as Engine, Conduit, or Steamroller as far as other economies are concerned, or is it a perpetrator of Flying Geese or of Sitting Ducks.

This all suggests that technological upgrading, a necessary aspect of the industrialisation putatively promoted by national developmental states, is no longer, even to the extent that it was, a linear step-by-step progression up the ladder of latecomer catch up. Industrial production is organised across global networks, through value chains that have mixed content and potential for spin-off, that do not necessarily neatly fit into uniform patterns. I could go into this in detail. But let me quote from one account of China's role (Haltmaier et al. 2007, p. 25):

> As China has moved up the value chain in recent years, increasing its presence in electronic high-tech exports in particular, there have also been shifts in the pattern of production in the other economies in the region. For instance, Japan and Korea have further increased their presence in the medium-tech automotive industry and Singapore has developed its biomedical sector. At the same time, the Philippines has increased its revealed comparative advantage in exports of electronic high-tech products, a large proportion of which are parts and components. However, our analysis of product displacement suggests that China's increasing export share has not reduced export growth for the other countries in the high-tech industries, although it has had a negative effect in the medium-tech and low-tech industries.

And, from another (Ahearne et al. 2006, p. 14):

> there is no doubt that China is displacing other Asian economies across a wide spectrum of markets. Not all of this displacement is symptomatic of competition. First, a significant portion of the final assembly of Asian-made products takes place in China.

As suggested, by reference to China which is simultaneously at top and bottom, this is symptomatic of no neat fit across countries in terms of stages of industrial development, with corresponding implications for industrial policy not simply targeting a step up the rung. It is so much a ladder that has been kicked away by neoliberalism, in the phrase so tellingly cited again and again by Ha-Joon Chang from the German protectionist, Friedrich List, as a whole sheaf of policies that are needed to negotiate an extraordinarily tricky and complex rock climb, with corresponding ties to the specificities of particular sectors and broader attention to developmental goals.

On the other hand, certainly compared to the post-war boom, when foreign direct investment was heavily concentrated in the hands of US multinational corporations, together with the UK as junior partner, there are now many different sources of FDI, including from within the South. This means that opportunities to deploy as well as to be exploited by FDI have expanded, alongside competition for it. But the conclusion to draw from the previous discussion of global production is that simple prognoses as enhanced opportunity versus enhanced competition as such are inadequate as they do not adequately address the complexities and diversities of global production, nor the broader national contexts and policy interventions that might render them both successful and developmental.

Let me now turn to financialisation, which some of you may have noticed I previously introduced surreptitiously. In brief, financialisation has involved: the phenomenal expansion of financial assets relative to real activity (by three times over the last thirty years); the proliferation of types of assets, from derivatives through to futures markets with a corresponding explosion of acronyms; the absolute and relative expansion of speculative as opposed to or at the expense of real investment; a shift in the balance of productive to financial imperatives within the private sector whether financial or not; increasing inequality in income arising out of weight of financial rewards; consumer-led booms based on credit; the penetration of finance into ever more areas of economic and social life such as pensions, education, health, and provision of economic and social infrastructure; the emergence of a neoliberal culture of reliance upon markets and private capital and corresponding anti-statism despite the extent to which the rewards to private finance have in part derived from state finance itself. Financialisation is also associated with the continued role of the US dollar as world money despite, at least in the current crisis, its deficits in trade, capital account, the fiscus, and consumer spending, and minimal rates of interest. I observe here, in passing and for future reference, that the policies adopted by the USA and some other developed countries have been exactly the opposite of those advised, or should that be imposed, on developing countries experiencing similar crises in the past. As Ha-Joon Chang has been at the forefront of arguing in the context of historical paths to development, those that have traversed it insist, "Do not do as we *did*, do as we say" to which should be added the nostrum, "Do not do as we *do*, do as we say".

However we define financialisation, its consequences have been: reductions in overall levels and efficacy of real investment as financial instruments and activities expand at its expense even if excessive investment does take place in particular sectors at particular times (as with the dotcom bubble of a decade ago); prioritising shareholder value, or financial worth, over other economic and social values; pushing of policies towards conservatism and commercialisation in all respects; extending influence of finance more broadly, both directly and indirectly, over economic *and* social policy; placing more aspects of economic and social life at the risk of volatility from financial instability and, conversely, placing the economy and social life at risk of crisis from triggers within particular markets (as with the food and energy crises that preceded the financial crisis). Whilst, then, financialisation is a single word, it is attached to a wide variety of different forms and effects of finance with the USA and the UK to the fore. And, even if exposed in acute form by the crisis, its expansion over the last few decades has been at the expense of the real economy despite otherwise extraordinarily favourable "fundamentals" for capitalism, including huge advance in technologies, in reserves of labour, in decline and defeat of progressive movements, and the triumph of neoliberalism. Over the last thirty years, capitalism has engineered a dream lottery ticket for itself. Yet, all it managed was low rates of growth compared to the post-war boom and, ultimately, a crisis of classic proportions.

This is the key to understanding the malaise of South African economy and society, once wedded to an understanding of it as historically and currently dominated by the Minerals-Energy Complex. What is this MEC? It is the specifically South African system of accumulation that has been centred on core sectors around, but more wide-ranging than, mining and energy, evolving with a character and dynamic of its own that has shifted over time. Its history and consequences can be traced back to the emergence of mining in the 1870s through to the present day. In the interwar and immediate post-war period, core MEC sectors drove the economy, furnishing a surplus for the protection and growth and, ultimately, incorporation of Afrikaner capital. State corporations in electricity, steel, transport and so on, represented an accommodation across the economic power of the mining conglomerates and the political power of the Afrikaners, an uneasy compromise of evolving fractions of classes and their interests forged through both state and market. The apartheid labour systems were less an accommodation than a common bond across capitals and against labour. But the divisions between Afrikaner and mining capitals precluded a more general strategy of industrial diversification out of core MEC sectors, leading to a partial vacuum in intermediate and capital goods capability, a failure to accrue economies of scale and scope other than in core MEC sectors, and an inefficient consumer goods industry surviving by protection upon demand.

At the economic level, if temporarily accepting the notion, these character-istics offer the most obvious similarities with, and differences from, the devel-opmental states of the East Asian economies (although their own experiences, and the reasons for them, should not be unduly homogenised). If South Africa has ever been a developmental state, it was so from the 1970s, given the close relationship between large-scale capital and the state. This was not a matter of state versus market, or even of state plus market, but of fractions of capital represented through both state and the market for the purposes of the most extreme forms of "labour market" oppression.

By the 1970s then, Afrikaner and mining-related capital had been suffi-ciently integrated for a common economic strategy to be adopted, as had always been the case for labour systems. But, with the collapse of the post-war boom and the Bretton Woods system based on gold at $35 per ounce, and the sharp rise in oil and energy prices, a huge premium attached to both gold and energy. As a result, an industrial strategy for diversification was scarcely considered let alone adopted. Instead, the 1970s witnessed an extraordinary state-led expansion of gold, other minerals and energy production. Into the 1980s, the crisis of apartheid also precluded a state and/or private strategy for industrial promotion. But, whilst the core MEC industries remained central to the economy, capital controls meant that profits generated internally that were not illegally transferred abroad, see below, were confined to accumula-tion within the South African economy itself. This gave rise both to further conglomeration across the economy but, first and foremost, to the expansion of a huge and sophisticated financial system as cause and consequence of the internationally confined, but domestically spread, reach of the South African conglomerates with Anglo-American in the lead.

The MEC is the system of accumulation that was inherited by post-apartheid South Africa. And it has survived more or less intact over the post-apartheid period. This is not to say it has remained unchanged, quite the opposite, just as it has experienced significant change in the past. Unfortunately, those changes have, however, reflected the extent to which South Africa is the exact opposite of a development state and has been driven further away from being so. In particular, the South African economy over the post-apartheid period has been driven by what might be termed a backlog in financialisation and globalisation that was inherited from the apartheid period. These have dominated both the low pace of domestic accumulation and the form and composition taken by the restructuring of the domestic economy. Whilst the MEC core sectors have strengthened, the fastest growing sector in the economy over the last twenty years has been finance and related services, now taking as much as 20% of GDP, although 40% of the population benefit from no financial services at all.

Now according to the efficient market hypothesis as far as those supporting financialisation are concerned, the role of financial markets is to provide for the efficient mobilisation and allocation of resources to investment. Has this been done by the South African financial system? Not at all, domestic levels of investment are running at half those generally acknowledged to be necessary for developmental state status. And where are all the resources going? Well, one answer has already been provided, they go into the financial sector itself. I exaggerate somewhat as, of course, some financial services are completely essential, like high security protection of the rewards and properties of the most unequal society in the world. But, essentially, far from adding 20% to GDP, financial services are *taking away* a quarter of GDP and cheekily suggesting that by doing so they *add* the equivalent to GDP. Across the world, as already mentioned, three times as many financial assets are now required to serve on unit of GDP than thirty years ago. If this were true of any other input, such as energy, steel, or whatever, we would be outraged. But finance gets away with it.

But the South African situation is even more serious and disturbing because this financialisation is not only associated, as elsewhere, with exaggerated rewards to those working within finance, and conducive to credit-based levels of consumption based on speculation in housing markets, it has been accompanied by unprecedented levels of capital flight, much of it totally illegal (and managed by large-scale corporations through transfer pricing – declaring value of exports from South Africa at a lower price than charged to importing countries). Illegal capital flight was certainly extensive during the apartheid period but it has attained new and dramatic heights subsequently, with capital flight exceeding 20% of GDP in peak years. This is, first and foremost, why South Africa has moved away from being a developmental state whose preconditions depend upon the use of domestically generated resources for attaining developmental goals. Until this issue is addressed, South Africa has no chance of being a developmental state other than in the utopian minds of those who dream of policies without the resources to implement them.

Unfortunately, far from addressing this problem, the record of post-apartheid governments has been at best to turn a blind eye, and at worst to facilitate it, as illegal capital flight has increasingly been legalised with a programme of relaxation of exchange controls. Recent developments indicate that this is worsening. Government only a year ago announced its intention to grant an amnesty for illegal capital flight upon payment of a 10% penalty, as a step towards removing all exchange controls. This is akin to announcing an amnesty for illegal firearm possession as the first step to removing all restrictions on possession. Why would anyone make use of the amnesty let alone reduce their use and possession of firearms. The South African Reserve Bank and the Treasury have been little short of scandalous in their failure to report upon and, one must suspect, pursue illegal capital flight, let alone take into account what impact it has had upon the economy. As far as these two hypocritical guardians of sound finance and austerity are concerned, it is as if capital flight does not exist, or as if it is a harmless and/or unpreventable, like possession of marijuana in the UK, illegal, tolerated and benign.

But capital flight ought to be seen as what is known as a class A drug in the UK as far as the South African economy and its potential to become a developmental state are concerned. For the influence of dealing in this crack-cocaine extends far beyond the admittedly devastating and debilitating drainage of resources from the economy. As a component part of globalisation and financialisation, capital flight places the economy on the cusp of instability, and this has had to be accommodated, and has even driven, macroeconomic policy to its advantage. Interest rates have been held high in order that short-term capital inflows (a source of volatility) can compensate for long-term outflows. And the exchange rate has been held at a high level with the effect of making capital outflows worth more in foreign currency to those who benefit from them, whilst making it ever more difficult to sustain both the exchange rate and economic growth.

This is so for the restructuring of domestic industry which has not been driven by the need to fill in the hollowed out industrial structure inherited from apartheid, with its limited capacity to build upon the MEC core strengths and diversify through capital and intermediate to more competitive and higher quality consumption goods. Rather the conglomerate structure has been dismantled to create sectoral monopolies whose profitability depends upon high prices and not productivity increase, the very antithesis of much needed three-high economy – high investment, high productivity and high wages. By the same token, industrial policy has itself been token, with some exceptions that tend to prove the rule, as with the auto industry. What has been notably absent is the commitment to secure long-term finance for investment in labour-intensive domestic production to meet domestic consumption of basic needs, thereby creating jobs, alleviating unemployment and addressing the backlog of provision and inequality inherited from apartheid. Again, with token if significant exceptions, inequality has strengthened post-apartheid.

Similar considerations apply in one way or another to each and every aspect of economic and social policy. They have been squeezed into the margins created by the triple whammy of MEC, financialisation, and globalisation. The one exception, of course, is BEE. There can be little doubt that a new elite has been created out of the form and content that restructuring and accumulation have taken in South Africa. Once again, from the perspective of the DSP, South Africa has moved away from its putative role as a developmental state, for BEE represents a fraction of capital that is almost entirely parasitical, adding nothing to the formulation let alone the implementation of developmental goals. Indeed, the impact of BEE has been much worse than this because it is conducive to an ethos, a skewed building of capacity and governance, a structure and hierarchy of institutions, indeed a politics and an ideology that is once more the antithesis to the creation of a democratic developmental state. Even if it were appropriate in the past to place faith in the emergence of a black national bourgeoisie as a source of developmentalism, that opportunity has long since passed in the current South African and global context. For it is one in which financial elites have both emerged and strengthened, at considerable cost to the vast majority who have been required to adjust to their pernicious impact upon economic and social functioning.

To put it pithily, and symbolically, developmental states do not run out of electricity, especially a mere decade after benefitting from massive excess capacity. The reasons for the power cuts were various but primarily reflect a nationalised utility left in limbo as the state refused to finance investment and commit to public ownership by the people for the people, and the domestic conglomerates refused to fund privatisation in the rush to free their resources from the domestic economy and being more than content to enjoy state-subsidised pricing and state responsibility for handling social protests. Meanwhile, renewable energy, in which South Africa could take a pioneering role, stagnates as it offers little by way of quick-fix rewards to an aspiring black bourgeoisie that can cherry pick mining leases, corporate fronting and the like.

I paint a bleak picture but one that I hope you find an appropriate assessment of current realities. Remarkably, the transition from apartheid in retrospect looks like the last throw of the dice of hopes for traditional third world revolution, associated as it was with a successful liberation movement, international solidarity, well-organised and politicised industrial trade unions and civic movements, and the Triple Alliance of COSATU, CPSA and ANC. What is striking is not so much the failure to make that revolution, even much by way of reform, but how rapidly its momentum was not only defeated but dissipated. This speaks volumes for the power of neoliberalism, overt and covert, vulgar and insidious. But all is by no means lost. Campaigns and organisations for alternatives can re-emerge, renew, unite and prosper. Perhaps NUMSA will be in the vanguard with Aporde alumni as intellectual figureheads. Whether this can and will be done under the banner of the developmental state is another matter, contingent upon how best to *unite* for alternatives without unduly compromising both outcomes and forward momentum.

It is crucial to be mindful that the turn to the state in the wake of the crisis, to rescue the banks, to promote public-private partnerships, and so on, is no more than an explicit demand upon the state to be developmental for private capital in general and for private finance in particular. Taking a long view, it may well be that the developmental state can serve as a stepping stone for radical and progressive reform but, equally, it could prove a potential pitfall for more progressive policies. The decisive issue will be who defines the development state, and how.

CHAPTER 8

Locating Industrial Policy in Developmental Transformation: Lessons from the Past, Prospects for the Future

Postscript as Personal Preamble

This postscript can be kept relatively short as the piece on which the Chapter is based was written relatively recently. The (relatively long) abstract gives a good indication of the content and motivation:

What can we learn from structural change of countries that successfully industrialised in the 20th and 21st century? This paper explains that current attempts at economic transformation of the structure of countries' economies, including industrial development, have to be analysed and understood within the shift to the new, financialised phase of capitalism and the imposition of neoliberal practices, interests and ideologies within countries and on their international economic and financial relations. Rather than reflecting an ideology of the reduction of the role of the state, neoliberalism has entailed the redirection and transformation of the control and role of the state in the provision of welfare, social security, industrial development and deregulation of trade, labour and finance as well as reorientation of both domestic macroeconomic policies and the global financial architecture.

The lessons that can be learned from studying late industrialising countries, such as the Asian Tigers, that had achieved relatively high levels of industrial transformation, have to take into account this context, including the analytical reduction, even implosion, of concepts such as development and industrial policy. Further, one has to understand the limitations of current mainstream economics approaches in the context of the redefined and degraded notions of development and the roles of the state that neoliberalism deployed defensively in response to ideas that developmental states played key roles in economic transformations of the late industrialisers.

First, we revisit the nature and role of industrial policy. Second, we situate these in relation to one another and what lessons we have learned from the developmental state paradigm and how we might take these lessons forward. And, third, we turn to the relationship between economic and social development. We are mindful, as already suggested, that neoliberalism, as the current stage of capitalism – now longer lasting than its "Keynesian" predecessor – is underpinned by financialisation, something that is increasingly acknowledged across the literature but which needs to be taken into account other than treating finance as one amongst many other factors.

Suffice it to add that the Chapter brings together the results and thinking from many of the major topics of my research: development, South Africa, the developmental state, neoliberalism, financialisation, and industrial and social policy. And, last, but by no means least, thanks to my co-author, Seeraj Mohamed, and to MISTRA for the opportunity to contribute to a volume on the South African economy and how it might be transformed. My work on South Africa has always been driven by the demands placed upon me by those seeking progressive policies. After a high point just before the ANC became a party of government in 1994, my role has been sharply diminished, reduced to occasional interventions. I tend to think the more I am needed, the less I am asked.

1   Introduction[1]

This Chapter discusses economic and industrial transformation within the context of the current stage of capitalism, which we both define as neoliberalism and see as fundamentally underpinned by, but not reducible to, financialisation. Rather than reflecting an ideology of the reduction of the role of the state, neoliberalism has entailed the redirection and transformation of the control and role of the state in the provision of welfare, social security, industrial development and deregulation of trade, labour and finance as well as reorientation of both domestic macroeconomic policies and the global financial architecture.[2] In other words, neoliberalism has entailed a shift in the

---

1   Originally appearing as Fine and Mohamed (2022) although heavily shortened as an introductory chapter for a volume on the South African economy, published by MISTRA, Fine and Mohamed (2023) within Mohamed et al. (eds) (2023). Hence frequent reference to South Africa in passing.

2   This Chapter brings together insights from much of our work across a wide range of issues, contributed over long periods of time. Many of these pieces offer literature reviews, including reference to our own earlier takes on the issues involved. Accordingly, we tend to restrict ourselves to citing more recent contributions from which reference to earlier work, including our own, can be accessed. In case of neoliberalism, see Fine and Saad-Filho (2016), Boffo et al.

boundaries of governance and the application of power within societies, which has particularly favoured interests of wealthy elites and domestic and foreign big businesses. We further contend that implementation of policies aimed at development and industrial policy have been subject to neoliberal reinterpretation and dilution, as concepts related to development and the developmental state have been degraded during their incorporation into mainstream economics and scholarly and policy thinking more generally.

In the context of development, the first phase of neoliberalism was in many respects pioneered by the Washington Consensus (WC) which stunted the industrialisation and transformation of developing countries, pushing them into policies favouring the power and interests of foreign businesses, especially the financial, and the corresponding domestic interests and activities to which they could be aligned.[3] As a result, at the level of ideology and policy discourses, the conceptualisation of development itself was degraded (to the idea of simply leaving things to the market) and industrial policy tended to disappear from the policy agenda if extensively pursued, albeit piecemeal and incoherently in practice, contingent on the exercise of evolving powers and interests.

The extent to which countries have been transformed by neoliberalism in general, and by financialisation in particular, has been highly differentiated even if the result of common (global) forces.[4] Both the incidence and impact of that incidence of financialisation have been subject to what is now recognised in the literature as being variegated. This Chapter explains that economic transformation of the structure of countries' economies, including industrial development, has to be analysed and understood within the shift to the new, financialised phase of capitalism and the imposition of neoliberal practices, interests and ideologies within countries and on their international economic and financial relations.

A natural starting point is the lessons that can be learned from studying late industrialising countries, such as the Asian Tigers, that had achieved relatively high levels of industrial transformation in the twentieth century. Doing

---

(2018) and Bayliss et al. (2024). Throughout there is much shortening and updating from Fine (2011). See also Fine (1997c-e) for earlier contributions in the South African context of the time, in relation to industrial policy, privatisation and what turned out to be lost opportunities in the South African steel industry and associated value chains.

3 For the phases of neoliberalism and their corresponding influence over development economics and policy, see Fine (2021 and 2024d).

4 There is now a huge literature on financialisation, by topic, discipline, definition and approach. See Mader et al. (eds) (2020) and Fine (2022) and, in context of development, Fine (2024e). For South Africa see collection edited by Ashman et al. (2018) for some coverage.

so entails departing from orthodoxy, especially its analytical reduction, even implosion, of concepts such as development and industrial policy that emanated from the WC. Further, one has to understand the limitations of current mainstream economics approaches in the context of the redefined and degraded notions of development and the roles of the state that neoliberalism has deployed defensively in response to ideas that developmental states played key roles in economic transformations of the late industrialisers.[5]

Prior to the WC, pioneered by the World Bank from the early 1980s, there used to be a two-fold conventional wisdom – that development depends upon industrialisation and industrialisation depends upon significant state intervention. Whilst the WC tended to accept the central role of industrialisation, contingent upon its being driven by market forces, it came down heavily against the role of the state in achieving it. With deindustrialisation across the developed world for a number of decades and, even with the WC giving way to the Post-Washington Consensus (PWC), there has been an increasing presumption not only that industrial policy is unnecessary, and even counterproductive, but also that industrialisation itself is superfluous as the tertiary sectors offers an alternative avenue for developmental success. The conventional wisdom with regard to finance prior to the WC was informed by the response, particularly of western developed countries, to reign in and stabilise finance after the Great Depression of the 1930s. The regulation of finance and international financial relations was reinforced with the implementation of a fixed exchange rate system and the endorsement of capital controls by the US and other western governments.[6] Regulation of finance and international financial flows was also seen as important for the macroeconomic policy sovereignty of the interventionist welfare states of the post-WW2 (World War Two) industrial countries and for their efforts to maintain stable exchange rates and to rebuild a liberal international trading order (Helleiner, 1994). The USA, to some extent prompted by the Cold War and attempts to counter growth of

---

5 For the latest developments in mainstream development economics, in context of nudging our way to development, see Fine et al. (2016) and, for the research and influence derived from the World Bank as knowledge bank, see Bayliss et al. (eds) (2011).

6 Helleiner (1994, p. 28) suggests, "Although the break with the liberal tradition in financial affairs was prompted by the 1931 crisis, it was part of a reaction against liberalism that had been growing throughout the industrial world since the late nineteenth century". He adds that even though liberalism in labour policy and international trade was challenged from the 1870s, the complexity of financial issues and their general absence from discussions in political and public forums allowed private and central bankers sympathetic to a liberal approach to finance to dominate international finance well into the 1920s. This dominance was seriously challenged after the financial crash and depression of the 1930s.

political support for the USSR, supported and even encouraged states to use capital controls to prevent capital flight and state intervention in finance to support the post-war recoveries of western Europe and Japan, including active state roles in influencing the allocation of finance in a manner consistent with state economic imperatives.[7]

With regard to countries that gained independence from colonialism after WW2, Amsden (2008, p. 95) says, "Nevertheless, unlike in the period after 1980, the United States did the developing world a great favor. It left it relatively alone – a new form of 'laissez-faire.' To create modern factories and skilled employment, the developing world could use unorthodox economic policies rather than laissez-faire". Industrial policy and adoption of import-substitution policies in developing countries, particularly the Asian Tigers, were supported by active state involvement in, and regulation of, financial markets and financial flows. State financial regulation increased state control over savings and direct state involvement in the allocation of finance towards industrialisation plans.

Whilst the WC may have shifted to its Post-Washington version, as indicated the idea of development itself became and has remained degraded. Economic transformation and structural change are seen merely as shifting the sectoral composition of the economy; and social policy is attached to providing safety nets, either explicitly in case of what were taken to be temporarily adverse circumstances, or in making up for deficiencies in provision of health, education, housing and so on. Deregulated financial markets are not seen as inevitably destabilising in and of themselves nor through resistance to, and/or avoidance of, (re)regulation and so causal of the misallocation of finance in economies. They are presented as more or less efficient, even imperative policy-manipulable vehicles for financing development and for sustaining developed economies (with massive levels of support following the Global

---

7   It is worth noting that the role of central banks has also much changed during the neo-liberal era. Not only were central banks important in the regulation of capital controls, including exchange controls, the historical role of almost all central banks was to support economic stability and direct support to industrial sectors. According to Epstein (2005, p. 3), "Throughout the early and recent history of central banking in the U.S., England, Europe, and elsewhere, financing governments, managing exchange rates, and supporting economic sectors by using "direct methods" of intervention have been among the most important tasks of central banking and, indeed, in many cases, were among the reasons for their existence. The neoliberal policy package currently proposed, then, is drastically out of step with the history and dominant practice of central banking throughout most of its history." Epstein (2009) provides case studies of the tools and policies used by central banks in developing countries to promote development.

Financial Crisis, GFC, being indicative of the lengths to which this is taken). Instead of being seen as driving contemporary capitalism, financial institutions have become misrepresented as merely (in)efficient intermediators and allocators of capital and, thereby, largely absent and blameless in erstwhile mainstream, neoliberal explanations of the problems that plague economies, such as macroeconomic instability, deindustrialisation, high unemployment, growing inequalities and the path to irreversible environmental damage and calamities.

This Chapter makes its contribution by restoring what had been so notably excised from the conception of (economic) development. As indicated, across scholarship, ideology and policy (and how they combine as a world vision), the WC so reduced the notion of development in scope and depth, that almost limited numbers of avenues have been opened up to compensate for these omissions, however minimally. As it were, the new neoliberal orthodoxy has created its own ragbag of heterodox alternatives, including the PWC and beyond. As captured by Mrs Thatcher's claim that her greatest achievement was New Labour, so the WC's greatest achievement has been both to constrain alternatives and the confidence with which they are put forward and to promote compromises to which they are attached in principle and in practice – all despite the transparent, and self-confessed deficiencies of the orthodoxy in the wake of the GFC; it could not but did happen, and we cannot put it right.

Much heterodoxy, then, and its central thrust, has compromised with the forward march of neoliberal scholarship. Much of this posturing, more or less removed from past and contemporary realities, has been caught in a two-fold pincer movement. One pinch has come from the mainstreaming of development economics, with an analytical framing around optimisation, (in)efficiency, equilibrium and the appropriate mix of institutions and policymaking to correct whatever market imperfections can be identified (this being the position of the PWC, with its WC predecessor and point of departure suggesting interventions would be worse than the imperfections given market-distorting rent-seeking). The other pinch has come from neoliberal ideology, especially with the demise of the Soviet bloc and its attachment to state ownership and planning, and the presumption that markets work well and state intervention does not.

What is so striking about these conventional wisdoms is the degree to which they depart from contemporary and past realities. The historical record shows that developmental success has always involved extensive state intervention and industrial development. As Ha-Joon Chang (2002) has neatly put it, advice based on the contrary is a denial not only of the developed countries' own pasts but also the pulling away of the ladder for those that would wish to follow – do not do as we did, do as we say. Further, the more recent examples of developmental success – the East Asian newly-industrialised countries, with Japan as the lead followed by South Korea, Taiwan, Singapore and so on – have all industrialised on the basis of extensive industrial policy. And, by even a short dose of realism, China is the latest example that proves this rule in bucket loads.

Significantly, in response to the WC, itself borne as the east Asian NICS' successes were coming to fruition, there was inspired a developmental state literature, the classics being Johnson (1982), Amsden (1989) and Wade (1990). These sought to demonstrate the role of industrial policy in bringing about industrialisation and industrial competitiveness. And, they were accompanied by another literature – although the two tended to reside in parallel with one another – around adjustment with a human face, in which it was argued that, whatever the questionable developmental success of WC policies, they were hitting the poorest hardest.[8]

These twin critiques of the WC had specific goals – to justify industrial policy on the basis of East Asian NICS' evidence and to show, working or not (as was demonstrably so), structural adjustments and stabilisation were disproportionately and absolutely hurting the already poor. As such, whilst each was compelling, and successful on its own terms and in its chosen goals, at the very least they needed to be combined to offer a rounded account of economic and social transformation. Whilst the WC may have shifted to its Post-Washington version (with questionable impact on policy in practice, other than to broaden the scope of coverage of policy appropriated by the World Bank),[9] as already, indicated the idea of development itself became degraded. Economic transformation or structural change became seen as merely shifting the sectoral composition of the economy; and social policy became attached to providing safety nets, either explicitly in case of what were taken to be temporarily adverse circumstances, or in making up for deficiencies in provision of health, education, housing and so on. Tellingly, neither WC nor PWC offered any clear or detailed conceptualisation of development itself, only the means by which to achieve its lack of specificity – respectively, leave everything to the market versus piecemeal correction of market and institutional imperfections.[10]

Unsurprisingly, such limitations of the mainstream have inspired more or less radical and constructive critical alternatives. A leading, and recent, contribution to the new heterodoxies that goes much further and deeper than most

---

8   For a retrospective, see Jolly (1991).
9   See Van Waeyenberge (2009).
10   See Fine and Van Waeyenberge (2006).

is the invaluable volume edited by Andreoni et al. (2021), covering both general principles and their application to South Africa in targeting economic trans-formation, and how both to understand and to achieve it. There are considera-ble resonances with our own approach, but there are also dissonances that we highlight here, partially and in brief, in order to bring out the distinctiveness of what we offer in breaking with incomplete reactions against the continu-ing influence, if not veiled strangleholds, of the (P)WC. Their volume appeals to the political settlement approach in which structures of interests, within evolving institutional contexts, determine outcomes in terms of more or less developmentally advantageous (re)distribution of rents from whatever poli-cies are adopted. This is, however, unduly negligent of the extent to which new (structures of) interests are formed: in the global context, we would emphasise the strengthening and emergence of financial elites; and, most notably, in the South African context, there is the newly formed role of big black business elites. In addition, seeing outcomes in terms of access to and appropriation of 'rents' either makes every rent sui generis in its own individual circumstances or, as is the case for the analysis in practice, unduly homogenises across what are different structures, processes, agencies and relations with, most obviously, financialisation and the appropriation of interest properly seen as distinct, for example, from both rents derived from (mineral) landed property or monop-oly profits from corporate control over competitiveness, patents or whatever. A further weakness, or absence is an understandable focus upon the cutting edge of industrial value added in the context of global value chains. But this leads to a neglect of the role played by more mundane domestic production of basic needs for domestic consumption, across clothing, food, housing, and so on and quite apart from public provision.

To address such issues of developmentalism, our own approach rests upon the more longstanding understanding of South Africa, in particular, as a national system of accumulation in a global context. The former has been specified as the Minerals-Energy Complex (MEC), with the latter now incor-porated into globalised, financialised neoliberalism, leading to the increas-ingly acknowledged presence of the MEC together with financialisation (each addressed by Andreoni et al. in passing) now to be newly termed as the Minerals-Energy and Financial Complex (MEFC).[11] This is indicative of both new political settlements *and* new partners in those newly constituted means

---

11   See Fine (2019b) for a recent and Fine and Rustomjee (1996) for the classic account. Unevenly and in embryonic form, the MERG (1994) report adopted the approach sug-gested here.

of settling, with some long-established and some dramatically emerging where previously they were absented or even non-existent.

But, in this Chapter, our concern is less with South Africa as such, and more with general principles. In this light, first, for contemporary conditions we revisit the nature and role of industrial policy. Then, we situate these in relation to one another and what lessons we have learned from the developmental state paradigm and how we might take these lessons forward. And, third, we turn to the relationship between economic and social development. We are mindful, as already suggested, that neoliberalism, as the current stage of capitalism – now longer lasting than its 'Keynesian' predecessor – is underpinned by finan-cialisation, something that is increasingly acknowledged across the literature but which needs to be taken into account other than treating finance as one amongst many other factors. In addition, it equally requires a burning of dual-isms rather than shifting emphasis from one side of them to another: whether it be macro and micro (or macro/micro as against an ill-defined and grab all for everything else, the meso); state (and other institutions more generally) and market; finance and the real economy; and the economic and the polit-ical (or social more generally). Identifying the nature of economic and social transformation, and how best to achieve it, requires a specification of evolving economic, political and ideological interests and how these are represented and fought out through the dualisms just listed rather than the latter being more or less harmoniously balanced against one another as independent, prime-moving factors. With these insights, we conclude by reassessing the role (to be) played by macro policy (as a product of a globalised, neoliberalised, financialised economy), and the prospects for forging a developmental state, transformative industrial policy and progressive social policy, drawing upon current analyses as critical point of constructive departure.

2   From Defining Industrial Policy ...

In relation to industrial policy, we begin by raising two questions. The first con-cerns how to define industrial policy. This is necessary in order to be able to assess, formulate, evaluate and reassess its role in policymaking (although this sequence of action cannot be taken for granted if industrial policy is made pri-marily to favour certain interests for then it is just done with minimal rationale and scrutiny). Defining industrial policy is also necessary in order to be able to address the second question; is industrial policy back on the agenda, especially in the wake of the Global Financial Crisis, GFC, of 2007/8, and the interven-tionist responses to the Covid pandemic, each of which has given a justifiable battering to the nostrum of leaving everything, from manufacturing, let alone finance through to healthcare, to the market (Wade, 2012).

Perversely, we are going to answer the second question before the first even though an answer to the first is needed to answer the second. This is because, with Wade, we consider that industrial policy has never been off the agenda, neoliberal and WC ideology to the contrary. Rather, industrial policy has remained extensive, with Wade himself suggesting that the USA (especially around military expenditure and innovation) has heavily supported industry and might even be considered a developmental state itself as a result.[12] More generally, searching on the technology, engineering and business literature – rather than mainstream economics – it is readily found how much (successful) industrial policy has been deployed other than in the world of neoliberal imaginaries. What has happened, though, is that it has become more acceptable to acknowledge and promote policy as industrial policy explicitly and openly and, in this sense, it is back on the agenda where previously it had been shunned. However, this does not turn the world back to where it was, either in word or deed. This reflects, even though industrial policy is more openly discussed, the ways of doing so are considerably more limited in scale and scope than previously (although, admittedly, there are new or revitalised issues especially around technology, the environment and finance). Indeed, it might even be argued that industrial policy has only been put back on the agenda in mainstream circles in order to contain rather than to promote it.[13] Further, if industrial policy were seriously back on the agenda, it would not only extend to policies that have not in general been restored (such as positively promoting state ownership and reversing privatisations other than those adopted because of extreme failures of the private sector) but serious attention would be paid to drawing lessons from developmental states and the role of industrial policy in their success. But, as will be seen below, the place of the developmental state in industrial policymaking has been eroded in terms of both its presence and its dilution where present.

Now, though, consider the question of defining industrial policy. Here, traditionally, consciously or otherwise, this has been done in two ways. The first

---

12   The idea of the hidden (US) developmental state derives from Block (2008). See also Rethel and Thurbon (2020).

13   This is the conclusion of Fine and Van Waeyenberge (2013) in response to Justin Lin's attempt to promote industrial policy at the World Bank, itself marked by its failure to gain much support from within despite his position as Chief Economist (Wade, 2012) – much as Stiglitz's push for change proved futile, leading to his (enforced) departure from the Bank.

is to define it very narrowly by reference to one or other particular aspect of policy affecting industrial performance, usually reflecting a particular intervention that is prominent or fashionable at the time for whatever reason. Unsurprisingly, given how many different policies and factors affect industrial performance, the list of potential industrial policies is extensive even if they only assume favoured prominence occasionally – a casual list includes trade policy, privatisation, competition, downsizing, regional development, technology, SMEs, entrepreneurship and business climate, the environment, human capital and management skills, finance for industry, and so on. In some respects, highlighting one or other of these allows the others to be ignored.

The point is that almost anything can be construed as industrial policy precisely because of so many influences on performance, including economic and social infrastructure and workers' wages and living conditions. This leads to the alternative definition of industrial policy as anything that affects industrial performance, the problem with this being that it does include so much. More usually, a stance is taken somewhere between these two extremes of one thing or everything, as suggested by Chang (1994) in defining industrial policy as those that are specifically designed to impact industry. The problem with this is that it excludes much that affects industry profoundly even though it was not intended to do so. In a nutshell, poor energy policy (and infrastructure more generally) may lead to power shortages and cuts that are disastrous for industry but might not count as (poor) industrial policy by this approach.

Our own view or definition of industrial policy is different and differently motivated, not least methodologically. The idea is not to have a more or less narrow definition of what affects industry, nor a template of factors to be ticked off or not as having been addressed in industrial policy (although this is essential). Rather, the nature, and hence definition, of industrial policy is to be accepted to be different by virtue of its context and specificity, whether by sector, country or circumstance – a recent dramatic illustration is policy for pharmaceuticals in light of the pandemic. This means that industrial policy should be inductively defined by how it is understood in situ by those implementing, assessing or seeking to contest and shift policy. This is very different from perceiving industrial policy as, for example, correcting market imperfections although it is compatible with such an approach however much valid is such a framing.

Such a perspective on industrial policy is well-illustrated when the stakes are high or significant changes are sought – post-war or post-apartheid (re)construction, for example – for, here, the context is, or should be, prominent and unavoidable. But, to facilitate a more concrete discussion, consider the case of trade policy. Here, there has been a conventional wisdom, reaching beyond proponents of the WC, that freer trade is good for development. Analytically, it is founded upon the policy of reducing what is called the effective protection rate (EPR) – a measure that assesses the impact upon (market) competitiveness by adjusting tariffs on outputs for those on inputs (if latter are larger, the sector becomes worse off). In practice, to deploy the EPR requires that it, first, be able to be well-defined so that it can, second, be measured (to check whether policy has lowered it) and, third, drawing the conclusion that reducing the EPR will be beneficial. Significantly, across mainstream studies (as reported in Deraniyagala and Fine, 2006),[14] the assumptions necessary to complete these three steps are mind-blowingly unacceptable. They include that: there are only two sectors of the economy; there is no unemployment at any time; there are no MNCs with inter-affiliate trade; all markets are fully competitive; there are no externalities and linkages across sectors; there are no economies of scale and scope; and there are no non-tradeables.[15]

In short, despite heavy acceptance across the discipline, as with much mainstream economics, the conditions under which its EPR prognostications are taken to be justified are totally unrealistic. But, in this case, from the definitional perspective on industrial policy adopted here, this exercise can be turned from critical negative to being constructive positive. For, what it demonstrates is that industrial policy does need to take into account interactions between sectors, employment levels, the roles of multinationals and monopolisation, etc., something that might appear to be little more than common sense and a touch of contact with contemporary economic and political realities – but for the deadweight of neoliberal ideologies concerning the virtues of an idealised world of free markets. To these considerations can also be added other goals of industrial policy such as environmental impact, issues of gender and race and poverty alleviation, employment generation, sources and application of finance, and technological change and skill enhancement. Whether and how these, and potentially other, factors impinge will need to be situated contextually in defining the goals and levers of industrial policy.

---

14   But see also Deraniyagala and Fine (2001) for a more wide-ranging critical assessment of trade policy prognostications, drawing positively for lessons from what are often mainstream empirical studies.

15   Note that the unacceptable conditions necessary for EPRs to be validly deployed are identical to those for comparative advantage. Perversely, those who rightly reject the conditions often depend upon the concept of comparative advantage (even though it cannot be defined) in terms of its (dynamic) creation, appealing to the very conditions that render it invalid (such as economies of scale and scope, technological change, etc). This includes Andreoni et al. (eds) (2021).

3   … to the Developmental State as Such

As is already apparent, what we will term the developmental state paradigm (DSP), emerged to prominence in the dual context of the economic successes of the east Asian newly-industrialised countries (NICs) and in opposition to the WC. It was at its strongest from the mid-1980s for a decade before it was eroded to some extent by the image-damage attached to the east Asian crisis of 1997 and the launch, around the same time, of the more state-friendly PWC, which, ironically, studiously ignored the DSP even though it was prompted in part by it due to the gathering dissatisfaction with the WC. We will return to the evolving status of the DSP later, if touching upon it from time to time in the interim, but we begin by bringing out its core features.[16]

First, and foremost, as mentioned, the DSP was inspired by establishing empirically the complete fallacy of the WC. The East Asian NICs are shown to have enjoyed *latecomer, catch-up industrialisation* with high growth in per capita income and movements up and across value chains as a result of substantial state intervention in general and targeted industrial policy in particular.

Second, unsurprisingly, the DSP departed theoretically from the WC in emphasising the importance of the positive role of non-market interventions and institutions, and of (the sources of) industrial policy in particular, drawing upon a framing that straddled the old or classic development economics (attending to the nature of, and conditions for, economic and social transformation) and appeal to the need to acknowledge and address market imperfections (as opposed to the new development economics, inspired by and underpinning the WC, that stressed the virtues of the market and relied exclusively upon the principles of mainstream economics).

Third, more specifically, the literature attached to the DSP can be more or less roughly divided into two schools. One, the 'economic' school, focuses on identifying the sorts of industrial policies that lead to success, drawing upon economies of scale and scope, targeting coordination upstream and downstream, ensuring finance for industry, expanding both domestic and export markets in sequence, providing essential infrastructure and so on.[17] The other,

---

16   On the DSP, see Fine (2013a), although the issue is covered in Fine and Rustomjee (1996), and most recently, Fine and Pollen (2018). For South Africa as a putative developmental state, see Ashman et al. (2013) and Fine (2013b and 2016a). For the stronger claims of the apartheid state as developmental, as opposed to post-apartheid, see Freund (2013 and 2018).

17   Such is the thrust of Chang's (2002) historical work, tracing the developmentalism of state intervention from Alexander Hamilton forward. It gives rise to a law of economics – wherever there is development, it will be seen to have been the result of a developmental

the 'political' school is less attentive to policy as such as opposed to interrogating what are the circumstances in which a state will be developmental rather than, say, corrupt and/or inefficient, that it is able to adopt developmental policies whatever they might be.[18]

Fourth, the scope of coverage of the DSP has been limited, especially for the economic school around the favoured east Asian NICs. This has two aspects. On the one hand, as its critics observe, successful case studies of state intervention to bring about industrialisation are self-selecting – maybe they would have succeeded in any case and for other reasons or despite the state, and what about all of the cases of failed state interventions. Accordingly, Africa has tended to be excluded from the DSP orbit.[19] On the other hand, as literally *underlined* above, the DSP has tended to confine itself to latecomer, catchup industrialisation. This begs the question of why the DSP is not applicable to both earlier and later stages of development, the transition from agrarian economies at one extreme and to the vanguard of industrialisation at the other (get in front of, not just catch-up level) as opposed to focusing exclusively on what are the intermediate stages of industrialisation. And, further, the preoccupation with industry reflects a narrow, if core, aspect of development with limited regard for health, education and welfare and for the role of labour (other than as 'human' capital).[20]

Fifth, the DSP is primarily if generally implicitly deeply wedded to what is termed methodological nationalism, in this case the idea that the problems of development are and can be confined to intra-national considerations. At most, the global counts as at most one factor amongst others to be taken into account rather than driving the conditions under which developmentalism may or may not be possible. Consider, for example, the counterfactual in which all national states succeeded in becoming developmental states. The world would be transformed beyond recognition, not least in terms of imperialism, US hegemony let alone the division between North and South. This is not to suggest that the global renders national developmentalism impossible, only

---

state! South Africa offers a perversion of the law, declaring itself a developmental state in the making as the Mbeki regime desperately sought to support itself ideologically in its death throes.

18   Thus, for example, Thurbon (2020) places considerable emphasis upon a developmental mindset.

19   See Mkandawire (2001) but also Mkandawire (2012) for South Africa's prospects.

20   Significantly, the pre-history of developmental states tends to be ignored, other than as a potential initial condition for success; for example, for South Korea, get yourself invaded by Japan to destroy your landlord class (and strategic US aid subsequently should not be overlooked).

that there are systemic forces at work that heavily influence what, and how it, can be realised. And, it should be added, these change over time alongside the international environment in both economic and political terms.

Sixth, within this methodological nationalism, the DSP adopts the same analytical framing of the WC, the better to be able to contest it – this is the dualism of state versus the market. The two sides of the dispute differ over relative emphasis on the role to be played by each and how state and market should be coordinated if at all.

Seventh, then, this is to overlook how the state and market are always heavily integrated with one another, but the relations and relative balance between the two are conditioned by how more fundamental economic, political and ideological (class or fractional) interests are formed and expressed through both state and market. In this respect, especially through the political school and empirical case studies, the DSP has tended to focus primarily on the capitalist class and its relations with the state, or even to reduce this to industry-ministry relations, at the expense of capital-labour relations and the role of labour at all other than as a factor of production.

3.1   The Evolution of the DSP

In short, in staggeringly successful opposition to the WC (on the basis of the experience of the East Asian NICs and beyond), the DSP established a sound, if incomplete, basis on which to construct alternative policies and to address the conditions under which they might be adopted. But from the mid-1990s, the DSP paradigm went into decline. There are a number of reasons for this. First was the damage inflicted by the Asian crisis of 1997/1998, and, even before that, denials that there ever was a miracle at all just accumulation of physical and human capital.[21] To the fore in this respect was the World Bank's (1993)

---

21   Such a position, initiated by Young (1993) and promulgated by Krugman (1994), was based on calculations of total factor productivity – as commonly deployed as it is well-known to be completely fallacious, Fine (2016b), and Felipe (1999) for an early critique of the TFP literature as applied to east Asia. The World Bank's (1993) Report on the NICs was funded by Japan at a time when it had become the world's leading donor of aid and was seeking activist industrial policy in the Asia-Pacific Rim in order to support labour-intensive assembly on the basis of its own capital-intensive domestic production. Japan must have been sadly disappointed with the Report (that set aside vast swathes of its own background papers) quite apart from the denial of Japan's own well-known history as the pioneering developmental state. For a recent, positive, assessment of the role of South Korean interventions in its Heavy and Chemical Industry, HCI, initiative, in shifting to heavy industry and promoting corresponding value chains, beyond the duration of the initiative itself, see Lane (2021).

own Report on the East Asian Miracle (EAM) which came to the remarkably contorted, self-serving conclusion that there had been substantial state intervention in the East Asian NICs, but this only did what the market would have done if the market had been working properly (and without implications for interventionism elsewhere).

Second, again before the Asian crisis itself, literature had begun to cast doubts on whether developmental states could be sustained because of the shifting balances of (class) power brought about by their success.[22] On the one hand, in the case of Latin American import-substituting industrialisation, it was argued that this brought about a strengthening of working class populism and its demands for higher wages and improved social provision at the expense of industrial competitiveness. On the other hand, for East Asia, the argument was more that the strengthening of corporate capital (chaebol in South Korea, for example), increasingly allowed it to defy government control and coordination – from directing who would invest in what (to ensure matched capacity within and across sectors), and who would not (to allow for economies of scale and scope), and in constraining speculative financial investments in particular. Significantly, then, the developmental state is confined to a limited window of opportunity but, analytically, this signals how the DSP set aside the evolving nature of economic (and political and ideological) interests underpinning developmentalism (or not) until forced to confront them by the apparent corrosive effect of shifting class relations on corresponding state-led developmentalism.

Third, each of these two assaults upon the DSP ultimately, and ironically, offered some paving stones along the way for the PWC which was more state-friendly in scholarly and ideological terms than its predecessor, basing itself on the need to identify and correct, where beneficial to do so, the incidence of institutional and market imperfections. Thus, whilst the criticisms and failings of the WC in developmental terms, with the DSP to the fore, persuaded the World Bank of the need for a change in scholarly and ideological postures, it proceeded as if the DSP simply did not exist with little or no reference to its contribution (and as if the EAM had squeezed out all there was to learn).

Subsequently, over the last two decades, the DSP has gone into decline and has been described as a failed buzz/fuzz word, as a result of its being used

---

22   See the 'death and end' literature, with more positive responses emphasing the continuing role of interventionism even if with erosion of the developmental state as such (Williams, ed. 2014; Haggard, 2015; Wade, 2017; Pirie, 2018; Wong, 2020; Rethel and Thurbon, 2020; and Hockmuth, 2022).

freely if casually and imprecisely.[23] More specifically, the DSP has been subject to being a port of call whenever and wherever there is any state intervention that can be interpreted as successful, most frequently at some microeconomic level as opposed to economic transformation in general and successful industrialisation in particular. With some exceptions, if primarily at the level of local economic development, the single most successful developmental state of the neoliberal era, China, has been studiously ignored or simply set aside as an exception rather than being drawn upon to learn developmental lessons, just as the DSP garnered a similar fate in the transition from the WC to the PWC.

4   Financialisation and Economic Structure

The changing relationship between finance and productive sectors occurs within a framework that is influenced not only by government ideology but also conflict and struggles within society (and, also with and within government). Evolving views and struggles over the role of the state in social provisioning, industrial development and macroeconomic and finance policies, including state influence over the allocation of finance, affect not only the structure but also the size of the productive and financial spheres of the economy. They also influence the level of commodification and privatisation in services and reproductive spheres of the economy. As economies become increasingly financialised, larger proportions of the nonfinancial spheres of the economy, including nonfinancial firms, households and public entities, are drawn into a context where their routine operations are increasingly influenced by financial motives and linked to financial activities. Fine (2022, p. 56) says:[24]

> For me, periodisation is based upon how economic restructuring and reproduction occurs in the accumulation and circulation of (surplus) value, and how that economic restructuring and reproduction is embedded within social restructuring and reproduction.

The impact of financialisation is not simple; it can lead to accumulation and also constrain it. This support for, or constraint on, accumulation will occur unevenly. As mentioned by Fine (2022, p. 57), "variegated financialisation is

---

23   See Cornwall and Eade (eds) (2010) for buzzwords and fuzzwords in the developmental lexicon. Their success and prominence generally depend, even as critical points of departure, upon their adoption by the World Bank.

24   And on social reproduction in this vein, see Fine (2020).

not just differentiation due to different variables and contexts being present but because of the complex interaction of underlying forces".

Widespread liberalisation and growth of finance were integral to the emergence of the neoliberal era and growing financialisation. As observed, it has also been an important component of the degradation of the concept of a development state, including the changed, reduced role of state involvement in promoting industrial transformation, economic development and redistributive social policies. The form of this financial liberalisation was affected by countries' specific internal political and economic dynamics during a particular historical period and its geopolitical circumstances. Therefore, external compulsion and internal choices of individual countries to liberalise finance, the extent to which they liberalised finance and their experience of financialisation over time, while affected by global factors, have to be considered on a case-by-case basis.

4.1   *Financial Liberalisation after the Bretton Woods Period*
The regulation of domestic financial markets and international financial relations, including cross-border financial activities, was a central function of developmental states. This role was easier when there was greater coordination of the global financial system by countries through the Bretton Woods arrangements during the post-WW2 era. However, the USA and Britain undermined the Bretton Woods arrangements in an effort to boost their financial sectors after they had lost ground to competition in global trade markets. The Bretton Woods arrangements, aimed at rebuilding economies after WW2, included an approach to finance, influenced by Keynes, that a stable global economy, and economic recovery within countries, required financial regulation within countries and of cross-border financial flows. In fact, the architects of the Bretton Woods agreement recognised that in order to rebuild the global trading system it was necessary to have a regulated, coordinated global financial architecture. According to Helleiner (1994), the USA made pragmatic political choices in support of embedded liberalism after WW2. However, the USA would drive an increasing imperialist and neoliberal global agenda as they intensified the Cold War, intervened in European politics, and made war in Korea and Vietnam. In part, the USA chose these actions to support the global expansion of their corporations, and it involved their efforts not to adjust their economy when government budget and current account deficits had grown.

Neoliberal policies did not support economic growth in the way that advocates of neoliberal policies suggest – by providing freedom from state constraints on private entrepreneurs to profit from their activities. The main proponents of neoliberal policies, including the USA and Britain, had faced increased industrial competition from Germany and Japan and later the newly industrialising countries of east Asia. These countries, particularly Japan and the Asian tigers, South Korea, Singapore, Malaysia, Indonesia, and the Philippines, had policies that were in many ways the opposite of those advocated by neoliberal economists (Amsden,1989; Woo-Cumings 1999; Chang, 2002; and Wade, 1990). They had activist developmental states that intervened in markets, directed the allocation of finance towards productive investments, and put in place industrial policies to support job creation and export orientation. Industrialisation and job creation were the main components of their strategies to address poverty. The state provided infrastructure not only for businesses to thrive but also to support household reproduction and education systems, which contributed to reducing poverty and improving labour productivity and skills development. Their financial and macroeconomic policies were supportive of these developmental goals and adjusted to these states' fiscal requirements. Their rapid economic growth and the direction of credit allocation by the developmental states meant that public finances stayed healthy.

The governments of the USA and Britain, faced with increasing competition in their countries' productive sectors, suffered from growing current account and fiscal deficits. Instead of adjusting their economies to support productivity and competitiveness in manufacturing, they looked for solutions to their balance of payments and government debt problems through their financial sectors. The rise of OPEC and the two oil crises of the 1970s, and the war in Vietnam, exacerbated these problems. They required foreign financial inflows to offset their negative current account balances. They also used increased tax earnings from their growing financial sectors to offset tax losses due to deindustrialisation (Block, 1977; and Panitch and Gindin, 2012). This turn towards finance in the USA and Britain, in response to loss of industrial competitiveness and associated balance of payments constraints, formed an important part of the link between increased financial liberalisation, increasingly integrated international financial markets and financialisation, and the growing dominance of neoliberal policies.

The US government had already experienced balance of payments pressures during the 1960s because of the Korean War and reduced industrial trade competitiveness. Instead of addressing their industrial competitiveness, the USA took advantage of charge of the global reserve currency to print more dollars to address their current account and budget deficits. By 1971, there was such a glut of dollars in global markets that the USA was forced to abandon its commitment to exchange dollars for gold, and so unilaterally undermined the fixed exchange rate global monetary system agreed upon at the Bretton Woods

Conference in 1944. Vernengo (2021) argues that the collapse of the Bretton Woods exchange rate arrangements, which was supported by large US businesses and banks that had become increasingly internationalised, led to the imposition of a global fiat currency system under the hegemony of the US dollar (which at that point had already been the global reserve currency).

As they became more dependent on finance and foreign capital inflows, both Britain and the USA pushed for deregulation of capital controls and rules with regard to foreign ownership of financial institutions to allow their financial sectors to grow and to be able to draw in financial flows from other countries to offset their trade deficits and poor real sector economic performances. The USA and British governments deregulated their own financial sectors. They also showed the world that they would turn a blind eye to the growing Eurodollar market, which helped multinational enterprises and individuals to contravene capital and exchange controls of their home countries. Large corporations of developed countries that expanded through internationalisation were eager to avoid capital controls and lobbied for deregulation and the growth of offshore capital markets. The response of countries to the breakdown in the Bretton Woods arrangements around capital controls was rapidly to deregulate their financial sectors and to remove capital controls.[25] Those that did not do so could face serious balance of payments difficulties because of the risk of large outflows of capital from their countries to other countries that had already deregulated their financial markets.

4.2   *Corporate Restructuring, Value Chains and Financialisation*[26]

The rhetoric of neoliberal ideology was that if government stepped aside and markets were freed from state distortion, and red tape on businesses were removed, then economies could thrive and grow. The actual historical experience was that much of the implementation of policies related to neoliberal ideology in the advanced capitalist countries was linked to their rapid liberalisation of financial markets and their interest in reshaping trade agreements and markets to suit their own businesses. The liberalisation of trade markets in developed countries at a time when the opening of the Indian and Chinese economies brought almost a billion low paid workers into the global labour market put further pressure on their industrial businesses. One response from the industrialised western countries' businesses to changes in the global economy was large-scale restructuring of their own industrial corporations and

---

25   Helleiner (1994) uses the term "competitive deregulation" to refer to the frenzy of capital account deregulation that occurred.

26   For this in the context of evolutionary economic geography, see Boschma (2021).

global value chains. They moved large parts of their production assembly processes abroad to developing countries, particularly in Asia, where wages and production costs were cheaper, but kept branding, design, technology development within their home countries (Mohamed, 2010). The large corporations of developed countries were also able to use their economic power and support from their states' geopolitical, including military, powers, to become lead corporations that dominated global value chains.

There have been two waves of growth of developing country firms into large MNEs. The first wave occurred during the 1970s and continued into the 1980s (see Kumar and McLeod, 1981; Wells, 1983; and Lall, 1983 for discussion of the first wave). Many of the first wave developing country MNEs grew out of the successful East Asian 'tiger' countries. The second wave of growth of developing country multinational enterprises occurred in a much more integrated and concentrated global economy where concentration and inter-firm influence occurred throughout value chains. Goldstein et al. (2006, p. 369) consider the recent growth in multinational enterprises from developing countries and conclude, "The emergence of a 'second wave' of developing-country multinational enterprises (MNEs) in a variety of industries is one of the characterising features of globalisation in the most recent years." The movement of developed country MNEs into developing countries to reduce costs and take advantage of growing markets created opportunities for growing developing country corporations.

In general terms, the second wave of developing country MNEs has been constrained by the form of globalisation since the 1980s and the influence of financialisation of the developed country lead firms on Global Value Chains (GVCs). Therefore, while many developing country corporations have been able to grow, it seems that they have more often than not had their growth constrained and been limited to the role of providers of raw materials and low value-added intermediate products and also low cost assembly. While each value chain will take on different forms and have different forms of governance, the general picture is one where there is an inequitable division of labour where financialisation allows rentiers to extract profits through lead corporations in global value chains. These rentiers pressure the lead corporations for high short-term returns on their investments. The lead corporations then govern the value chains to ensure that they capture most of the profits by squeezing the other parts of the value chain. Froud et al. (2014, p. 47) illustrate the difference between the first and second waves in the auto sector, and include the impact of financialisation on this second wave:

When the Japanese sold cars in the United States in the 1970s and 1980s, the contest was a productionist one between compact nationally enclosed supply chains in Japan and Detroit with lower wages sustaining Japanese advantage so that firms like Toyota could reinvest profits and grow market share as they built their own brands. The position in the 2000s is complicated by financialisation and long trans-Pacific supply chains where power is often wielded by US firms which act as proxies for the stock market and boost profits by multiple tactics which include control of design, consumer marketing and the use of contract power to take profits at the expense of margins in their Chinese suppliers.

4.3   *Financialisation of Nonfinancial Corporations*

Increasing offshore operations and reorganisation of global value chains were not the only way in which developed country large corporations responded to declining profits, changes in the competitive environment and the deregulation and growth of finance. During the post-WW2 period many of these large, developed country industrial corporations, in key sectors such as auto, shipbuilding, and chemicals, had high profits and were able to use retained profits to reinvest in growing their businesses. According to Crotty (2002) global oligopoly market structures in these sectors reduced the likelihood of cut-throat price competition and helped to maintain a stable environment for the profitability of these corporations. Stability was important for these large global players because expansion of these businesses required large long-term sunk costs in investments in sectors where scale and technology of operations determined profitability and survival. However, these stable oligopoly market structures broke down as a result of a changed competitive environment towards increasing cutthroat price competition at the expense of profits. As a result, large nonfinancial corporations did not earn adequate profits to reinvest to maintain competitiveness but were forced to raise more finance in financial markets.

This increased dependence on financial markets coincided with the rise of the hostile takeover and the shareholder value movements in the USA and their global spread. The shareholder value movement was driven by activist shareholders and led by institutional investors which, as a result of deregulation, had access to more money to invest and fewer restrictions on where to invest, demanding higher levels of short-term returns for their investments. Non-financial corporations, pressured to raise profits, turned towards financial activities to raise their returns. This increasing reliance on financial activities to provide the short-term returns demanded by shareholders is described as the financialisation of non-financial corporations (Crotty, 2002; and Froud et al. 2007). Financialisation, however, was a broader process that underpinned the spread and dominance of neoliberalism.[27] As with neoliberal ideology the spread of financialisation, and its nature and impacts, has been uneven across the world and even across different sectors within countries. For example, on the African continent, South Africa and larger economies such as Nigeria and Egypt have become more financialised but countries whose financial markets and businesses are less integrated into global markets have lower levels of financialisation overall (Karwowski and Stockhammer, 2017).

| 5 | Neoliberalism, Financial Liberalisation and Financialisation in Developing Countries |

Hujo (2021, p. 346) describes the impact of neoliberal policies on developing countries:

> Developing countries were even harder hit by the systemic overhaul in the 1980s. State-led development strategies promoting full employment and public social services adopted by developmentalist governments concerned with catching-up (typically represented by Latin America and East Asia), as well as by newly independent states striving to overcome the legacies of colonialism (typically represented by sub-Saharan Africa), were replaced with stabilization and structural adjustment policies (SAP), what was later called the Washington Consensus.

The damage to developing countries caused by Structural Adjustment Programmes 'imposed' by the WC will not be covered here as it is well documented (see for example, Beckman, 1992; Chang, 2002; Cornia et al. 1987; and Mkandawire and Soludo, 1998). Industrial policy and adoption of import-substitution policies in developing countries, particularly the Asian Tigers, was supported by active state involvement in, and regulation of, financial markets and cross-border financial flows. The role of the state in finance extended to increased state control over savings, development finance institutions, as well as state influence over allocation of finance by private financial institutions

---

27   UNCTAD (2020, p. vi), discussing what is needed for 'sustainable recovery' after the COVID-19 pandemic, provides a succinct appraisal of the impact of financialisation and the pursuit of neoliberal policies and their role in widespread declines in productivity and aggregate demand, financial fragility and related weakening of resilience to crises within countries before the pandemic.

towards national industrialisation plans, use of capital and exchange controls, and management of exchange and interest rates (Woo-Cumings, 1999;
Epstein and Grabel, 2007; and Eichengreen, 2008). Increased state control over
developing country financial institutions and allocation of finance was crucial
to break from the inherited colonial powers and imperial banks shaping of
financial systems to support wealth extraction from colonies and to service
colonial and settler businesses and populations (Mohamed, 2014). Mainstream
economists used the term 'financial repression' to dismiss state regulation and
involvement in finance as distortionary and argued that it starved poor developing countries of savings and capital required for investment (McKinnon,
1973; and Shaw, 1973). The WC called for the liberalisation of financial markets,
and within the PWC era at least post-GFC, while recognising that unregulated
finance and capital flows could lead to volatility, proposed continued laborali-
sation of finance and at best temporary use of capital controls within a mainstream approach to macroeconomic policy (see for example, IMF, 2012).

During the 1980s and 1990s many developing countries were involved
in sweeping financial liberalisation, removal of capital controls and also
notably establishment and rapid expansion of stock markets (Singh, 1997).
Liberalisation of finance initially led to massive surges of capital inflows
through foreign bank lending in the 1980s. For, after the 1980s international
debt crisis, surges of capital into developing countries occurred largely through
short-term portfolio capital flows. Palma (2000) reports, "no matter how hard
financially-liberalised LDCs have tried in the last quarter of a century to deal
with the problem of sudden and massive surges in capital inflows, they have
ended up in a financial crisis". Palma's study shows that different developing
countries absorbed surges in capital inflows differently. The role of financial
institutions, nonfinancial corporations and the state all influenced how surges
in capital inflows were used in the host economies. For example, in Brazil much
of the short-term foreign capital flows were sterilised; in Thailand and the
Philippines they were directed towards financial and real estate speculation
and debt-driven consumption; and in South Korea much of it was (unwisely)
used to finance uncoordinated and excessive long-term fixed investments by
the private sector.

Volatile short-term capital flows create systemic financial instability related
to the potential for panic and capital flight out of countries by foreigners and
residents. It is also associated with macroeconomic fragility as surges in short-
term flows affect key macroeconomic variables, notably the exchange rate and
movements in both the current account and financial accounts of the balance
of payments, and it affects dynamics and sentiment in domestic financial markets, including private and sovereign debt markets. And, as many governments

of developed country states realised after WW2, open capital markets reduce macroeconomic policy sovereignty to implement redistributive welfare, infrastructural and industrial development programmes, for fear of market fright and capital flight. Liberalisation of capital controls has led to speculative booms and busts in stock markets that caused allocation of capital away from long-term productive investments. Currency and maturity mismatch risks make short-term capital flows unsuited for long-term investments in industry and productive sectors.

The liberalisation of cross-border capital flows is not a form of financialisation as such but has been a catalyst for increased financial activities, 'deepening' financial markets and financialisation in many countries. This is the case particularly where these flows have been absorbed into speculation in financial and real estate markets and increasing household debt. The increased flows have intensified the use of derivatives, including securitisation of debt. Over the past two decades, they have increased the influence of foreign institutional investors over domestically-listed firms. Developed country institutional investors have been at the vanguard of the shareholder value movement and demanded higher, short-term returns on their portfolio flows (Lazonick and O'Sullivan, 2000). Developing country institutional investors have followed this practice. In fact, institutional investors of both developed and developing countries have expanded as global capital flows have risen and they have also increasingly diversified their portfolios out of their host countries (Pazarbaşıoğlu et al. 2007; and Fichtner, 2020).

Even though finance and the power of institutional investors has grown during the neoliberal era, the role of the state (and its potentially enhanced role) in the allocation of finance, financial market formation and regulation should not be dismissed or underappreciated. Finance operates under conditions and laws decided by the state. The extent to which countries have become neoliberalised, the extent of financialisation and the role and influence of finance occurs within parameters set by the state. The experience with increased numbers of financial crises since the start of the neoliberal era shows that neoliberalisation of finance and financial markets requires, or at least induces, an active role of the state. Helleiner (1994), writing before the Asian financial crisis of 1997, made the point that neoliberalism and financial market deregulation has not led to a smaller role for the state. The role of the state has grown as it changed from regulation to avert financial crises to cleaning up and bailing out finance after crises. And these remain after the GFC but also complemented by the wish to avert contagion for which the possibility of capital controls has been tentatively mooted.

Experience after the GFC has confirmed that inadequately regulated finance requires a more active and larger role for the state. States are also able to influence the evolution of the financial system within a country through financial market formation and the structure and regulation of institutions involved in trading and price formation of financial instruments. This regulation and governance include the role of the state and state ownership and control over these institutions and creation and transacting within these markets. A good example is provided by Petry et al. (2023) who give an indication of how variegated are both capital markets and the processes by which those markets contribute to financialisation in developing countries. They examine how different approaches to regulation of securities exchanges in certain increasingly financialised developing countries affect the shape and outcomes in capital markets. They find that there is a continuum with some states choosing greater degrees of neoliberalisation (of finance). They point out that, "there is clear variation in the extent to which the quest for private profit is allowed to reign freely in these capital markets", p. 158. They also make the important point that profit creation does not have to be the only function of financial markets but that they can also be organised to facilitate broader state objectives.

6   Developmentalism within the Neoliberal Era

In taking forward lessons for economic transformation from our discussion of the global/macro context, industrial policy and the DSP, we highlight the following. First is to specify the nature of contemporary, global capitalism, not least as the context within which national policymaking is proposed and implemented with corresponding outcomes. Here, as emphasised in our introduction, we point to the role of globalised production as well as the neoliberalisation of economic and social reproduction, something which renders current circumstances considerably different than those that prevailed during the golden age of the DSP. More specifically, neoliberalism has been underpinned by financialisation, and the associated proliferation and accumulation of financial assets without this necessarily leading to satisfactory levels of effective investment in either public or private sectors, quite apart from rendering the (global) economy susceptible to (financial) crises. And the presence and strength of financial interests have been considerably enhanced with corresponding effects felt across economy, politics, ideology and cultures.

Indeed, the vast majority of the burgeoning literature on financialisation across heterodox political economy and the social sciences, even if negligible within mainstream economics, has emphasised not only too much finance but, equally, the more finance there is the worse are a whole range of economic and social dysfunctions. The core reason for this is that financialisation is strongly attached to (the interests of) short-term speculative finance at the expense of longer-term productive or other functional goals. Given just how much expansion there has been of financial markets, with the spread of asset types, alongside poor economic and social performance relative to the postwar golden age, it is hardly surprising that there should be simple correlations between growing finance and poorer performance, especially in the wake of the GFC. However, we would emphasise that the association of financialisation with, for example, lesser real in favour of speculative investment is far from universal. Financialisation can also be associated with what might be termed the political economy of excess, most obvious in the expansive reliance upon fossil fuels as well as over-supply and maldistribution of food (with as many suffering malnutrition through obesity as undernutrition across the globe).

This points to a deeper insight concerning financialisation. It is not only that it can have differentiated effects across sectors of activity but the mechanisms by which it does so are themselves highly differentiated, just as is the incidence and impact of finance from sector to sector and from country to country. This is the first light in which we can upgrade, or update, the DSP. Certainly, the success of the east Asian NICS depended upon targeted finance and support from the state in conformity with industrial policies adopted but this was not seen as particularly problematic in terms of potential obstacles posed by financial interests themselves.[28] The situation in contemporary capitalism is very different, with the deregulation of financial markets, and limited and ineffective reregulation in the wake of the GFC, as opposed to state command over, and direction of, financial resources in support of concerted policymaking. Significantly, the glaring developmental success of China has been based upon unprecedentedly large-scale reliance upon bank finance of productive investments but such finance has been directed by the state in pursuit of its designated policies.

In short, developmentalism will depend upon taking command of financial resources in order to guarantee appropriate levels of investment in appropriate directions in conformity with targeted policy. Paradoxically, in what might be termed the third phase of neoliberalism,[29] and despite its ideology to the

---

28   At least until the South Korean chaebol, for example, sought to engage in speculative and international financial markets in conflict with state policy, some considering this to underpin the Asian financial crisis of 1997/98.

29   The first phase might be shorthanded by the moniker, shock therapy, and the second by Third Wayism (with financialisation as a common motif). In a South African context, these phases have tended to overlay one another, see Fine (2016a and 2019b).

contrary, closer relations have been forged between the state, finance and private enterprise in the attempt to rekindle profitable growth through such collaborations, with economic and social infrastructure to the fore.[30] Illustrative has been the rise of Public Private Partnerships.[31] These need to be built upon and expanded but by substituting developmental goals for speculative or other profitmaking.

Such initiatives point to a second aspect for upgrading the DSP, and that is to extend its scope beyond industrial policy as such to other sectors of the economy, even if industrialisation as such is taken to be as central to economic and social transformation. But that is not to denigrate the role to be played by agriculture, services and economic and social infrastructure. One reason to incorporate these into the DSP is because there is both convergence and overlap between them and 'industry', especially in light of new technologies. Manufacturing can both subcontract and incorporate services; agriculture is (increasingly) industrialised; and social and economic infrastructure is vital for industrial performance from research and development through energy and transport to a healthy, housed and educated workforce.

As observed, one of the major limitations of the DSP has been its neglect of social policy. Significantly, this neglect, as Mkandawire (2010, p. 50) observes, is complemented by the presumption that developmental states no longer offer the potential on which to construct social policy let alone to include it as part of the developmental state:

> One quite remarkable feature of the new social policy focused on MDGs ... is that the status and the requisite capacity of the state differ radically from the historical 'success stories'. Thus far, these policies are tethered to the demise of the 'developmental state', both as a reality and as an aspiration.

In response, first, as observed, there is no need to treat social policy as different from industrial policy as outlined previously, once recognising that social policy does itself offer general or horizontal and social provision. The education, housing and health systems are imperative for industrial performance and industrial policy neglects them at its peril. Second, by the same token, even if often primarily within the public sector, social is akin to industrial policy because it is sectoral, using inputs through a chain of provision to provide

---

30   For this in the context of the DSP and its latest incarnation as piecemeal intervention, see
       Bohrt et al. (2020).

31   See Gideon and Unterhalter (eds) (2020).

outputs even if these might be designated as public goods (and subject to various degrees of commercialisation including privatisation).

Until the WC, mainstream social policy was dominated by the idea of creating and/or improving a welfare state, as an aspect of developmental modernisation. It had its counterpart in critical literature in terms of whether welfare provision was adopted to be functional for the capitalist economy (in material and legitimising roles) or as a response to working class struggle to ameliorate conditions under capitalism (the so-called political economy of the welfare state). Over the period of neoliberalism, these traditions have been lost and two new orthodoxies have emerged. One is the welfare regimes approach associated with Esping-Andersen in which three ideal types (liberal, Scandinavian and authoritarian) are uncomfortably retro-fitted to developed countries and then, even more uncomfortably, extrapolated to developing countries where the lack of (retro-)fit between ideal types and empirical realities is cruelly exposed (whatever their legitimacy across different social policy programmes within developed countries). In short, the welfare regime approach does not work for developing countries, is insensitive to differences across sectors, and does not form the basis for developmental or transformative policy since policy is caught within a designated regime with no apparent escape clause![32]

The second now less than novel approach to social policy is associated with the new welfare economics which has taken neoliberal antipathy to welfare (and its own commitment to privatisation and user charges) as point of departure to see welfare provision as a game in which the state and citizen strategise in relation to one another on the basis of different information and objectives (meeting minimum standards of living at minimum cost for the state, for example, but maximising income for minimum work by the individual). This approach is deficient in two respects. On the one hand, in specifying social policy as a response to individual risk and vulnerability, it overlooks the systemic and enduring nature of economic and social reproduction, treating social policy as if it were the response to short-term shocks as opposed to a component part of development itself. On the other hand, like the welfare regime approach even if based on universal deductive principles (merit goods, optimisation, market imperfections, etc) as opposed to ideal types, the new welfare economics is insensitive to the contextual differences that mark both countries and policies in terms of individual aspects of welfare provision. Child education means different things in different places at different levels of development, and is also provided and poses challenges that differ by context.

---

32   See Fine (2016c and 2017).

The issue, then, is how to deal with the specificity of particular elements of social policy, in terms of their diversity of causes, content and consequences, without losing grip of the bigger pictures of economic and social reproduction within which they are embedded.

For the latter, pioneered by UNRISD, emphasis has been on locating welfare provision within the framework of the developmental welfare state. This has the advantage of foregrounding systemic change in targeting development, welfare and the role of the state. The approach also remains sufficiently open to be able to accommodate different aspects and trajectories to development and welfare provision.

Where does this leave the promotion of social policy and alternative public sector provision into the future?[33] Initially, we can draw two general lessons. First, there is a need to insulate public provision from financialisation (the direct or indirect effects of turning provision into a financial asset however near or distant). Privatisation does incorporate finance directly with provision becoming subject to the vagaries of stakeholder value on the stock market; subcontracting does it indirectly as the firms involved require their own financial imperatives to be observed. In short, the vulnerability of public sector provision to erosion and distortion is a consequence of the absence of broader supportive institutions and policies in the wake of three or more decades of neoliberalism. Alternative public sector provision, and new, broader policy capacities, and corresponding means and sources of finance, must be built in tandem in the differentiated context of specific locations and of what is being provided, across the water, health, energy, transport, housing systems, etc.[34]

---

33   For an interesting take on neoliberal social policy, see Laruffa (2021), "the promotion of social policy ... is largely informed by logics that make this agenda compatible with the epistemological and distributive aspects of the neoliberal framework: the application of the economic rationale and the cost–benefit logic to all domains of society and the protection (if not the promotion) of the interests of the economic and financial elites. Hence, contrary to the widespread assumption that promoting social policy is enough to overcome neoliberalism, this study corroborates the view that it is insufficient to focus on social policy generosity: it is necessary to investigate also the underlying rationale and goals informing social policy promotion, interrogating the extent to which these challenge the epistemological and distributive core of neoliberalism."

34   See Bayliss and Fine (2021), and the beginnings of the corresponding system of provision approach applied to public provision can be found in an introductory section to the MERG Report on social and economic infrastructure which was not published but is available as Fine (1996a).

7   Concluding Remarks

Drawing on both developmental experience and developmental scholarship, we have attempted in this Chapter to push for a more critical and rounded approach to economic and social transformation, especially in light of the reduced and skewed terms and content in which the issue has been confined despite the varieties of responses to the extremes of neoliberalism that have been prompted by its unavoidable travails, from GFC, the environment to pandemic ... and beyond. But we are equally mindful that this remains a necessary if academic exercise. There is a view, held with greater or lesser conviction, that economists rule the policy world, even beyond the economic, and the demise of Keynesianism and interventionism more generally, and the corresponding rise of various versions of monetarism, are closely reflected in neoliberal policymaking.

Our view is different, placing much less emphasis on the role of economists as such. When Mrs Thatcher first pioneered the British version of monetarism, it was intellectually inspired by one or two academic economists held in low regard by their peers, with 364 professors signing a letter to the Times deploring the policies involved. If we still remain convinced of the influence of academic scribblers, consider two other major issues of our time. One is the environment, where we can only be astonished by the extent to which well-established climate science continues to be ignored in the breach in practice. The other is social policy where, for most academic practitioners, the Scandinavian model of welfarism remains the gold standard even though it is being eroded on its own turf, with privatisation, commercialisation and austerity the order of the day. We might also add, to put it polemically, that South Korea had no idea it was a developmental state until told so by western social scientists, and its success, and subsequent "death", were based upon the absence and then presence of ATKEs, American-trained Korean economists, respectively.[35] In Japan, its period of developmentalism was also marked by the absence of (western) economists, other than Marxists!

The point then is not that academic endeavour is without influence or even futile. But it has to be placed within the context of which ideas are liable to be picked up and acted upon in contemporary conditions. Here, neoliberalism has done its work in ways that have gone far beyond the world of ideas. The supposed rolling back of the state in deference to the market has been nothing of the sort. Rather, the state has continued to be highly interventionist if

---

35   ATKE became an acronym as students sought their training abroad with the orthodoxy.

more attuned to the needs of capital in general and of finance, and financialisation, in particular. What has been rolled back are the institutions, and the powers that informed them, associated with more progressive policymaking, not least with the decline in the strength and influence of trade unions. And, subsequently, what has been rolled out are more centralised, authoritarian and closed forms of governance in which the revolving doors between politics, policymaking, commerce and the media have come to the fore together with more or less maverick and corrupt leaderships as progressive forms of (institutional and popular) checks and balances have been eroded.[36]

It follows that the prospects for developmental transformation in progressive directions involves building and rebuilding progressive movements for change, in detail across specific issues and in coordination with one another. Where these opportunities will arise, and how successful they can be, remains uncertain. But opportunities will derive from what will be the increasing inadequacies of globalised, financialised, neoliberalised economic and social reproduction, and the increasingly transparent deployment of the state to promote the interests of the few at the expense of the many.

---

36   For how this has impacted upon the South African developmental state, or lack of one, in the context of BEE, see Mabasa (2020).

References

Adams, A. (1993) "Food Insecurity in Mali: Exploring the Role of the Moral Economy", *IDS Bulletin*, vol 24, no 4, pp. 41–51.

Agénor, P. and P. Montiel (1996) *Development Macroeconomics*, Princeton: Princeton University Press.

Agosin, M. and R. Ffrench-Davis (1995) "Trade Liberalization and Growth: Recent Experiences in Latin America", *Journal of InterAmerican Studies and World Affairs*, vol 37, no 3, pp. 9–58.

Ahearne, A., J. Fernald, P. Loungani and J. Schindler (2006) "Flying Geese or Sitting Ducks: China's Impact on the Trading Fortunes of other Asian Economies", Board of Governors of the Federal Reserve System, International Finance Discussion Papers, no 887.

Akerlof, G. (1970) "The Market for 'Lemons': Quality Uncertainty and the Market Mechanism", *Quarterly Journal of Economics*, vol 84, no 3, pp. 488–500.

Akerlof, G. (1984) *An Economic Theorist's Book of Tales*, Cambridge: Cambridge University Press.

Akerlof, G. (1990) "George A. Akerlof", in Swedberg (ed.) (1990), pp. 61–77.

Akerlof, G. and R. Kranton (2000) "Economics and Identity", *Quarterly Journal of Economics*, vol 115, no 3, pp. 71–53.

Allen, G. (1986) "Famines: the Bowbrick-Sen Dispute and Some Related Issues", *Food Policy*, vol 11, no 3, pp. 259–63.

Amariglio, J. and D. Ruccio (1998) "Postmodernism, Marxism, and the Critique of Modern Economic Thought", in Prychitko (ed.) (1998), pp. 1–18.

Amsden, A. (1989) *Asia's Next Giant: South Korea's Late Industrialisation*, Oxford: Oxford University Press.

Amsden A. (2008) "The Wild Ones: Industrial Policies in the Developing World", in Narcis and Stiglitz (eds) (2008), pp. 95–118.

Anderson, J. (1995) "Tariff Index Theory", *Review of International Economics*, vol 3, no 2, pp. 156–173.

Anderson, J. (1998) "Effective Protection Redux", *Journal of International Economics*, vol 44, no 1, pp. 21–44.

Anderson, J. and J. Neary (1996) "A New Approach to Evaluating Trade Policy", *Review of Economic Studies*, vol 63, no 1, pp. 107–125.

Andreoni, A., P. Mondliwa, S. Roberts and F. Tregenna (eds) (2021) *Structural Transformation in South Africa: the Challenges of Inclusive Industrial Development in a Middle-Income Country*, Oxford: Oxford University Press.

Argyrous, G. (1992) "Kuhn's Paradigms and Neoclassical Economics", *Economics and Philosophy*, vol 8, no 2, pp. 231–48.

Argyrous, G. (1994) "Kuhn's Paradigms and Neoclassical Economics: Reply to Dow", *Economics and Philosophy*, vol 10, no 1, pp. 123–26.

Arrow, K. (1951) *Social Choice and Individual Values*, New Haven: Yale University Press.

Ashman, S. and B. Fine (2013) "Neo-Liberalism, Varieties of Capitalism, and the Shifting Contours of South Africa's Financial System", *Transformation*, no 81/82, pp. 145–78.

Ashman, S., B. Fine and E. Karwowski (2018) "Introduction to the Special Section 'Financialization in South Africa'", *Competition and Change*, vol 22, no 4, pp. 383–87.

Ashman, S., B. Fine and S. Newman (2010a) "The Developmental State and Post-Liberation South Africa", in Misra-Dexter and February (eds) (2010), pp. 23–45.

Ashman, S., B. Fine and S. Newman (2010b) "The Crisis in South Africa: Neoliberalism, Financialization and Uneven and Combined Development", in Panitch et al. (eds) (2010), pp. 174–95.

Ashman, S., B. Fine and S. Newman (2011) "Amnesty International?: the Nature, Scale and Impact of Capital Flight from South Africa", *Journal of Southern African Studies*, vol 37, no 1, pp. 7–25.

Ashman, S., B. Fine and S. Newman (2013) "Systems of Accumulation and the Evolving South African MEC", in Fine et al. (eds) (2013), pp. 245–67.

Aston, T. and C. Philpin (eds) (1985) *The Brenner Debate: Agrarian Class Structure and Economic Development in Pre-Industrial Europe*, Cambridge: Cambridge University Press.

Aswichayono, H., K. Bird and H. Hill (1996) "What Happens to Industrial Structure When Countries Liberalise?", *Journal of Development Studies* vol 32, no 3, pp. 340–363.

Atkinson, A. (1970) "On the Measurement of Inequality", *Journal of Economic Theory*, vol 2, no 3, pp. 244–63.

Aw, B. and G. Batra (1998) "Technological Capability and Firm Efficiency in Taiwan", *World Bank Economic Review*, vol 12, no 1, pp. 59–79.

Aw, B. and A. Hwang (1995) "Productivity and the Export Market: A Firm-Level Analysis", *Journal of Development Economics*, vol 47, no 2, pp. 313–32.

Balakrishnan, R. and C. Grown (1999) "Foundations and Economic Knowledge", in Garnett (ed.) (1999), pp. 124–38.

Balassa, B. (1988) "Interests of Developing Countries in the Uruguay Round", *World Economy*, vol 11, no 1, pp. 39–54.

Balasubramanyam, V. and S. Lall (eds) (1991) *Current Issues in Development Economics*, London: Macmillan.

Baldwin, R. (1992) "Are Economists' Traditional Trade Policy Views Still Valid?", *Journal of Economic Literature*, vol XXX, no 2, pp. 804–29.

Bandyopadhyay, S. (1996) "Growth, Welfare and Optimal Trade Taxes: A Fallacy of Composition", *Journal of Development Economics*, vol 50, no 2, pp. 369–80.

Barbour, I. (1980) "Paradigms in Science and Religion", in Gutting (ed.) (1980), pp. 223–45.

Bardhan, P. (1989) "General Introduction", in Bardhan (ed.) (1989), pp. 3–29.

Bardhan, P. (1995) "The Contribution of Endogenous Growth Theory to the Analysis of Development Problems: An Assessment", in Behrman and Srinivisan (eds) (1995), pp. 2984–88.

Bardhan, P. (ed.) (1989) *The Economic Theory of Agrarian Institutions*, Oxford: Clarendon Press.

Basant, R. (1993) "R&D, Foreign Technology Purchase and Technology Spillovers on Indian Industrial Productivity", Maastricht: United Nations University Institute for New Technologies, https://digitallibrary.un.org/record/223528.

Basu, K., P. Pattanaik and K. Suzumura (eds) (1995) *Choice, Welfare, and Development: A Festschrift in Honour of Amartya K. Sen*, Oxford: Clarendon Press.

Bates, R., A. Greif, M. Levi, J.-L. Rosentahl and B. Weingast (1998) *Analytic Narratives*, Princeton: Princeton University Press.

Bayliss, K. and B. Fine (2021) *A Guide to the Systems of Provision Approach: Who Gets What, How and Why*, Basingstoke: Palgrave MacMillan.

Bayliss, K. and B. Fine (2024) "Locating the World Bank: the Unmaking and Remaking of Development Economics in Its Shifting Vision", in Vetterlein and Schmidtke (eds) (2024), forthcoming.

Bayliss, K. and B. Fine (eds) (2008) *Whither the Privatisation Experiment? Electricity and Water Sector Reform in Sub-Saharan Africa*, Basingstoke: Palgrave Macmillan.

Bayliss, K., B. Fine, M. Robertson and A. Saad-Filho (2024) "Reports of My Death Are Greatly Exaggerated: the Persistence of Neoliberalism in Britain", *European Journal of Social Theory*, vol 27, no 4, 2024, pp. 540–60.

Bayliss, K., B. Fine and E. Van Waeyenberge (eds) (2011) *The Political Economy of Development: the World Bank, Neoliberalism and Development Research*, London: Pluto.

Bebbington, A., S. Guggenheim, E. Olson and M. Woolcock (2004) "Grounding Discourse in Practice: Exploring Social Capital Debates at the World Bank", *Journal of Development Studies*, vol 40, no 5, pp. 33–64.

Becker, G. (1990) "Gary S. Becker", in Swedberg (ed.) (1990), pp. 27–46.

Becker, G. (1996) *Accounting for Tastes* Cambridge: Harvard University Press.

Beckman, B. (1992) "Empowerment or Repression?: the World Bank and the Politics of Adjustment", in Gibbon et al. (eds) (1992), pp. 83–105.

Behrman, J. and T. Srinivisan (eds) (1995) *Handbook of Development Economics*, vol 3B, Oxford: Elsevier.

Bell, M. and K. Pavitt (1992) "Accumulating Technological Capability in Developing Countries", Supplement to, *World Bank Economic Review*, pp. 257–81.

Bernhofen, D (1977) "Strategic Trade Policy in a Vertically related Industry", Review of International Economics, vol 5, no 3, pp. 429–33.

Bernstein, M. (1999) "Economic Knowledge, Professional Authority, and the State: the Case of American Economics during and after World War II", in Garnett (ed.) (1999), pp. 103–23.

Bhagwati, J. (1993) India's Economy: the Shackled Giant, Oxford: Clarendon Press.

Bhattacharjea, A. (1995) "Strategic Tariffs and Endogenous Market Structures: Trade and Industrial Policies under Imperfect Competition", Journal of Development Economics, vol 47, no 2, pp. 287–312.

Bhorat, H., A. Hirsch and R. Kanbur (eds) (2014) Oxford Companion of South African Economics, Oxford: Oxford University Press.

Biel, R. (2000) The New Imperialism: Crisis and Contradictions in North-South Relations, London: Zed Books.

Biggs, S. (2008) "The Lost 1990s? Personal Reflections on a History of Participatory Technology Development", Development in Practice, vol 18, no 4–5, pp. 489–505.

Bilal, S. (1998) "Political Economy Considerations on the Supply of Trade Protection in Regional Integration Agreements", Journal of Common Market Studies, vol 36, no 1, pp. 1–31.

Blaug, M. (1975) "Kuhn versus Lakatos, or Paradigms versus Research Programmes in the History of Economics", History of Political Economy, vol 7, no 4, pp. 399–433.

Blaug, M. (1980) "The Methodology of Economics: or How Economists Explain", Cambridge: Cambridge University Press.

Blaug, M. (1998a) "Disturbing Currents in Modern Economics," Challenge, vol 41, no 3, pp. 11–34.

Blaug, M. (1998b) "The Problems with Formalism: Interview with Mark Blaug", Challenge, vol 41, no 3, pp. 35–45.

Block, F. (1977) The Origins of International Economic Disorder: a Study of United States International Monetary Policy from World War II to the Present, Berkeley, CA: UCLA Press.

Block, F. (2008) "Swimming against the Current: the Rise of a Hidden Developmental State in the United States", Politics and Society, vol 36, no 2, pp. 169–206.

Boffo, M., B. Fine and A. Saad-Filho (2018) "Neoliberal Capitalism: the Authoritarian Turn", in Panitch and Albo (eds) (2018), pp. 247–70.

Bohrt, M., D. Graizbord and P. Heller (2020) "Toward a Spatial Measure of Twenty-First-Century Developmental State Capacity", Sociology of Development, vol 6, no 2, pp. 250–74.

Boileau, M. (1996) "Growth and the International Transmission of Business Cycles", International Economic Review, vol 37, no 4, pp. 737–56.

Boschma, R. (2021) "Global Value Chains from an Evolutionary Economic Geography Perspective: a Research Agenda", Papers in Evolutionary Economic Geography, no

21.34, Utrecht University, https://www.researchgate.net/publication/355929162 _Global_Value_Chains_from_an_Evolutionary_Economic_Geography_perspective _a_research_agenda.

Bowbrick, P. (1986) "The Causes of Famine: a Refutation of Professor Sen's Theory", *Food Policy*, vol 11, no 2, pp. 105–24.

Bowbrick, P. (1987) "Rejoinder: the Causes of Famine", *Food Policy*, vol 12, no 1, pp. 5–9.

Bowles, S. and H. Gintis (1993) "The Revenge of Homo Economicus: Contested Exchange and the Revival of Political Economy", *Journal of Economic Perspectives*, vol 7, no 1, pp. 83–102.

Boylan, T. and P. O'Gorman (1995) *Beyond Rhetoric and Realism in Economics: towards a Reformulation of Economic Methodology*, London: Routledge.

Braga, H. and L. Wilmore (1991) "Technological Imports and Technological Effort: an Analysis of their Determinants in Brazilian Firms", *Journal of Industrial Economics*, vol 39, no 4, pp. 421–32.

Brainard, S. and D. Martimort (1997) "Strategic Trade Policy with Incompletely Informed Policymakers", *Journal of International Economics*, vol 42, no 1–2, pp. 33–66.

Brander, J. and B. Spencer (1985) "Export Subsidies and Market Share Rivalry", *Journal of International Economics*, vol 18, no 1/2, pp. 83–100.

Bronfenbrenner, M. (1971) "The 'Structure of Revolutions' in Economic Thought", *History of Political Economy*, vol 3, no 1, pp. 136–51.

Buchanan, J. (1984) "Politics without Romance: a Sketch of Positive Public Choice Theory and its Normative Implications", in Buchanan and Tollison (eds) (1984), pp. 11–22.

Buchanan, J. and R. Tollison (eds) (1984) *The Theory of Public Choice II*, Ann Arbor: University of Michigan Press.

Bush, R. (1996) "The Politics of Food and Starvation", *Review of African Political Economy*, no 68, pp. 169–95.

Calvo, G., R. Findlay, P. Kouri and J. de Macedo (eds) (1989) *Debt, Stabilisation and Development: Essays in the Honour of Carlos-Diaz Alejandro*, New York: Basil Blackwell.

Cameron, J. (2000) "Amartya Sen on Economic Inequality: the Need for an Explicit Critique of Opulence", Journal of International Development, vol 12, no 7, pp. 103–45.

Carmen, R. (2000) "Prima Mangiare, Poi Filosofare", *Journal of International Development*, vol 12, no 7, pp. 1019–30.

Carrier, J. and D. Miller (eds) (1998) *Virtualism: the New Political Economy*, London: Berg.

Cawe, A. and K. Mabasa (eds) (2020) *Beyond Tenderpreneurship: Rethinking Black Business and Economic Empowerment*, Johannesburg: Mapungubwe Institute for Strategic Reflection (MISTRA).

Chandra, R. (2024) *Reflections on the Future of Capitalism: from Karl Marx to Amartya Sen*, London: Palgrave MacMillan.

Chang, H.-J. (1994) *The Political Economy of Industrial Policy*, Basingstoke: Macmillan.

Chang, H.-J. (2002) *Kicking Away the Ladder – Development Strategy in Historical Perspective*, London: Anthem Press.

Chang, H.-J. (ed.) (2001) *Joseph Stiglitz and the World Bank: the Rebel Within*. London: Anthem Press.

Chase, R. (1983) "The Kuhnian Paradigm Thesis as a Dialectical Process and Its Application to Economics", *Rivista Internazionale di Scienze Economiche e Commerciali*, vol xxx, no 9, pp. 809–28.

Chen, L. and J. Devereux (1997) "Trade Neutrality: a Clarification", *Journal of Developing Areas*, vol 31, no 3, pp. 357–66.

Chen, T. and D. Tang (1987) "Comparing Technical Efficiency among Import Substituting and Export-Oriented Foreign Firms in a Developing Country", *Journal of Development Economics*, vol 26, no 2, pp. 277–89.

Clerides, S., S. Lach and J. Tybout (1998) "Is Learning by Exporting Important? Micro-Dynamic Evidence from Colombia, Mexico and Morocco", *Quarterly Journal of Economics*, vol CXIII, no 3, pp. 903–47.

Coats, A. (1969) "Is There a 'Structure of Scientific Revolutions' in Economics?", *Kyklos*, vol 22, no 2, pp. 289–96.

Coats, A. (ed.) (1996) *The Post-1945 Internationalization of Economics, History of Political Economy*, vol 28 (Supplement), Durham, NC: Duke University Press.

Coe, D., E. Helpman and W. Alexander (1995) "North-South R&D Spillovers", CEPR Discussion Paper, no 1133, Centre for Economic Policy Research, London.

Collier, P. and N. Sambanis (eds) (2005a) *Understanding Civil War: Evidence and Analysis, Volume 1: Africa*, Washington, DC: World Bank, http://hdl.handle.net /10986/7437.

Collier, P. and N. Sambanis (eds) (2005b) *Understanding Civil War: Evidence and Analysis, Volume 2: Europe, Central Asia, and Other Regions*, Washington, DC: World Bank, http://documents.worldbank.org/curated/en/373981468308066282/Europe -Central-Asia-and-other-regions.

Connell, R. (1997) "Why Is Classical Theory Classical?", *American Journal of Sociology*, vol 102, no 6, pp. 1511–57.

Corbridge, S. (2002) "Development as Freedom: the Spaces of Amartya Sen", *Progress in Development Studies*, vol 2, no 3, pp 183–217.

Corbridge, S. (2006) "Amartya Kumar Sen", in Simon (ed.) (2006), pp. 230–35.

Corbridge, S. (2007) "The (Im)possibility of Development Studies", *Economy and Society*, vol 36, no 2, pp. 179–211.

Cornia, G., R. Jolly and F. Stewart (1987) *Adjustment with a Human Face: Protecting the Vulnerable and Promoting Growth. Vol. 1: a Study by UNICEF*, London: Oxford University Press.

Cornwall, A. and D. Eade (eds) (2010) *Deconstructing Development Discourse: Buzzwords and Fuzzwords*, Warwickshire: Practical Action Publishing.

Cramer, C. (2006) *Civil War Is not a Stupid Thing: Accounting for Violence in Developing Countries*, London: Hurst.

Creane, A. (1998) "Ignorance Is Bliss as Trade Policy", *Review of International Economics*, vol 6, no 4, pp. 616–24.

Crotty, J. (2002) "The Effects of Increased Product Market Competition and Changes in Financial Markets on the Performance of Nonfinancial Corporations in the Neoliberal Era", Political Economy Research Institute, University of Massachusetts, Amherst Working Paper no 44.

Dahlman, C. and N. Fonseca (1987) "Technological Dependence and Technological Capability: the Case of the USIMINAS Steel Plant in Brazil", in Katz (ed.) (1987), pp. 154–82.

Damodaran, S., S. Gupta, S. Mitra and D. Sinha (eds) (2023) *Development, Transformations and the Human Condition: Volume in Honour of Professor Jayati Ghosh*, New Delhi: Routledge, forthcoming.

Dasgupta, P. (1993) *An Inquiry into Well-Being and Destitution*, Oxford: Clarendon Press.

Dasgupta, P. (2001) *Human Well-Being and the Natural Environment*, Oxford: Oxford University Press.

Dasgupta, P. and D. Ray (1990) "Adapting to Undernourishment: the Biological Evidence and Its Implications", in Drèze and Sen (eds) (1990a), pp. 191–246.

Dauncey, E., V. Desai and R. Potter (eds) (2024) *The Companion to Development Studies*, London: Routledge.

Davies, S. (1993) "Are Coping Strategies a Cop Out?", *IDS Bulletin*, vol 24, no 4, pp. 60–72.

de Melo, J. and A. Sapir (eds) (1991) *Trade Theory and Economic Reform: Essays in the Honour of Bela Balassa*, Oxford: Basil Blackwell.

de Melo, J. and S. Robinson (1982) "Trade Adjustment Policies and Income Distribution in Three Archetype Developing Countries", *Journal of Development Economics*, vol 10, no 1, pp. 67–92.

de Moraes, I. (2023) "The Concept of Developmental State Revisited", *Brazilian Journal of Political Economy*, vol 43, no 4, pp. 813–36.

De Vroey, M. (1975) "The Transition from Classical to Neoclassical Economics: a Scientific Revolution", *Journal of Economic Issues*, vol IX, no 3, pp. 415–39.

de Waal, A. (1990) "A Reassessment of Entitlement Theory in the Light of Recent Famines in Africa", *Development and Change*, vol 21, no 3, pp. 469–90.

de Waal, A. (1991) "Logic and Application: a Reply to S.R. Osmani", *Development and Change*, vol 22, no 3, pp. 597–608.

de Waal, A. (1993) "War and Famine in Africa", *IDS Bulletin*, vol 24, no 4, pp. 52–59.

Deane, K., J. Chukwuma, and L. Lombardozzi (2023) "COVID-19 in an African Context: What the Pandemic Has Taught Us About the Development Economics Curriculum and the Need for Reform", in Yusuf et al. (eds), pp. 49–68.

Decker, S., W. Elsner and S. Flechtner (2018) (eds) *Advancing Pluralism in Teaching Economics*, London: Routledge.

Deraniyagala, S. and B. Fine (2001) "New Trade Theory versus Old Trade Policy: a Continuing Enigma", *Cambridge Journal of Economics*, vol 25, no 6, pp. 809–25. See Chapter 5.

Deraniyagala, S. and B. Fine (2006) "Kicking away the Logic: Free Trade Is neither the Question nor the Answer for Development", in Jomo and Fine (eds) (2006), pp. 46–67.

Deraniyagala, S. and H. Semboja (1999) "Technology Upgrading and Trade Liberalisation in Tanzania", in Lall (ed.) (1999), pp. 112–47.

Desai, M. (2001) "Amartya Sen's Contribution to Development Economics", *Oxford Development Studies*, vol 29, no 3, pp. 213–24.

Devereux, M. and K. Lee (1999) "Endogenous Trade Policy and Gains from International Financial Markets". *Journal of Monetary Economics,* vol 43, no 1 pp 35–39.

Devereux, S. (1993a) *Theories of Famine*, Hemel Hempstead: Wheatsheaf/Harvester.

Devereux, S. (1993b) "Goats before Ploughs: Dilemmas of Household Response Sequencing During Food Shortages", *IDS Bulletin*, vol 24, no 4, pp. 52–59.

Devereux, S. and T. Naerra (1996) "Drought and Survival in Rural Namibia", *Journal of Southern African Studies*, vol 22, no 3, pp. 421–40.

Dornbusch, R. (1992) "The Case for Trade Liberalisation in Developing Countries", *Journal of Economic Perspectives*, vol 6, no 1, pp. 69–85.

Dow, S. (1985) *Macroeconomic Thought: a Methodological Approach*, Oxford: Basil Blackwell.

Dow, S. (1994) "Kuhn's Paradigms and Neoclassical Economics", *Economics and Philosophy*, vol 10, no 1, pp. 119–22.

Drèze, J. and A. Sen (2002) *India: Development and Participation*, Delhi: Oxford University Press.

Drèze, J. and A. Sen (1989) *Hunger and Public Action*, Oxford: Clarendon.

Drèze, J. and A. Sen (eds) (1990a) *The Political Economy of Hunger, Volume 1: Entitlement and Well-Being*, Oxford: Clarendon.

Drèze, J. and A. Sen (eds) (1990b) *The Political Economy of Hunger, Volume 2: Famine Prevention*, Oxford: Clarendon.

Drèze, J. and A. Sen (eds) (1990c) *The Political Economy of Hunger, Volume 3: Endemic Hunger*, Oxford: Clarendon.

Duffield, M. (1993) "NGOs, Disaster Relief and Asset Transfer in the Horn: Political Survival in a Permanent Emergency", *Development and Change*, vol 24, no 1, pp. 131–57.

Duffield, M. (1994) "The Political Economy of Internal War: Asset Transfer, Complex Emergencies and International Aid", in Macrae and Zwi (eds) (1994), pp. 50–69.

Durkin, J. (1997) "Perfect Competition and Endogenous Comparative Advantage", *Review of International Economics*, vol 5, no 3, pp. 401–11.

Dyson, T. (1993) "Demographic Responses to Famines in South Asia", *IDS Bulletin*, vol 24, no 4, pp. 17–26.

Eaton, J. and G. Grossman (1986) "Optimal Trade and Industrial Policy Under Oligopoly", *Quarterly Journal of Economics*, vol 101, no 2, pp. 383–406.

Edigheji, O. (ed) (2010) *Constructing a Democratic Developmental State in South Africa: Potentials and Challenges*, Cape Town: Human Sciences Research Council Press.

Edwards, S. (1993) "Openness, Trade Liberalization, and Growth in Developing Countries", *Journal of Economic Literature*, vol XXXI, no 3, pp. 1358–93.

Edwards, S. (1997) "Trade Policy, Growth, and Income Distribution", *American Economic Review*, vol 87, no 2, pp. 205–210.

Eichengreen, B. (2008) *Globalizing Capital: a History of the International Monetary System*, Princeton: Princeton University Press.

Epstein, G. (2005) "Central Banks as Agents of Economic Development", Political Economy Research Institute, University of Massachusetts at Amherst, Working Paper no 104.

Epstein, G. (2009) "Post-war Experiences with Developmental Central Banks: the Good, the Bad and the Hopeful", G-24 Discussion Paper no 54, Geneva: United Nations Conference on Trade and Development.

Epstein, G. and I. Grabel (2007) "Financial Policy Training Module", International Poverty Centre, UNDP, Brasilia. http://www.ipc-undp.org/pub/IPCTrainingModule3.pdf.

Erasmo, V. (2024) "Who Are the Capability Theorists?': a Tale of the Origins and Development of the Capability Approach", *Cambridge Journal of Economics*, vol 48, no 3, pp. 425–50.

Ethier, W. (1982) "National and International Returns to Scale in the Modern Theory of International Trade", *American Economic Review*, vol 72, no 3, pp. 389–405.

Evans, P. (2014) "The Developmental State: Divergent Responses to Modern Economic Theory and the Twenty-First-Century Economy", in Williams (ed.) (2014), pp. 220–40.

Evenson, R. and L. Westphal (1995) "Technological Change and Technology Strategy", in Behrman and Srinivisan (eds) (1995), pp. 2209–99.

Fasenfest, D. (ed.) (2022) *Marx Matters*, Leiden: Brill.

Febrero, R. and P. Schwartz (eds) (1995) *The Essence of Becker*, Stanford: Hoover Institution Press.

Felipe, J. (1999) "Total Factor Productivity Growth in east Asia: a Critical Survey", *Journal of Development Studies*, vol 35, no 4, pp. 1–41.

Fichtner, J. (2020) "The Rise of Institutional Investors", in Mader et al. (eds) (2020), pp. 265–75.

Fikkert, R. (1993) "Complementary Technology Imports and Domestic R&D", Princeton University, mimeo.

Fine, B. (1975) "Individual Liberalism in a Paretian Society", *Journal of Political Economy*, vol 83, no 6, pp. 82–96.

Fine, B. (1982) *Theories of the Capitalist Economy*, London: Edward Arnold.

Fine, B. (1985) "A Note on the Measurement of Inequality and Interpersonal Comparison", *Social Choice and Welfare*, vol 1, no 4, pp. 273–75.

Fine, B. (1992) *Women's Employment and the Capitalist Family*, London: Routledge.

Fine, B. (1993) "Resolving the Diet Paradox", *Social Science Information*, vol 32, no 4, pp. 669–87.

Fine, B. (1994a) "Towards a Political Economy of Food", *Review of International Political Economy*, vol 1, no 3, pp. 519–45.

Fine, B. (1994b) "Towards a Political Economy of Food: a Response to My Critics", *Review of International Political Economy*, vol 1, no 3, pp. 579–86.

Fine, B. (1995) "Towards a Political Economy of Anorexia?", *Appetite*, vol 24, pp. 231–42.

Fine, B. (1996a) "Some Perspectives on the Provision of Social and Economic Infrastructure", Prepared for, but not presented at, Workshop for South African Policy Makers, June, 1996, https://eprints.soas.ac.uk/32961/1/MERGINTR.docx.

Fine, B. (1996b) "A Formal Note on New Theories of International Trade and Development", *Journal of International Development*, vol 8, no 6, pp. 805–11.

Fine, B. (1997a) "The New Revolution in Economics", *Capital and Class*, no 61, Spring, pp. 143–48.

Fine, B. (1997b) "Entitlement Failure?", *Development and Change*, vol 28, no 4, pp. 617–47. See Chapter 2.

Fine, B. (1997c) "Industrial Policy and South Africa: a Strategic View", NIEP Occasional Paper Series, no 5, Johannesburg: National Institute for Economic Policy.

Fine, B. (1997d) "Privatisation and the Restructuring of State Assets in South Africa: a Strategic View". NIEP Occasional Paper Series no 7, Johannesburg: National Institute for Economic Policy.

Fine, B. (1997e) "Vertical Relations in the South African Steel Industry". NIEP Occasional Paper Series no 13, Johannesburg: National Institute for Economic Policy, originally a report for NUMSA Investment Company, December.

Fine, B. (1998a) *Labour Market Theory: the Case for Political Economy*, London: Routledge.

Fine, B. (1998b) *Diet, Health and Information: the World of Food*, London: Routledge.

Fine, B. (1999) "Competition and Market Structure Reconsidered", *Metroeconomica*, vol 50, no 2, pp. 194–218. See Chapter 6.

Fine, B. (2000) "Endogenous Growth Theory: a Critical Assessment", *Cambridge Journal of Economics*, vol 24, no 2, pp. 245–65, a shortened and amended version of identically titled, SOAS Working Paper no 80, February 1998.

Fine, B. (2001a) *Social Capital versus Social Theory: Political Economy and Social Science at the Turn of the Millennium*, London: Routledge.

Fine, B. (2001b) "Amartya Sen: a Partial and Personal Appreciation", Centre for Development Policy Research, School of Oriental and African Studies, University of London, Discussion Paper, no 1601.

Fine, B. (2001c) "Economics Imperialism as Kuhnian Revolution?", *International Papers in Political Economy*, vol 8, no 3, pp. 1–58.

Fine, B. (2002a) *The World of Consumption: the Material and Cultural Revisited*, London: Routledge.

Fine, B. (2002b) "Globalisation and Development: the Imperative of Political Economy", Paper for the Conference "Towards a New Political Economy of Development: Globalisation and Governance", Sheffield, July.

Fine, B. (2002c) "It Ain't Social, It Ain't Capital and It Ain't Africa", *Studia Africana*, no 13, pp. 18–33.

Fine, B. (2002d) "'Economic Imperialism': a View from the Periphery", *Review of Radical Political Economics*, vol 34, no 2, pp. 187–201.

Fine, B. (2002e) "Economics Imperialism and the New Development Economics as Kuhnian Paradigm Shift", World Development, vol 30, no 12, pp. 2057–70. See Chapter 4.

Fine, B. (2002f) "Economics and Ethics: Amartya Sen as Point of Departure", Paper presented to the World Bank ABCDE Conference, Oslo, July, https://view.off iceapps.live.com/op/view.aspx?src=https%3A%2F%2Feprints.soas.ac.uk%2F6 606%2F1%2Fsenidea.doc, published as revised in Fine (2004b).

Fine, B. (2003) "Beyond the Developmental State: towards a Political Economy of Development", in Hirakawa et al. (eds) (2003), (in Japanese), pp. 21–43, with English version in Lapavitsas and Noguchi (eds) (2005), pp. 17–33.

Fine, B. (2004a) "Examining the Idea of Globalisation and Development Critically: What Role for Political Economy?", *New Political Economy*, vol 9, no 2, pp. 213–31.

Fine, B. (2004b) "Economics and Ethics: Amartya Sen as Point of Departure", *The New School Economic Review*, vol 1, no 1, pp. 151–62. See Chapter 3.

Fine, B. (2004c) "Addressing the Critical and the Real in Critical Realism", in Lewis (ed.) (2004), pp. 202–26.

Fine, B. (2006a) "Joseph Stiglitz", in Simon (ed.), pp. 247–51.

Fine, B. (2006b) "The Developmental State and the Political Economy of Development", in Jomo and Fine (eds) (2006), pp. 101–122.

Fine, B. (2007) "State, Development and Inequality: the Curious Incidence of the Developmental State in the Night-Time", paper presented to Sanpad Conference, Durban, June 26–30, www.networkideas.org/ideasact/jan09/PDF/Fine.pdf.

Fine, B. (2008a) "The Minerals-Energy Complex is Dead: Long Live the MEC?", Amandla Colloquium, eprints.soas.ac.uk/5617/.

Fine, B. (2008b) "Engaging the MEC: Or a Lot of My Views on a Lot of Things", paper for MEC workshop at University of KwaZulu-Natal, Durban, June, eprints.soas.ac.uk/5813/ in shortened version as "Engaging the MEC: Or a Few of My Views on a Few Things", *Transformation*, no 71, 2010, pp. 26–49.

Fine, B. (2009) "Development as Zombieconomics in the Age of Neo-Liberalism", *Third World Quarterly*, vol 30, no 5, pp. 885–904.

Fine, B. (2010a) "From the Political Economy of Development to Development Economics: Implications for Africa?", in Padayachee (ed.) (2010), pp. 60–82.

Fine, B. (2010b) *Theories of Social Capital: Researchers Behaving Badly*, London: Pluto.

Fine, B. (2010c) "Can South Africa Be a Developmental State?", in Edigheji (ed.) (2010), pp. 169–82.

Fine, B. (2010d) "The Developmental State?", in Maharaj et al. (eds) (2010), pp. 101–124.

Fine, B. (2011) "Locating the Developmental State and Industrial and Social Policy after the Crisis", UNCTAD, The Least Developed Countries Report 2011: *the Potential Role of South-South Cooperation for Inclusive and Sustainable Development*, Background Paper No. 3, https://eprints.soas.ac.uk/13440/3/Fine_unctadnotrack.pdf.

Fine, B. (2012a) "Chronicle of a Developmental Transformation Foretold: South Africa's National Development Plan in Hindsight", *Transformation*, no 78, pp. 115–32.

Fine, B. (2012b) "Assessing South Africa's New Growth Path: Framework for Change?", *Review of African Political Economy*, vol 39, no 134, pp. 551–68.

Fine, B. (2013a) "Beyond the Developmental State: an Introduction", in Fine et al. (eds) (2013), pp. 1–32.

Fine, B. (2013b) "Beyond the Developmental State", *African Communist*, no 186, pp. 40–54. See Chapter 7.

Fine, B. (2013c) "Economics – Unfit for Purpose: the Director's Cut", SOAS Department of Economics Working Paper Series, no 176, https://eprints.soas.ac.uk/14605/, revised and shortened to appear as, "Economics: Unfit for Purpose", *Review of Social Economy*, vol LXXI, no 3, 2013, pp. 373–89.

Fine, B. (2016a) "Across Developmental State and Social Compacting: the Peculiar Case of South Africa", ISER Working Paper, no 2016/1, Grahamstown: Institute of Social and Economic Research, Rhodes University, https://eprints.soas.ac.uk/34148/1/iserwp.pdf.

Fine, B. (2016b) *Microeconomics: a Critical Companion*, London: Pluto.

Fine, B. (2016c) "The Systemic Failings in Framing Neo-liberal Social Policy", in Subaset (ed.) (2016), pp. 159–77.

Fine, B. (2017) "The Continuing Enigmas of Social policy", in Ye (ed.) (2017), pp. 29–60.

Fine, B. (2018a) "*Collective Choice and Social Welfare*: Economics Imperialism in Action and Inaction", *Ethics and Social Welfare*, vol 12, no 4, pp. 393–99.

Fine, B. (2018b) "In and Against Orthodoxy: Teaching Economics in the Neoliberal Era", in Decker et al. (eds) (2018), pp. 78–94.

Fine, B. (2019a) "A Note on the Relationship between Additive Separability and Decomposability in Measuring Income Inequality", SOAS Department of Economics Working Paper, no 224, https://eprints.soas.ac.uk/31281/1/economics-wp224.pdf.

Fine, B. (2019b) "Post-Apartheid South Africa: It's Neoliberalism, Stupid!", in Reynolds et al. (eds) (2019), pp. 75–95.

Fine, B. (2020) "Framing Social Reproduction in the Age of Financialisation", in Santos and Teles (eds) (2020), pp. 257–72.

Fine, B. (2021) "Situating PPPs", in Gideon and Unterhalter (eds), pp. 26–38.

Fine, B. (2022) "From Marxist Political Economy to Financialisation or Is It the Other Way about?", in Fasenfest (ed.) (2022), pp. 43–66.

Fine, B. (2023a) "Social Capital: the Indian Connection", in Damodaran et al. (eds) (2023), forthcoming.

Fine, B. (2023b) "Mathematical Economics as Aid or Obstacle to Heterodox Economists?: a Personal Experience", Special Issue for Duncan Foley and Anwar Shaikh, *New School Economic Review*, vol 12, pp. 21–29.

Fine, B. (2023c) "Discrimination through Bargaining Structures: Gender Bias in the National Coal Board and British Coal", *Historical Studies in Industrial Relations*, vol 44, no 1, pp. 63–74.

Fine, B. (2024a) *Economics Imperialism and Interdisciplinarity: before the Watershed; Critical Reconstructions of Political Economy*, Volume 1, Leiden: Brill, and Chicago: Haymarket.

Fine, B. (2024b) *Economics Imperialism and Interdisciplinarity: the Watershed and after; Critical Reconstructions of Political Economy*, Volume 2, Leiden: Brill, and Chicago: Haymarket.

Fine, B. (2024c) *Cliometrics as Economics Imperialism: across the Watershed; Critical Reconstructions of Political Economy*, Volume 3, Leiden: Brill, and Chicago: Haymarket.

Fine, B. (2024d) "The Vagaries and Volatilities of Mainstream Development Economics: a Personal Account", in Meramveliotakis and Manioudis (eds) (2024), pp. 13–28.

Fine, B. (2024e) "Financialisation and Development", in Dauncey et al. (eds) (2024), pp. 387–92.

Fine, B. (2025) *In and against Development: the World Bank behind the Looking Glass; Critical Reconstructions of Political Economy*, Volume 6, Leiden: Brill, and Chicago: Haymarket.

Fine, B., M. Heasman, and J. Wright (1996) *Consumption in the Age of Affluence: the World of Food*, London: Routledge.

Fine, B., D. Johnston, A. Santos and E. Van Waeyenberge (2016) "Nudging or Fudging: the World Development Report 2015", *Development and Change*, vol 47, no 4, pp. 640–63.

Fine, B., C. Lapavitsas and J. Pincus (eds) (2001) *Development Policy in the Twenty-First Century: beyond the Post-Washington Consensus*, London: Routledge.

Fine, B. and E. Leopold (1993) *The World of Consumption*, London: Routledge.

Fine, B. and P. Mendes Loureiro (2020) "A Note on the Relationship between Additive Separability and Decomposability in Measuring Income Inequality", *Review of Social Economy*, vol 80, no 4, pp. 550–65.

Fine, B. and P. Mendes Loureiro (2021) "From Social Choice to Inequality-Decomposition: In the Spirit of Arrow and Atkinson by Way of Sen and Shorrocks", *International Review of Applied Economics*, vol 35, no 1, pp. 765–91.

Fine, B. and D. Milonakis (2009) *From Economics Imperialism to Freakeconomics: the Shifting Boundaries between Economics and Other Social Science*, London and New York: Routledge.

Fine, B. and S. Mohamed (2022) "Locating Industrial Policy in Developmental Transformation: Lessons from the Past, Prospects for the Future", SOAS Department of Economics Working Paper, no 246, London: SOAS University of London. See Chapter 8.

Fine, B. and S. Mohamed (2023) "Locating Industrial Policy in Developmental Transformation: Lessons from the Past, Prospects for the Future", Mohamed et al. (eds), pp. 22–58.

Fine, B. and A. Murfin (1984a) *Macroeconomics and Monopoly Capitalism*, Brighton: Wheatsheaf.

Fine, B. and A. Murfin (1984b) "The Political Economy of Monopoly and Competition: a Critique of Monopoly and Stagnation Theory", *International Journal of Industrial Organisation*, vol 2, no 2, pp. 133–46.

Fine, B., A. Petropoulos and H. Sato (2005) "Beyond Brenner's Investment Overhang Hypothesis: the Case of the Steel Industry", *New Political Economy*, vol 10, no 1, pp. 43–64.

Fine, B. and G. Pollen (2018) "The Developmental State Paradigm in the Age of Financialisation", in Hyland and Munck (eds) (2018) pp. 211–27.

Fine, B. and Z. Rustomjee (1996) *The Political Economy of South Africa: from Minerals-Energy Complex to Industrialisation*, London: Hurst, and Johannesburg: Wits University Press.

Fine, B. and A. Saad-Filho (2016) "Thirteen Things You Need to Know about Neoliberalism", *Critical Sociology*, vol 43, no 4–5, pp. 685–706.

Fine, B., J. Saraswati and D. Tavasci (eds) (2013) *Beyond the Developmental State: Industrial Policy into the 21st Century*, London: Pluto.

Fine, B. and C. Stoneman (1996) "The State and Development: an Introduction", *Journal of Southern African Studies*, vol 22, no 1, pp. 5–26.

Fine, B. and E. Van Waeyenberge (2006) "Correcting Stiglitz: from Information to Power in the World of Development", in Leys and Panitch (eds) (2005), pp. 146–68.

Fine, B. and E. Van Waeyenberge (2013) "A Paradigm Shift that Never Was: Justin Lin's New Structural Economics", *Competition and Change*, vol 17, no 4, pp. 355–71; for longer version, "A Paradigm Shift that Never Will Be?: Justin Lin's New Structural Economics", with E. Van Waeyenberge, SOAS Department of Economics Working Paper Series, no 179, 2013, https://eprints.soas.ac.uk/16707/.

Fischer, R. and P. Serra (1996) "Income Convergence within and between Countries", *International Economic Review*, vol 37, no 3, pp. 531–51.

Freund, B. (2013) "A Ghost from the Past: the South African Developmental State of the 1940s", *Transformation*, no 81/82, pp. 86–114.

Freund, B. (2018) *Twentieth Century South Africa: a Developmental History*, Cambridge: Cambridge University Press.

Frey, B. (1999) *Economics as a Science of Human Behaviour: towards a New Social Science Paradigm*, extended second edition of that of 1992, Boston: Kluwer Academic Publishers.

Froud, J., S. Johal, A. Leaver and K. Williams (2007) *Financialization and Strategy: Narrative and Numbers,* New York: Routledge.

Froud, J., S. Johal, A. Leaver and K. Williams (2014) "Financialization across the Pacific: Manufacturing Cost Ratios, Supply Chains and Power", *Critical Perspectives on Accounting,* vol 25, no 1, pp. 46–57.

Fuerst, T. and K. Kim (1997) "Two Part Trade Policy under Imperfect Competition", *Review of International Economics*, vol 5, no 1, pp. 63–71.

Fujita, M. and P. Krugman (2004) "The New Economic Geography: Past, Present and the Future", *Regional Science*, vol 83, no 1, pp. 139–164.

Fung, K. (1995) "Rent Shifting and Rent Sharing: a Re-examination of the Strategic Industrial Policy Problem", *Canadian Journal of Economics*, vol XXVIII, no 2, pp. 450–62.

Gallagher, M. (1991) *Rent Seeking and Economic Growth in Africa*, Boulder: Westview Press.

Garnett, R. (1999) "Economics of Knowledge: Old and New", in Garnett (ed.) (1999), pp. 1–16.

Garnett, R. (ed.) (1999) *What Do Economists Know?: New Economics of Knowledge*, London: Routledge.

Gasper, D. (1993) "Entitlements Analysis: Relating Concepts and Contexts", *Development and Change*, vol 24, no 4, pp. 679–718.

Gasper, D. (2000) "Amartya Sen on Inequality, Human Well-Being, and Development as Freedom", *Journal of International Development*, vol 12, no 7, pp. 989–1001.

Gasper, D. (2002) "Is Sen's Capability Approach an Adequate Basis for Considering Human Development?", Institute of Social Studies, The Hague, Working Paper Series, no 360.

Gasper, D. and J. Cameron (2000) "Assessing and Extending the Work of Amartya Sen", *Journal of International Development*, vol 12, no 7, pp. 985–88.

Gibbon, P., Y. Bangura and A. Ofstad (eds) (1992) *Authoritarianism, Democracy and Adjustment: the Politics of Economic Reform in Africa*, Uppsala: Scandinavian Institute of African Studies.

Gideon, J. and E. Unterhalter (eds) (2020) *Critical Reflections on Public Private Partnerships*, London: Routledge.

Giri, A. (2000) "Rethinking Human Well-Being: a Dialogue with Amartya Sen", *Journal of International Development*, vol 12, no 7, pp. 1003–18.

Goldstein, A., S. Bonaglia and J. Mathews (2006) "Accelerated Internationalization by Emerging Multinationals: the Case of White Goods", *Journal of World Business*, vol 42, no 4, pp. 369–83.

Gordon, D. (1965) "The Role of the History of Economic Thought in the Understanding of Modern Economic Theory", *American Economic Review*, vol 55, no 2, pp. 119–27.

Gore, C. (1993) "Entitlement Relations and 'Unruly' Social Practices: a Comment on the Work of Amartya Sen", *Journal of Development Studies*, vol 29, no 3, pp. 429–60.

Gould, D. and R. Ruffin (1995) "Human Capital, Trade, and Economic Growth", *Weltwirthschaftliches Archiv*, vol 131, no 3, pp. 425–45.

Gray, L. and M. Kevane (1993) "For Whom Is the Rural Economy Resilient – Initial Effects of Drought in Western Sudan", *Development and Change*, vol 24, no 1, pp. 159–76.

Greenaway, D. (1991) "New Trade Theories and Developing Countries", in Balasubramanyam and Lall (eds) (1991), pp. 156–70.

Greenaway, D., W. Morgan and P. Wright (1997) "Trade Liberalization and Growth in Developing Countries: Some New Evidence", *World Development*, vol 25, no 11, pp. 1885–92.

Greenaway, D., W. Morgan and P. Wright (1998) "Trade Reform, Adjustment and Growth: What Does the Evidence Tell Us?", *Economic Journal*, vol 108, no 3, pp. 1547–64.

Greenaway, D. and D. Sapsford (1994) "What Does Liberalisation Do for Exports and Growth?", *Weltwirtschaftliches Archiv*, vol 130, no 1, pp. 152–74.

Grossman, G. and E. Helpman (1991) *Innovation and Growth in the Global Economy*, Cambridge: MIT Press.

Grossman, G. and H. Horn (1988) "Infant Industry Protection Reconsidered: the Case of International Barriers to Entry", *Quarterly Journal of Economics*, vol CIII, no 4, pp. 767–87.

Gutting, G. (ed.) (1980) *Paradigms and Revolutions: Applications and Appraisals of Thomas Kuhn's Philosophy of Science*, Notre Dame: Notre Dame University Press.

Haddad, L., J. Hoddinott and H. Alderman (1994) *Intrahousehold Resource Allocation: an Overview*, Policy Research Working Paper, no 1255, Poverty and Human Resources Division, Washington: World Bank.

Haddad, M. (1993) "How Trade Liberalization Affected Productivity in Morocco", World Bank, Policy Research Working Paper, no 1096.

Haggard, S. (2015) "The Developmental State Is Dead: Long Live the Developmental State!", in Mahoney and Thelen (eds) (2015), pp. 39–66.

Haltmaier, J., S. Ahmed, B. Coulibaly, R. Knippenberg, S. Leduc, M. Marazzi, and B. Wilson (2007) "The Role of China in Asia: Engine, Conduit, or Steamroller?", Board of Governors of the Federal Reserve System, International Finance Discussion Papers, no 904.

Harriss, J. (2001) *Depoliticizing Development: the World Bank and Social Capital*, New Delhi: Leftword Books.

Harvey, D. (2003) *The New Imperialism*, Oxford: Oxford University Press.

Harvey, D. (2005) *A Brief History of Neoliberalism*, Oxford: Oxford University Press.

Helleiner, E. (1994) *States and the Reemergence of Global Finance: from Bretton Woods to the 1990s*, Ithaca, NY: Cornell University Press.

Helleiner, G. (1992) "Introduction", in Helleiner (ed.) (1992), pp. 1–17.

Helleiner, G. (ed.) (1992) *Trade Policy, Industrialisation and Development*, Oxford: Clarendon Press.

Helleiner, G. (ed.) (1994) *Trade Policy and Industrialization in Turbulent Times*, London: Routledge.

Hildyard, N. (1998) *The World Bank and the State: a Recipe for Change?*, London: Bretton Woods Project.

Hirakawa, H., M. Noguchi and M. Sano (eds) (2003) *Beyond Market-Driven Development: A New Stream of Political Economy of Development*, Tokyo: Nihon Hyoron Sha, in Japanese.

Hockmuth, K. (2022) "The Developmental Sources of South Korean Neoliberalism", *Fudan Journal of the Humanities and Social Sciences*, vol 11, pp. 41–61.

Hodgson, G. (2001) *How Economics Forgot History: the Problem of Historical Specificity in Social Science*, London: Routledge.

Hodgson, G. and H. Rothman (1999) "The Editors and Authors of Economics Journals: a Case of Institutional Oligopoly?", *Economic Journal*, vol 109, no 453, pp. F165–86.

Hoff, K., A. Braverman and J. Stiglitz (1993) "Preface" in Hoff et al. (eds) (1993), pp. I–XIII.

Hoff, K., A. Braverman and J. Stiglitz (eds) (1993) *The Economics of Rural Organisation: theory, Practice, and Policy*, New York: Oxford University Press.

Holm, P. (1997) "Vertically Integrated Oligopoly and International Trade Policy", *Canadian Journal of Economics*, vol XXX, no 1, pp. 194–207.

Hout, W. and J. Hutchison (eds) (2022) *Handbook on Governance and Development*, Cheltenham: Edward Elgar.

Huff, W., G. Dewit and C. Oughton (2001) "Credibility and Reputation Building in the Developmental State: a Model with East Asian Applications", *World Development*, vol 29, no 4, pp. 711–24.

Hujo, K. (2021) "Social Protection and Inequality in the Global South: Politics, Actors and Institutions", *Critical Social Policy*, vol 41, no 3, pp. 343–63.

Hyland, M. and R. Munck (eds) (2018) *Handbook on Development and Social Change*, Cheltenham: Edward Elgar.

International Monetary Fund (2012) "The IMF's Institutional View on Capital Flows in Practice", https://www.imf.org/external/np/g20/pdf/2018/073018.pdf.

Jackson, C. (2002) "Disciplining Gender", *World Development*, vol 30, no 3, pp. 497–509.

Jaspars, S. and H. Young (1995) "Malnutrition and Poverty in the Early Stages of Famine – North Dafur, 1988–90", *Disasters*, vol 19, no 3, pp. 198–215.

Jaspars, S. and L. Kuol (2024) "Famine and Food Security: New Trends and Systems or Politics as Usual? An Introduction", *Disasters*, DOI: 10.1111/disa.12669, forthcoming.

Jie-A-Joen, C. (1997) *Strategic Trade Policy, Multinational Firms, and Vertically Related Industries*, Amsterdam: Thesis Publishers.

Johnson, C. (1982) *MITI and the Japanese Miracle*, Stanford: Stanford University Press.

Jolly, R. (1991) "Adjustment with a Human Face: a UNICEF Record and Perspective on the 1980s", *World Development*, vol 19, no 12, pp. 1807–21.

Jomo, K. and B. Fine (eds) (2006) *The New Development Economics: after the Washington Consensus*, Delhi: Tulika, and London: Zed Press.

Kanbur, R. (2002) "Economics, Social Science and Development", *World Development*, vol 30, no 3, pp. 477–86.

Kanbur, S. (1990) "Global Food Balances and Individual Hunger: Three Themes in an Entitlements-Based Approach", in Sen and Drèze (eds) (1990a), pp. 53–78.

Kaneda, M. (1995) "Industrialization under Perfect Foresight – a World Economy with a Continuum of Countries", *Journal of Economic Theory*, vol 66, no 2, pp. 437–62.

Karp, L. and J. Perloff (1995) "Why Industrial Policies Fail: Limited Commitment", *International Economic Review*, vol 36, no 4, pp. 887–905.

Karsten, S. (1973) "Dialectics and the Evolution of Economic Thought?", *History of Political Economy*, vol 5, no 2, pp. 399–419.

Karwowski, E. and E. Stockhammer (2017) "Financialisation in Emerging Economies: a Systematic Overview and Comparison with Anglo-Saxon Economies", *Economic and Political Studies*, vol 5, no 1, pp. 60–86.

Katrak, H. (1997) "Developing Countries' Imports of Technology, In-House Technological Capabilities and Efforts: an Analysis of the Indian Experience", *Journal of Development Economics*, vol 53, no 1, pp. 67–83.

Katz, J. (ed.) (1987) *Technology Generation in Latin American Manufacturing Industries*, London: Macmillan.

Keen, D. (1994) *The Benefits of Famine: a Political Economy of Famine and Relief in Southwestern Sudan, 1983–1989*, Princeton: Princeton University Press.

Keller, W. (1996) "Absorptive Capacity: On the Creation and Acquisition of Technology in Development", *Journal of Development Economics*, vol 49, no 1, pp. 199–228.

Kenny, C. and D. Williams (2001) "What Do We Know about Economic Growth? Or, Why Don't We Know Very Much?", *World Development*, vol 29, no 1, pp. 1–22.

Khalil, E. (1987) "Kuhn, Lakatos, and the History of Economic Thought", *International Journal of Social Economics*, vol 14, no 3, pp. 118–31.

Kierkowski, H. (ed.) (1984) *Monopolistic Competition and International Trade*, Oxford: Oxford University Press.

Konopelko, E. (2023) *Factors behind the Introduction and Design of a National Minimum Wage Policy: with Application to South Africa*, unpublished Phd, SOAS University of London.

Krueger, A. (1986), "Aid in the Development Process", *World Bank Research Observer*, vol 1, no 1, pp. 57–78.

Krueger, A. (1997) "Trade Policy and Economic Development: How We Learn", *American Economic Review*, vol 87, no 1, pp. 1–22.

Krueger, A. (1998) "Why Trade Liberalisation is Good for Growth", *Economic Journal*, vol 108, no 3, pp. 1513–22.

Krugman, P. (1984) "Import Protection as Export Protection", in Kierkowski (ed.) (1984), pp. 180–93.

Krugman, P. (1986) *Strategic Trade Policy and the New International Economics*, Cambridge: MIT Press.

Krugman, P. (1989) "New Trade Theories and Less Developed Countries", in Calvo et al. (eds) (1989), pp. 73–100.

Krugman, P. (1992) "Toward a Counter-Counterrevolution in Development Theory", *World Bank Economic Review*, Supplement (Proceedings of the Annual Bank Conference on Development Economics), pp. 15–39.

Krugman, P. (1994) "The Myth of Asia's Miracle", *Foreign Affairs*, vol 73, no 6, pp. 62–8.

Krugman, P. and R. Elizondo (1996) "Trade Policy and the Third World Metropolis", *Journal of Development Economics*, vol 49, no 1, pp. 137–150.

Kuhn, T. (1970) *The Structure of Scientific Revolutions*, Chicago: Chicago University Press, second edition with postscript, original of 1962.

Kumar, M. and K. McLeod (eds) (1981) *Multinationals from Developing Countries*, Lexington, MA: Lexington Books.

Kunin, L. and F. Weaver (1971) "On the Structure of Scientific Revolutions in Economics", *History of Political Economy*, vol 3, no 2, pp. 391–97.

Kuznets, S. (1971) *Economic Growth of Nations: Total Output and Production Structure*, Cambridge: Harvard University Press.

Lakatos, I. and A. Musgrave (eds) (1970) *Criticism and the Growth of Knowledge*, Cambridge: Cambridge University Press.

Lall, S. (1983) *The New Multinationals: the Spread of Third World Enterprises*, Chichester Wiley.

Lall, S. (1998) "Exports of Manufactures by Developing Countries: Emerging Patterns of Trade and Location", *Oxford Review of Economic Policy*, vol 14, no 2, pp. 54–73.

Lall, S. (ed.) (1999) *The Technological Response to Import Liberalisation in Sub-Saharan Africa*, London: Macmillan.

Lane, N. (2021) "Manufacturing Revolutions: Industrial Policy and Industrialization in South Korea", SoDa Laboratories Working Paper Series, no 2021–10, Monash Business School, http://soda-wps.s3-website-ap-southeast-2.amazonaws.com/RePEc/ajr/sod wps/2021-10.pdf, *Quarterly Journal of Economics*, forthcoming.

Laruffa, F. (2021) "Studying the Relationship between Social Policy Promotion and Neoliberalism: the Case of Social Investment", *New Political Economy*, vol 27, no 2, pp. 1–17.

Latsch, W. and P. Robinson (1999) "Technology Upgrading in Post-Liberalisation Zimbabwe", in Lall (ed.) (1999), pp. 148–206.

Lau, M. and H. Wan (1994) "On the Mechanism of Catching Up", *European Economic Review*, vol 38, no 3–4, pp. 952–63.

Lawson, T. (1997) *Economics and Reality*, London: Routledge.

Lazear, E. (2000) "Economic Imperialism", *Quarterly Journal of Economics*, vol 115, no 1, pp. 99–146.

Lazonick, W. and M. O'Sullivan (2000) "Shareholder Value as a New Ideology of Corporate Governance", *Economy and Society*, vol 29, no 1, pp. 13–35.

Leahy, D. and J. Neary (1996) "International R&D Rivalry and Industrial Strategy without Government Commitment", *Review of International Economics*, vol 4, no 3, pp. 322–38.

Lee, F. and S. Harley (1998) "Peer Review, the Research Assessment Exercise and the Demise of Non-Mainstream Economics", *Capital and Class*, no 66, pp. 23–51.

Lee, J. (1995) "Capital Goods Imports and Long-Run Growth", *Journal of Development Economics*, vol 48, no 1, pp. 91–110.

Lee, N. (1992) "Market Structure and Trade in Developing Countries", in Helleiner (ed.) (1992), pp. 89–121.

Lestringant, F. (1997) *Cannibals: the Discovery and Representation of the Cannibal from Columbus to Jules Verne*, Berkeley: University of California Press.

Lewis, P. (ed.) (2004) *Transforming Economics: Perspectives on the Critical Realist Project*, London: Routledge.

Leys, C. and L. Panitch (eds) (2005) *Telling the Truth, Socialist Register*, 2006, London: Merlin Press.

Lindbeck, A. (2000) "The Sveriges Riksbank (Bank of Sweden) Prize in Economic Sciences in Memory of Alfred Nobel, 1969–1998", www.nobel.se/economics/artic les/lindbeck/index.html.

Lucas, R. (1988) "On the Mechanics of Economic Development", *Journal of Monetary Economics*, vol 22, no 1, pp. 3–42.

Mabasa, K. (2020) "The Developmental State and Black Economic Empowerment: Lessons from East Asian Capitalist Models", in Cawe and Mabasa (eds) (2020), pp. 121–47.

Macrae, J. and J. Zwi (1994) "Famine, Complex Emergencies and International Policy in Africa: an Overview", in Macrae and Zwi (eds) (1994), pp. 6–36.

Macrae, J. and J. Zwi (eds) (1994) *War and Hunger: Rethinking International Responses to Complex Emergencies*, London: Zed Books.

Mader, P., D. Mertens and N. van der Zwan (eds) (2020) *The Routledge International Handbook of Financialization*, Abingdon: Routledge.

Maharaj, B., A. Desai and P. Bond (eds) (2010) *Zuma's Own Goal: Losing South Africa's 'War on Poverty'*, Trenton, NJ: Africa World Press, Inc.

Mahoney, J. and R. Thelen (2015) (eds) *Advances in Comparative-Historical Analysis (Strategies for Social Inquiry)*, Cambridge: Cambridge University Press.

Marangos, J. (2009) "The Evolution of the Term 'Washington Consensus'", *Journal of Economic Surveys*, vol 23, no 2, pp. 350–84.

Masterman, M. (1970) "The Nature of a Paradigm", in Lakatos and Musgrave (eds) (1970), pp. 59–90.

McCloskey, D. (1986) *The Rhetoric of Economics*, Brighton: Wheatsheaf.

McKay, A. and C. Milner (1997) "Strategic Trade Policy, Learning by Doing Effects and Economic Development", *World Development*, vol 25, no 11, pp. 1893–1900.

McKinnon, R. (1973) *Money and Capital in Economic Development*, Washington DC: Brooking Institute.

McPherson, M. (1995) "The Hazards of Small Firms in Southern Africa", *Journal of Development Studies*, vol 32, no 1, pp. 31–54.

Meramveliotakis, G. and M. Manioudis (eds) (2024) *Sustainable Economic Development Perspectives from Political Economy and Economics Pluralism*, London: Routledge.

MERG (1994) Making Democracy Work: a Framework for Macroeconomic Policy in South Africa, New York: Oxford University Press, https://eprints.soas.ac.uk/14614/1 /MERG.pdf.

Milonakis, D. and B. Fine (2009) *From Political Economy to Economics: Method, the Social and the Historical in the Evolution of Economic Theory*, London: Routledge.

Miranda, J., R. Torres and M. Ruiz (1998) "The International Use of Antidumping – 1987–1997", *Journal of World Trade*, vol 32, no 5, pp. 5–71.

Misra-Dexter, N. and J. February (eds) (2010) *Testing Democracy: Which Way Is South Africa Going?*, Institute for a Democratic South Africa, Cape Town: ABC Press.

Mitra, A. (1982) "The Meaning of Meaning", *Economic and Political Weekly*, vol XVII, no 13, March 27, pp. 488–89.

Mkandawire, T. (2001) "Thinking about Developmental States in Africa", *Cambridge Journal of Economics*, vol 25, no 3, pp. 289–314.

Mkandawire, T. (2010) "How the New Poverty Agenda Neglected Social and Employment Policies in Africa", *Journal of Human Development and Capabilities*, vol 11, no 1, pp. 37–55.

Mkandawire, T. (2012) "Building the African State in the Age of Globalisation: the Role of Social Compacts and Lessons for South Africa", Mapungubwe Institute for Strategic Reflection, Inaugural Annual Lecture, MISTRA, https://mistra.org.za/mistra-media/building-the-african-state-in-the-age-of-globalisation-the-role-of-social-compacts-and-lessons-for-south-africa/.

Mkandawire, T. and C. Soludo (eds) (1998) *Our Continent, Our Future: African Perspectives on Structural Adjustment*, Dakar: Council for the Development of Social Science Research in Africa, with International Development Research Centre and Africa World Press.

Mohamed, S. (2010) "The State of the South African Economy", in Southall et al. (eds) (2010), pp. 39–64.

Mohamed, S. (2014) "Banking and Credit Markets" in Bhorat et al. (eds) (2014), pp. 178–84.

Mohamed, S., A. Ngoma and B. Baloyi (eds) (2023) *The Evolving Structure of South Africa's Economy: Faultlines and Futures*, Johannesburg: MISTRA.

Moore, M. (1999) "Politics against Poverty?: Global Pessimism and National Optimism", *IDS Bulletin*, vol 30, no 2, pp. 33–46.

Morgan, J. (2024) "Economics Imperialism Then and Now: Ben Fine on the Changing Relationship between Economics and the Other Social Sciences", *Contributions to Political Economy*, forthcoming, https://doi.org/10.1093/cpe/bzae012.

Mosley, P., J. Harrigan and J. Toye (1991) *Aid and Power: the World Bank and Policy-Based Lending*, London: Routledge.

Murphy, E. (2013) *The Evolution of Trade Theory: an Exercise in the Construction of Surrogate or Substitute Worlds?*, unpublished Phd, SOAS University of London.

Narcis, S. and J. Stiglitz (eds) (2008) *The Washington Consensus Reconsidered: towards a New Global Governance*, London: Oxford University Press.

Nas, T. and M. Odekon (eds) (1991) *Economics and Politics of Turkish Liberalisation*, London: Associated Universities Press.

Nelson, R. (1981) "Research on Productivity Growth and Differences: Dead Ends and New Departures", *Journal of Economic Literature*, vol 19, no 3, pp. 1029–64.

Nielsen, P. and J. Morgan (2005) "No New Revolution in Economics? Taking Thompson and Fine Forward", *Economy and Society*, vol 34, no 1, pp. 51–75.

Nishimuzu, M. and J. Page (1991) "Trade Policy, Market-Orientation and Productivity in Industry", in de Melo and Sapir (eds) (1991), pp. 246–64.

Nishimuzu, M. and S. Robinson (1984) "Trade Policy and Productivity in Semi-Industrialised Countries", *Journal of Development Economics*, vol 16, no 1/2, pp. 177–206.

Nobel (2001) "Markets with Asymmetric Information. Advanced Information", https://www.nobelprize.org/prizes/economic-sciences/2001/advanced-information/.

Nolan, P. (1993) "The Causation and Prevention of Famines: a Critique of A.K. Sen", *Journal of Peasant Studies*, vol 21, no 1, pp. 1–28.

Nolan, P. and J. Sender (1992) "Death Rates, Life Expectancy and China's Economic Reforms: a Critique of A.K. Sen", *World Development*, vol 20, no 9, pp. 1279–1303.

Ocampo, J. (1986) "New Developments in Trade Theory and LDCs", *Journal of Development Economics*, vol 22, no 1, pp. 129–70.

Ocampo, J. and L. Taylor (1998) "Trade Liberalisation in Developing Economies: Modest Benefits but Problems with Productivity Growth, Macro Prices, and Income Distribution", *Economic Journal*, vol 108, no 3, pp. 1523–46.

O'Donnell, K. (2023) "Canteen Workers' Wages and Collective Bargaining in British Coal", *Historical Studies in Industrial Relations*, vol 44, no 1, pp. 75–89.

Ohyama, M. and R. Jones (1995) "Technology Choice, Overtaking and Comparative Advantage", *Review of International Economics*, vol 3, no 2, pp. 224–34.

Okawa, M. (1997) "A General Equilibrium Approach to the Non-Equivalence of Tariffs and Quotas under International Duopoly", *Japanese Economic Review*, vol 48, no 2, pp. 156–65.

Olson, M. and S. Kähkönen (2000) "Introduction: the Broader View", in Olson and Kähkönen (eds) (2000), pp. 1–36.

Olson, M. and S. Kähkönen (eds) (2000) *A Not-So-Dismal Science: a Broader View of Economies and Societies*, Oxford: Oxford University Press.

Onafowora, O., O. Owoye and A. Nyatepe-Coo (1996) "Trade Policy, Export Performance and Economic Growth: Evidence from Sub-Saharan Africa", *Journal of International Trade and Economic Development*, vol 5, no 3, pp. 341–60.

Onis, Z. (1991) "Organisation of Export-Led Industrialisation: the Turkish Foreign Trade Companies in Comparative Perspective", in Nas and Odekon (eds) (1991), pp. 73–100.

Ormerod, P. (1994) *The Death of Economics*, London: Faber & Faber.

Osang, T. and A. Pereira (1996) "Import Tariffs and Growth in a Small Open Economy". *Journal of Public Economics,* vol 60, no 1, pp 45–47.

Osmani, S. (1990) "Nutrition and the Economics of Food: Implications of Some Recent Controversies", in Sen and Drèze (eds) (1990a), pp. 247–96.

Osmani, S. (1991) "Comments on Alex de Waal's 'A Reassessment of Entitlement Theory in the Light of Recent Famines in Africa'", *Development and Change*, vol 22, no 3, pp. 587–96.

Osmani, S. (1995) "The Entitlement Approach to Famine: an Assessment", in Basu et al. (eds) (1995), pp. 253–94.

Pack, H. (1992) "Technology Gaps Between Industrial and Developing Countries", Supplement to *World Bank Economic Review*, pp. 283–302.

Pack, H. and L. Westphal (1986) "Industrial Strategy and Technological Change", *Journal of Development Economics*, vol 22, no 1, pp. 87–128.

Padayachee, V. (ed.) (2009) *The Political Economy of Africa*, London: Routledge.

Pal, D. and M. White (1998) "Mixed Oligopoly, Privatization, and Strategic Trade Policy", *Southern Economic Journal*, vol 65, no 2, pp. 264–81.

Palma, G. (2000) "The Three Routes to Financial Crises: the Need for Capital Controls", New York, Schwartz Center for Economic Policy Analysis (SCEPA), Working Paper no 2000–17, The New School, http://www.economicpolicyresearch.org/scepa/publi cations/workingpapers/2000/cepa0318.pdf.

Panitch, L. and G. Albo (eds) (2018) *A World Turned Upside Down?, Socialist Register, 2019*, London: Merlin Press.

Panitch, L. and S. Gindin (2012) *The Making of Global Capitalism: the Political Economy of American Empire*, London & New York: Verso.

Papageorgiou, D., A. Choksi and M. Michaely (eds) (1991) *Liberalising Foreign Trade*, Oxford: Basil Blackwell.

Patnaik, U. (1991) "Food Availability and Famine: a Longer View", *Journal of Peasant Studies*, vol 19, no 1, pp. 1–25.

Pazarbaşıoğlu, C., M. Goswami and J. Ree (2007) "The Changing Face of Investors", *Finance and Development*, vol 44, no 1, https://www.imf.org/external/pubs/ft/fandd /2007/03/pazar.htm.

Petry, J., K. Koddenbrok and A. Nölke (2023) "State Capitalism and Capital Markets: Comparing Securities Exchanges in Emerging Markets", *Environment and Planning A: Economy and Space*, vol 55, no 1, pp. 143–64.

Pirie, I. (2018) "Korea and Taiwan: the Crisis of Investment-led Growth and the End of the Developmental State", *Journal of Contemporary Asia*, vol 48, no 1, pp. 133–58.

Pissarides, C. (1997) "Learning by Trading and Returns to Human Capital in Developing Countries", *World Bank Economic Review*, vol 11, no 1, pp. 17–21.

Prasch, R. (1996) "Reassessing the Theory of Comparative Advantage", *Review of Political Economy*, vol 8, no 1, pp. 37–55.

Prychitko D. (ed.) (1998) *Why Economists Disagree: an Introduction to the Alternative Schools of Thought*, Albany: SUNY Press.

Pursell, G. (1990) "Industrial Sickness, Primary and Secondary: the Effects of Exit Constraints on Industrial Performance", *World Bank Economic Review*, vol 4, no 1, pp. 104–14.

Qizilbash, M. (2002) "On Ethics and the Economics of Development", paper presented to the World Bank ABCDE Conference, Oslo, July.

Ragkousis, A. (2024) "Amartya Sen as a Neoclassical Economist", *Journal of Economic Issues*, vol 58, no 1, pp. 24–58.

Raikes, P. (1988) *Modernising Hunger: Famine, Food Surplus and Farm Policy in the EEC and Africa*, London: CIIR.

Ram, N. (1990) "An Independent Press and Anti-Hunger Strategies: the Indian Experience", in Sen and Drèze (eds) (1990a), pp. 146–90.

Rangasami, A. (1985) "'Failure of Exchange Entitlements' Theory of Famine: a Response", *Economic and Political Weekly*, vol 20, no 41, Oct 12, pp. 1747–54, and no 42, Oct 19, pp. 1797–1801.

Reddy, S. (1999) "Dynamic Comparative Advantage and the Welfare Effects of Trade", *Oxford Economic Papers*, vol 51, no 1, pp 15–39.

Rethel, L. and E. Thurbon (2020) "Introduction: Finance, Development and the State in East Asia", *New Political Economy*, vol 25, no 3, pp. 315–19.

Reynolds, J., B. Fine and R. van Niekerk (eds) (2019) *Race, Class and the Post-Apartheid Democratic State*, Pietermaritzburg: University of KwaZulu-Natal Press.

Riezman, R. and J. Wilson (1997) "Political Reform and Trade Policy", *Journal of International Economics*, vol 42, no 1–2, pp. 67–90.

Rivera-Batiz, L. and P. Romer (1991) "International Trade with Endogenous Technological Change", *European Economic Review*, vol 35, no 4, pp. 971–1001.

Roberts, M. and J. Tybout (1991) "Size Rationalisation and Trade Exposure in Developing Countries", The World Bank Working Paper Series, no 594.

Rodrik, D. (1992) "The Limits of Trade Policy Reform in Developing Countries", *Journal of Economic Perspectives*, vol 6, no 1, pp. 87–105.

Rodrik, D. (1994) "Coordination Failures and Government Policy: a Model with Application to East Asia and Eastern Europe", Columbia University, mimeo, published in *Journal of International Economics*, vol 40, no 1–2, 1996, pp. 1–22.

Rodrik, D. (2007) *One Economics, Many Recipes*, Princeton: Princeton University Press.

Rodrik, D. and F. Fouroutan (1998) "Why Is Trade Reform So Difficult in Africa?", *Journal of African Economies*, vol 7, Supplement, pp. 10–36.

Romer, P. (1992) "Two Strategies for Economic Development: Using Ideas and Producing Ideas", Supplement to *World Bank Economic Review*, pp. 63–91.

Rostow, W. (1957) "The Interrelation of Theory and Economic History", *Journal of Economic History*, vol 17, no 4, pp. 509–23.

Rostow, W. (1960/1990) *The Stages of Economic Growth: a Non-Communist Manifesto*, Cambridge: Cambridge University Press, third revised edition, 1990.

Ruttan, V. (1998) "The New Growth Theory and Development Economics: a Survey", *Journal of Development Studies*, vol 35, no 2, pp. 1–26.

Sachs, J. (2005) *The End of Poverty: How We Can Make It Happen in Our Lifetime*, London: Penguin.

Santos, A. and N. Teles (eds) (2020) *Financialisation in the European Periphery: Work and Social Reproduction in Portugal*, London: Routledge.

Schmalensee, R. (1992) "Sunk Costs and Market Structure: a Review Article", *Journal of Industrial Economics*, vol XL, no 2, 125–34.

Schuurman, F. (2000) "Paradigms Lost, Paradigms Regained?: Development Studies in the Twenty First Century", *Third World Quarterly*, vol 21, no 1, pp. 7–20.

Seaman, J. (1993) "Famine Mortality in Africa", *IDS Bulletin*, vol 24, no 4, pp. 27–32.

Sen, A. (1970/2017) *Collective Choice and Social Welfare*, London: Penguin for second edition.

Sen, A. (1977) "Rational Fools: a Critique of the Behavioral Foundations of Economic Theory", *Philosophy and Public Affairs*, vol 6, no 4, pp. 317–44.

Sen, A. (1981) *Poverty and Famines*, Oxford: Clarendon Press.

Sen, A. (1985) *Commodities and Capabilities*, Amsterdam: North-Holland.

Sen, A. (1986) "The Causes of Famine: a Reply", *Food Policy*, vol 11, no 2, pp. 125–32.

Sen, A. (1987a) "Reply: Famine and Mr. Bowbrick", *Food Policy*, vol 12, no 1, pp. 10–14.

Sen, A. (1987b) *On Ethics and Economics*, Oxford: Blackwell.

Sen, A. (1989) "Food and Freedom", *World Development*, vol 17, no 6, pp. 769–81.

Sen, A. (1992) "Life and Death in China", *World Development*, vol 20, no 9, pp. 1305–312.

Sen, A. (1993) "The Causation and Prevention of Famines: a Reply", *Journal of Peasant Studies*, vol 21, no 1, Oct, pp. 29–40.

Sen, A. (1995) "Rationality and Social Choice", *American Economic Review*, vol 85, no 1, pp. 1–24.

Sen, A. (1999a) *Development as Freedom*, Oxford: Oxford University Press.

Sen, A. (1999b) "The Possibility of Social Choice", *American Economic Review*, vol 89, no 3, pp. 349–78.

Sen, A. (ed.) (1970) *Growth Economics: Selected Readings*, London: Penguin.

Serulnikov, S. (1994) "When Looting Becomes a Right – Urban Poverty and Food Riots in Argentine", *Latin American Perspectives*, vol 21, no 3, pp. 69–89.

Shaw, E. (1973) *Financial Deepening in Economic Development*, New York: Oxford University Press.

Siegfried, J. and W. Stock (1999) "The Labor Market for New Ph.D. Economists, with Comments from R. Ehrenberg", *Journal of Economic Perspectives*, vol 13, no 3, pp. 115–34.

Simon, D. (ed.) (2006) *Fifty Key Thinkers on Development*, London: Routledge, second edition, 2019.

Singh, A. (1997) "Financial Liberalisation, Stock Markets and Economic Development", *Economic Journal*, vol 107, no 442, pp. 771–82.

Sleuwaegen, L., R. Belderbos and C. Jie-a-Joen (1998) "Cascading Contingent Protection and Vertical Market Structure", *International Journal of Industrial Organization*, vol 16, no 6, pp. 697–718.

Soludo, C. (1998) "Trade Policy Reforms and Supply Responses in Africa", African Development in a Comparative Perspective, Working Paper, no 6, UNCTAD.

Solway, J. (1994) "Drought as a Revelatory Crisis – an Exploration of Shifting Entitlements and Hierarchies in the Kalahari, Botswana", *Development and Change*, vol 25, no 3, pp. 471–95.

Southall, R., D. Pillay, P. Naidoo and J. Daniel (2010) (eds) *New South African Review 1: Development or Decline*, Johannesburg: Wits University Press.

Standing, G. (2000) "Brave New Worlds?: a Critique of Stiglitz's World Bank Rethink", *Development and Change*, vol 31, no 4, pp. 737–63.

Stanfield, R. (1974) "Kuhnian Scientific Revolutions and the Keynesian Revolution", *Journal of Economic Issues*, vol VIII, no 1, pp. 97–109.

Steel, W. and L. Webster (1992) "How Small Firms in Ghana Responded to Adjustment", *World Bank Economic Review*, vol 6, no 3, pp. 423–38.

Stewart, F. (1991) "A Note on Strategic Trade Theory and the South", *Journal of International Development*, vol 3, no 5, pp. 467–84.

Stiglitz, J. (1989) "Markets, Market Failures and Development", *American Economic Review*, vol 79, no 2, pp. 197–202.

Stiglitz, J. (1991) "Another Century of Economic Science", *Economic Journal*, vol 101, no 1, pp. 134–41.

Stiglitz, J. (1993) "Post-Walrasian and Post-Marxian Economics", *Journal of Economic Perspectives*, vol 7, no 1, pp. 109–14.

Stiglitz, J. (1994) *Whither Socialism?*, Cambridge: MIT Press.

Stiglitz, J. (1998a) "More Instruments and Broader Goals: Moving Toward the Post-Washington Consensus", The 1998 WIDER Annual Lecture, January 7th, Helsinki, reproduced in Chang (ed.) (2001), pp. 17–56.

Stiglitz, J. (1998b) "Towards a New Paradigm for Development: Strategies, Policies and Processes", Prebisch Lecture, UNCTAD, Geneva, reproduced in Chang (ed.) (2001), pp. 57–93.

Stiglitz, J. (2001) "An Agenda for the New Development Economics. Paper to UNRISD meeting on 'The Need to Rethink Development Economics'", Cape Town, September, http://www.unrisd.org/engindex/research/rethink.htm

Stiglitz, J. (2002a) "Ethics, Economic Advice, and Economic Policy." mimeo, revised from paper presented at the Interamerican Development Bank, Washington, D.C., December.

Stiglitz, J. (2002b) *Globalization and Its Discontents*, New York: W.W. Norton.

Stiglitz, J. (2010) *The Stiglitz Report: Reforming the International Monetary and Financial Systems in the Wake of the Global Crisis*, New York: the New Press.

Stiglitz, J. and K. Hoff (1999) "Modern Economic Theory and Development", Symposium on Future of Development Economics in Perspective, Dubrovnik, 13–14th May.

Subaset, T. (ed.) (2016) *The Great Financial Meltdown: Systemic, Conjunctural or Policy Created?*, Cheltenham: Edward Elgar.

Sumner, A. (2024) "Unity in Diversity? Reflections on Development Studies in the Mid-2020s", *European Journal of Development Research*, https://doi.org/10.1057/s41 287-024-00636-x, forthcoming.

Suppe, P. (1977) *The Structure of Scientific Theories*, Urbana: University of Chicago Press, second edition.

Sutton, J. (1991) *Sunk Costs and Market Structure: Price Competition, Advertising, and the Evolution of Concentration*, Cambridge: MIT Press.

Swedberg, R. (ed.) (1990) *Economics and Sociology, Redefining Their Boundaries: Conversations with Economists and Sociologists*, Princeton: Princeton University Press.

Swift, J. (1993) "Understanding and Preventing Famine and Famine Mortality", *IDS Bulletin*, vol 24, no 4, Oct, pp. 1–16.

Tarr, D. (1992) "Rent-Seeking and the Benefits of Price and Trade Reform in Poland: the Automobile and Colour Television Cases", World Bank, mimeo.

Teubal, M. (1992) "Food Security and 'Regimes of Accumulation': the Case of Argentina", ISS Working Papers, no 123.

Thurbon, E. (2020) "The Future of Financial Activism in Taiwan? The Utility of a Mindset-centred Analysis of Developmental States and their Evolution", *New Political Economy*, vol 25, no 3, pp. 320–36.

Tommasi, M., and K. Ierulli (eds) (1995) *The New Economics of Human Behaviour*, Cambridge: Cambridge University Press.

Toulmin, S. (1972) *Human Understanding: the Collective Use and Evolution of Concepts*, Princeton: Princeton University Press.

Toye, J. (1993) *Dilemmas of Development*, Oxford: Blackwell.

Turner, B. (1987) *Medical Power and Social Knowledge*, London: Sage Publications.

Tybout, J. (1992) "Linking Trade and Productivity", *World Bank Economic Review* vol 6, no 2, pp. 189–211.

Tybout, J., J. de Melo and V. Corbo (1991) "The Effects of Trade Reform on Scale and Technical Efficiency: New Evidence from Chile", *Journal of International Economics*, vol 31, no 3/4, pp. 231–50.

Tybout, J. and M. Westbrook (1995) "Trade Liberalization and the Dimensions of Efficiency Change in Mexican Manufacturing Industries", *Journal of International Economics*, vol 39, no 1/2, pp. 53–78.

UNCTAD (2011) *The Least Developed Countries Report 2011: the Potential Role of South-South Cooperation for Inclusive and Sustainable Development*, Geneva: UNCTAD.

UNCTAD (2020) *Trade and Development Report. From Global Pandemic to Prosperity for All: Avoiding Another Lost Decade*, Geneva: United Nations.

Unwin, T. (2007) "No End to Poverty", *Journal of Development Studies*, vol 43, no 5, pp. 929–53.

van de Klundert, T. and S. Smulders (1996) "North-South Knowledge Spill-Overs and Competition: Convergence versus Divergence", *Journal of Development Economics*, vol 50, no 2, pp. 213–32.

van Long, N. and A. Soubeyran (1997) "Cost Heterogeneity, Industry Concentration and Strategic Trade Policies", *Journal of International Economics*, vol 43, no 1–2, pp. 207–20.

Van Waeyenberge, E. (2007) *Exploring the Emergence of a New Aid Regime: Selectivity, Knowledge and the World Bank*, Unpublished PhD thesis, SOAS, University of London.

Van Waeyenberge, E. (2009) "Selectivity at Work: Country Policy and Institutional Assessments at the World Bank", *European Journal of Development Research*, vol 21, no 5, pp. 792–810.

Velthuis, O. (1999) "The Changing Relationship between Economic Sociology and Institutional Economics: from Talcott Parsons to Mark Granovetter", *American Journal of Economics and Sociology*, vol 58, no 4, pp. 629–49.

Vernengo, M. (2021) "The Consolidation of Dollar Hegemony after the Collapse of Bretton Woods: Bringing Power Back", *Review of Political Economy*, vol 33, no 4, pp. 529–51.

Vetterlein, A. and T. Schmidtke (eds) (2024) *The Elgar Companion to the World Bank*, Cheltenham: Edward Elgar, forthcoming.

Von Braun, J., T. Teklu and P. Webb (1993) "Famine as the Outcome of Political Production and Market Failures", *IDS Bulletin*, vol 24, no 4, pp. 73–79.

Wade, R. (1990) *Governing the Market: Economic Theory and the Role of Government in East Asian Industrialisation*, Princeton: Princeton University Press.

Wade, R. (2001) "Showdown at the World Bank", *New Left Review*, no 7, pp. 124–137.

Wade, R. (2012) "Return of Industrial Policy?", *International Review of Applied Economics,* vol 26, no 2, pp. 223–39.

Wade, R. (2017) "The Developmental State: Dead or Alive?", *Development and Change*, vol 49, no 2, pp. 518–46.

Walde, K. (1996) "Proof of Global Stability, Transitional Dynamics, and International Capital Flows in a Two-Country Model of Innovation and Growth", *Journal of Economics*, vol 64, no 1, pp. 53–84.

Ward, B. (1972) *What's Wrong with Economics?*, New York: Basic Books.

Watts, M. (1991) "Entitlements or Empowerment? Famine and Starvation in Africa", *Review of African Political Economy*, no 51, pp. 9–26.

Watts, M. (1994) "What Difference Does Difference Make?", *Review of International Political Economy*, vol 1, no 3, pp. 563–70.

Watts, M. and H. Bohle (1993) "The Space of Vulnerability: the Causal Structure of Hunger and Famine", *Progress in Human Geography*, vol 17, no 1, pp. 43–67.

Waverman, L. and S. Murphy (1992) "Total Factor Productivity in Automobile Production in Argentina, Mexico, Korea and Canada", in Helleiner (ed.) (1992), pp. 279–310.

Wells, L. (1983) *Third World Multinationals: the Role of Foreign Direct Investment from Developing Countries*, Cambridge, MA: MIT Press.

Westerhout, E. (1995) "Trade Policies, Imperfect Competition and Endogenous Growth", *De Economist*, vol 143, no 1, pp 15–40.

Wiegratz, J., P. Behuria, C. Laskaridis, L. Pheko, B. Radley and S. Stevano (2023) "Common Challenges for All? A Critical Engagement with the Emerging Vision for Post-pandemic Development Studies", *Development and Change*, https://doi.org/10.1111/dech.12785, forthcoming.

Williams, M. (ed.) (2014) *The End of the Developmental State?*, London: Routledge.

Williamson, O. (1993) "Contested Exchange versus the Governance of Contractual Relations", *Journal of Economic Perspectives*, vol 7, no 1, pp. 103–108.

Woldemeskel, G. (1990) "Famine and the Two Faces of Entitlement: a Comment on Sen", *World Development*, vol 18, no 3, pp. 491–95.

Wong, K. and K. Chow (1997) "Endogenous Sequencing in Strategic Trade Policy Games under Uncertainty", *Open Economies Review*, vol 8, no 4, pp. 353–69.

Wong, P. (2020) "State–Market–Society Alliance: the Evolving Nature of the '21st-century Developmental State'", WIDER Working Paper, no 2020/103, https://www.wider.unu.edu/publication/state%E2%80%93market%E2%80%93society-alliance.

Woo-Cumings, M. (ed.) (1999) *The Developmental State*, Ithaca, NY: Cornell University Press.

Wood, A. and C. Ridao-Cano (1999) "Skill, Trade and International Inequality", *Oxford Economic Papers*, vol 51, no 1, pp. 89–119.

World Bank (1990) *Report on Adjustment Lending II: Policies for the Recovery of Growth, Document R90099*, Washington: World Bank.

World Bank (1993) *The East Asian Miracle: Economic Growth and Public Policy: a World Bank Policy Research Report*, Oxford: Oxford University Press.

Wright, D. (1998) "Strategic Trade Policy and Signalling with Unobservable Costs", *Review of International Economics*, vol 6, no 1, pp. 105–19.

Ye, I. (ed.) (2017) *Towards Universal Health Care in Emerging Economies: Opportunities and Challenges*, London: Palgrave MacMillan.

Young, A. (1993) "Lessons from the East Asian NICs: a Contrarian View", NBER Working Paper, no 4482, https://ssrn.com/abstract=227317.

Young, L. (1996) "World Hunger – A Framework for Analysis", *Geography*, vol 81, no 351, 'part 2, pp. 97–110.

Yusuf, A., C. Morelli and O. Feraboli (eds) (2023) *Post-Crash Economics and the Covid Emergency in the Global Economy: Interdisciplinary Issues in Teaching and Research*, London: Palgrave MacMillan.

Zhang, W. (1994) "Knowledge, Growth and Patterns of Trade", *Annals of Regional Science*, vol 28, no 3, pp. 285–303.

Ziss, S. (1997) "Strategic Trade Policy and Vertical Structure", *Review of International Economics*, vol 5, no 1, pp. 142–52.

Index

www.ingramcontent.com/pod-product-compliance
Lightning Source LLC
LaVergne TN
LVHW021549230526
839611LV00034B/455